Grammar for Everyday Use

Ona Low

Collins ELT: London and Glasgow

Collins ELT
8 Grafton Street
London W1X 3LA

10 9 8 7 6 5 4 3 2

First published 1986
Reprinted 1986

Printed in Great Britain by William Collins Sons and Co Ltd

ISBN 0 00 370640 0

Design and cover by Jacky Wedgwood.
Illustrations by Mike Strudwick.
Index by Jill Cooke.

Contents

Introduction

Here are a few of the many reasons for wanting to learn another language:

- to be able to speak and understand it while on holiday
- to speak, write and understand it while living and possibly working in the country where it is spoken
- to use it in professional discussions, negotiations, conferences and on social occasions either during visits abroad or at home with visitors from abroad, when business, scientific, technical, artistic topics and matters of general interest are likely to be subjects of conversation
- to qualify to act as an interpreter, translator, guide or to work as a hotel employee or shop assistant in a tourist area
- to teach it
- to communicate with guests, friends and acquaintances
- to pass examinations
- to read books for information or pleasure
- to pass the time enjoyably in an evening class

As an international language, English is used by (among others) air crews and airport staff, ships' personnel and amateur radio enthusiasts. Above all it serves as a means of communication between speakers of other differing languages.

Spoken communication

Most of these suggested motives for learning involve speaking and understanding what has been said and both of these activities present special difficulties for very many learners, who are happy enough when, with a dictionary within easy reach, they can take their time considering the printed word or how they can best express themselves in writing. The ability to carry on an effective conversation in a foreign language during which useful information can be exchanged and decisions made involves quick thinking and concentration together with practice and training in achieving proficiency in each of the various aspects of language learning.

An ability to express ideas clearly, convincingly and fully depends on each and all of the following aspects of language learning:

a Constant practice in understanding and making active use of a wide range of vocabulary (especially words, phrases and idioms that are in everyday use in present-day speech) when talking about general topics and also those specialist subjects that you may need to deal with in connection with your job or particular interest.

b A sound knowledge of basic grammar, word order, prepositional usage and structural features in general which will enable you to create whatever kind of sentence you need to express your meaning most effectively.

c A pronunciation that is clear and correct enough to ensure easy understanding together with enough feeling for intonation to be able to convey politeness and interest.

(The above aspects of communication can best be acquired by listening to and imitating native speakers, either in person or on tape.)

d The confidence that is developed by ample practice in the creative expression of ideas, free from any inhibiting fear of making mistakes. Mistakes may be common enough at first and they may or may not be corrected, as the teacher thinks best. Many of them you will recognise yourself as you make them and realise where you need to be careful: others are valuable because you can learn from your teacher's correction. Do your best to avoid mistakes but don't let the fear of making them make you afraid of trying to say what you want to.

As you gain confidence you will enjoy expressing your ideas, even when you are alone and if you make as much use as possible of expressions you have learned in class or from this book, mistakes should gradually disappear.

The aims of this book

a To provide a sound knowledge of English grammar and language usage to enable students to create effectively whatever kind of sentences they need to express their ideas and feelings.

b To introduce a wide range of present-day vocabulary in context. There is some slight emphasis on words, phrases and idioms that will be of special use to holidaymakers and travellers, businessmen and other professional people in discussing and entertaining, guides and other tourist industry personnel, housewives, teachers and students in general.

c To give advice and material useful in dealing with common situations politely and effectively and in understanding shades of meaning and feeling in what is heard.

d To offer very considerable practice in using all the above material in expressing ideas freely and creatively and in dealing with situations.

A note on the grammar

Grammatical terms and explanations are those normally associated with what is sometimes described as 'traditional' grammar. It is possible that some of the various recent approaches to this subject are more accurate, comprehensive and/or efficient in some of their aspects, but among other things the terms used are likely to be unfamiliar to the average teacher of English in many countries who probably feels more at home with the 'traditional' approach. The variety of new approaches is in itself somewhat daunting and for present purposes the old and familiar is more than adequate.

Specialists in grammar may regret certain simplifications and omissions, but in fact the form of explanations and amount of detail are determined by the needs of the average student and his/her capacity for concentration, absorption and memorising.

On the other hand, the responsibility for covering sufficiently even those aspects of grammar and usage that are essential for understanding and effective application has resulted in a very considerable amount of material from which teachers may need to select at their discretion.

Level

This book is intended for:

a Students with a basic knowledge of English who are moving towards an intermediate (possibly Cambridge First Certificate) level. The spoken responses suggested by the Practice material could be supplemented or replaced by written ones. Teachers of students at this level will probably wish to select and grade the material in conformity with the needs of their class.

b Intermediate to advanced students who need practice in expressing themselves creatively and fluently in the spoken language.

c Businessmen, scientists, doctors, technicians, interpreters, guides, personnel catering for tourists and others who, in the course of their jobs, travels and overseas residence, have to communicate with native English-speakers or others who share English as a common language.

Suggestions to teachers

Very many students are hesitant about expressing their ideas even in their own language and need a good deal of encouragement and practice in doing so in a foreign one. It is with this problem in mind that the following suggestions for presentation of the material are made.

Introduction of the learning material

The grammatical and other learning material is first presented by the teacher, probably with the help of the blackboard and with additional explanations (according to class level) and examples suggested both by the teacher and class members. In a single-language class there may be useful comparisons with related usage in the native language. An obvious example might be the past simple and present perfect tenses with their contrasting uses in English and a number of other languages.

Introduction of the practice material

The nature of the practice material can be explained, with special reference to the preceding learning material, and vocabulary and other special points can be discussed. One or two of the responses could be considered and discussed but, as explained below, most of these are suggested by the students after individual preparation.

Practice preparation at home

The class are then given the practice material to prepare for the next lesson. It is true that this is a *learning* rather than a *natural* situation but it is fully justified by the fact that:

1 the boredom of blank minds and interminable pauses which accompany the demand for immediate responses is avoided
2 the students have adequate time to think over what they have learned and to apply it to the responses they prepare
3 the responses are given by individual students selected in turn with pauses for other students to suggest alternatives. Mistakes can be corrected (with explanations from the teacher where desirable) and possibly more effective ideas can be added by the teacher. In this way each student has made an attempt, and has discovered whether he/she is right or wrong, and whether he/she has grasped the material being studied.

Discussion

The ideas expressed may stimulate discussion and it is up to the teacher to decide how much time can be given to this and what use can be made of it. In any case it should not be allowed to slide into the students' own language. How long it lasts must depend on how much teaching time is available and how useful the discussion is. In most cases it could go on for a minute or so before the teacher draws attention to the next sentence.

Correction The amount of correction and explanations and practice of the corrections made must depend on the discretion of the teacher, who will bear in mind that mistakes will be the result of:

1 the student's carelessness or concentration on other things: in other words, the student need not have made the mistake
2 ignorance, confusion, misunderstanding, own-language interference, over-reaching his/her language ability etc.

Correction in the first case is often unnecessary as the student may realise the mistake as soon as he/she has made it and correction takes up time unnecessarily. However, it may serve as a useful reminder both to the perpetrator and to the rest of the class and thus provide an opportunity to ram the point home.

Correction of the second case will probably depend on:

1 whether it can be useful to the class as a whole – the mistake may for example involve a confusion of the meanings of similar words (such as **bring, take, fetch**) which can be suitably dealt with at this point, and referred back to later.
2 whether the student involved asks for help (*Is it all right to say . . .?*)
3 the level of the mistake, as for example when a student reveals ignorance of something he/she has supposedly mastered long before.

In general it should be remembered that the aim of the responses is to encourage confidence and fluency: intelligent and useful correction can be valuable but it should interfere as little as possible with the promotion of these two essential achievements.

Revision Students will probably wish to record more suitable alternative responses in their files and exercise books, though they should be discouraged from using their course book for recording both these and their own original ideas and suggestions.

If time allows at the beginning of the following lesson, it is well worthwhile to use the unmarked course book to recall and revise the responses that have already been suggested. This will encourage the students to look through their corrected and recorded answers after the lesson (as otherwise they rarely do). The repetition is itself a valuable form of revision and is above all useful in securing genuine fluency as the responses are likely to be unhesitating. The whole exercise will normally take up no more than five or at the very most ten minutes of the lesson.

Part 1

Contents Verb tenses and verbal constructions

Section A Present simple and continuous tenses

Section B Past simple and past continuous tenses, **used to**

Section C Perfect tenses

Section D Future and conditional tenses

Section E Revision of tenses, reported speech

Section F Infinitives and participles

Section G Gerunds, clauses after certain verbs, **make** and **do, have** something **done**

Section A Present simple and continuous tenses

1 The present simple

Main uses

a To express a HABITUAL ACTION:
An action that happens ALL THE TIME, OFTEN, SOMETIMES, or NEVER is usually expressed by this tense.

A bookseller sells books.
A librarian doesn't sell them; he only lends them.
I often make mistakes.
As he has poor sight, he never drives in the dark.

Notes

1 Word order with adverbs of frequency:
He always/usually/never speaks English.
He doesn't always/normally/ever speak English.

2 Note the idiomatic use of the present continuous with **always** to express a habitual action, usually with some feeling, in particular annoyance.
He's always asking silly questions.

b In a few cases, to express FUTURE ARRANGEMENTS:
This form is often used in connection with travel arrangements, especially those appearing in a timetable, and in this case probably refers to habitual actions.
The train/boat/plane leaves at ten tomorrow morning.

c To express an ACTION THAT IS HAPPENING NOW, in the case of verbs which rarely or never have a present continuous form. These include **see, hear, smell, taste, know, say, believe, realise, want, seem** and **appear.** Other verbs are listed in Part 1, Section A5.
He says he wants to see you immediately.
I don't know what to do now.
I hope he realises we're here.

Notes

1 Distinguish between: *I think/believe he lives near here.*
and: *He always frowns when he is thinking.*

2 In the case of the verbs **see, hear, smell** and **taste**, the verb is often preceded by **can.**
Can you see that aeroplane?
I can hear somebody outside.

d 1 Instead of a future form in certain TIME CLAUSES (see Part 1, Section D5):
I'll tell you more when we meet.

2 Instead of the future form in certain CONDITIONS:
If he gets a university place he'll study medicine.

Practice

Affirmative answers

Answer these questions in complete sentences, using in your answer a present simple tense form.

EXAMPLE
When do people usually give presents to friends?
They usually give presents to friends on birthdays and at Christmas.

1 What do you do when you have a bad headache?
2 Which shoe do you normally put on first?
3 Do you always tip the waiter or only if he gives good service?
4 What do you usually say when you meet a friend in the street?
5 Why do Greenlanders rarely buy summer clothes?
6 How often does a clock strike thirteen?
7 How long do you think a flight from London to Paris takes?
8 What size shoes do you take?
9 What is one thing you know about the moon?
10 Do you walk to school or do you come by bus or car?
11 What colour do you most often wear?
12 At what age do you think children need most attention from their mothers?

Affirmative and negative answers

a Which of the following does a secretary often/sometimes/seldom do? Which of them doesn't she do?

1 get annoyed with her boss
2 shout at her boss
3 type letters
4 feel tired
5 answer the telephone
6 write appointments in her diary
7 do overtime
8 have dinner with her boss
9 file correspondence
10 earn more than her boss
11 change her job
12 marry her boss
13 ask for a rise
14 cook meals for the office staff
15 change her typewriter ribbon
16 receive visitors
17 take down dictation
18 make cups of tea

b Which of these things do you do every day, and which don't you do so often? If you don't do the action every day, say how often you do it.

EXAMPLES
read a newspaper
I read a newspaper every day.
write out a cheque
I don't write out a cheque every day. I only occasionally write out a cheque.

Here are some useful expressions:
every second day **once/twice/three times a week**
now and again **when I feel like it**
when I've got nothing else to do
sometimes **seldom** **never**
The last three can come before a verb. (See above, Note 1 under Main Uses **a.**)

1 get up before seven o'clock
2 shave
3 go for a walk
4 have an egg with your breakfast
5 drink instant coffee
6 wash up the breakfast things
7 daydream
8 listen to the weather forecast on the radio
9 play table tennis
10 go shopping
11 quarrel with your relations
12 decide to change your job or course of study
13 feel depressed
14 lose your temper

Asking questions

a An absent-minded intermediate or even an advanced student can on occasion make a mistake in framing the present simple question form. A lot of practice is needed before the change in word order and the introduction of **do/does** becomes completely automatic.

EXAMPLES
The subject is often short: *Do you sell string, please? What time does the museum open?*
but may be much longer: *Does that woman who's sitting alone at that table over there by the service door know you, by any chance?*

Here is some information about Kurt Kurheim:

Kurt Kurheim works as a bank clerk in the centre of Cologne. He lives (with his wife and eight children, three dogs, two cats and a hamster) in a large old house which belongs to the bank manager. His wife takes the three eldest children to school in their estate car so Kurt travels to work by underground train. His daily journey takes about half an hour but his single ticket costs very little. A friend usually gives him a lift home. Kurt leaves home (often in a great hurry) shortly before half past seven and gets to the bank just before eight. Fortunately he lives only a hundred metres from the nearest underground station. In February Kurt and his wife usually go to Bavaria for a week's skiing while the children stay with their grandparents in Cologne so that they don't miss school.

Ask as many questions about the passage as you can think of, using in each a present simple form, and starting with any of the following suitable interrogatives: **what? where? what kind of work? how many? which? how? why? how long? how much? what time? when? how far? who? whom? do/does?**
Get another student to provide a suitable answer.

EXAMPLES
What does Kurt do for a living?
He works as a bank clerk.
What kind of house does he live in?
He lives in a large, old one.
Who owns the house he lives in?
His boss owns it.

b Suggest questions introducing present simple forms to which the words and phrases numbered below could be answers. Vary the subjects of the questions, and try not to use the pronoun **you** too often.

EXAMPLE
About £5,000.
How much does a medium priced car cost nowadays?

1 At eight o'clock.
2 When they are sixty or sixty-five.
3 At the seaside.
4 Because I like it.
5 Platform four.
6 About a dozen.
7 In the White House.
8 Because I don't want to.
9 Once a year.
10 S - M - I - T - H - E.
11 About seventy kilos.
12 A Rolls-Royce.
13 About an hour.
14 In autumn.

c You are asking in your hotel for information about a guided tour of London. What questions do you ask in order to find out the following facts?

1 the tour departure point (start)
2 the departure time
3 the duration of the tour (last)
4 places of interest visited
5 cost
6 languages the guide is likely to speak
7 how to reserve a place in the coach and buy tickets

Can you think of any more questions you might want to ask?

---

2 Has, have (has got, have got)

With the meanings:

1 own: *Jane's got a motor scooter.*

2 be in charge of or control of: *He's got a well-paid job.*

3 have as part of oneself: *Most cats have got yellow eyes.*
The news reader has got a bad cold.

In speech, **has/have** as a main verb is usually followed by **got**.

NEGATIVES
1 *Jane hasn't got a car yet; she can't afford one.*
2 *We haven't got much time left.*
3 *You really haven't got much sense.*

QUESTIONS
1 *Have you got a cigarette you can let me have?*
2 *How much time have we got?*
3 *Why haven't those trees got any leaves on their upper branches?*

With other meanings **has/have** frequently replace other verbs in certain everyday expressions. In this case, **do/does** are used in negative and question forms.

have a meal (**eat**)
have a good time (**spend**)
have an exciting journey (**make**)
have something to drink/a cup of tea
have an interesting life (**lead**)
have a sleep/a break/a holiday/an English lesson etc.

Note
Compare: *I haven't got any cigarettes.* (**possess**)
with: *I don't have a cigarette with my coffee.* (**smoke**)

AFFIRMATIVE *He always has lunch between one and two.*

NEGATIVE *He doesn't have cheese after lunch.*

QUESTION *Does he have a rest after lunch?*

Note
In American usage negative and interrogative **do/does** are normal with all meanings of the verb **have. have got** is mainly British.

Practice

a Abigail the waitress is busy serving lunches in the Belvedere Restaurant. Which of the following: has she got? hasn't she got? does she have? doesn't she have?

EXAMPLES
long conversations with her favourite customers
She doesn't have long conversations with her favourite customers.
a cigarette in her mouth
She hasn't got a cigarette in her mouth.

1 a good memory
2 a university degree in law
3 free time between noon and two o'clock
4 comfortable shoes on
5 a lot to do, waiting on the many customers
6 a rich husband at home
7 a cup of tea before she starts work
8 aching feet at the end of the day
9 time off during the lunch hour
10 an expensive gold watch on her wrist
11 lunch with some of the diners
12 her dog with her
13 a scarf over her head
14 a cheerful expression on her face

b Ask questions, which the other students will answer, introducing **have you got?** or **do you have?**

EXAMPLES
Do you have a lot of free time?
No I don't. I've always got a lot to do.

Have you got any cigarettes on you?
No, I haven't. I don't smoke.

3 Can, should/ought to, must, have to

Meanings **a can**

1 Have the ability to:
We can all read and write, but can we all think clearly? I can't think clearly when I feel strongly.

Note
The verb **be able to** may replace **can** when it has the above meaning.

2 Colloquially, in place of **may**, expressing a request or permission:
Can I leave early today? Certainly you can.

3 To express willingness:
Can you help me? Yes, indeed I can.

4 As a form of assurance:
You can just leave everything to me.

5 In making a suggestion:
We can take some sandwiches with us.

6 Occasionally to express an impatient order:
You can just be quiet and do as you're told.

Practice

Suggest what you or someone else can say in each of the following situations. Add any information and ideas needed. Use **can** in your answer.

EXAMPLES
A travel guide is making suggestions to a group of tourists about how to spend an evening in the town they're visiting.
You can go to one of the two cinemas, though I'm afraid the films are in Spanish, and there's a very pleasant café you can visit.
A neighbour is looking after your cat while you're on holiday. She assures you that the animal will be well cared for.
Don't you worry about her, Mrs Mogg. You can be sure she's all right with me.

1 A policeman is asking you for your name and address.
2 You're suggesting what to take Aunt Matilda when you visit her in hospital.
3 Maureen's room is very untidy and Mother is telling her what to do about it.
4 A salesman is expressing willingness to deliver goods to your home at a certain time.
5 You're asking someone about his ability to play a certain game.
6 A shopkeeper is assuring somebody that something he is selling will give good service.

b can't

1 Lack of ability:
I'm sorry, I can't understand you.

2 When forbidding an action (= **may not**):
You can't park here, in front of my gate.

3 In making a suggestion:
Can't we ask the bank for a loan?

4 When making a request, often with annoyance or special need:
Can't you be a little quieter?
Can't I possibly have it by tomorrow?

5 Expressing disbelief:
You can't be hungry already, after such an enormous meal!

6 Indicating that something is impossible:
You can't go shopping this afternoon – the shops are closed.

Practice

Suggest what you or some other person might say in each of the following situations. Add any information and ideas needed. Use **can't** in your answer.

EXAMPLES
You're telling someone not to carry a suitcase. Why?
You can't carry that suitcase. It's far too heavy.
A suggestion about where to have lunch and why.
Can't we have lunch outside? It's such a lovely day.

1 Why it's impossible for somebody to go swimming this afternoon. (a rough sea)
2 You're expressing your inability to understand something. What and why?
3 You have been discussing for some time where to spend the following free day and what to do.
4 One of your family breaks a plate, the second one that day. You're angry about it.
5 Someone has said that an acquaintance gets a large salary. You're expressing your disbelief. Why don't you believe it?
6 You're explaining why it's impossible for you to take any photographs.
7 You're telling somebody not to smoke in a certain place. Why?
8 For no apparent reason a student always comes late and disturbs the class. Without much hope the teacher requests him not to do this.

---

c **should/ought to**

1 To express a duty:
I should take more exercise. (but I probably won't)

2 To express a right to something:
I should get more money for all the work I do. (I have the right to it, but . . .)

3 To suggest a possibility:
He should be home by now. (We expect this, but we are not quite sure.)

Notes
1 **ought to** can replace **should** in each of the above cases:
I ought to take . . . I ought to get . . . He ought to be. . .
2 The use of these verbs may involve a negative implication, as indicated after each example. The negative forms **shouldn't** and **oughtn't to** very often suggest that the person speaking or being spoken to is unlikely to make any change.
I really shouldn't smoke so much. (It's bad for me, but . . .)
You shouldn't eat so many sweets. (but mother is pessimistic)

d **must**

1 Expresses a personal feeling of obligation or necessity:
I must write that letter before I go to bed tonight.
You must be quieter.

2 Indicates what in the circumstances appears a strong probability:
He must be over eighty. He served in the First World War.

Note
For **must** with a following perfect form, see Part 1, Section C2.

e **must not/need not**
1 **must not** = it is forbidden:
Passengers must not cross the line.

2 **need not, don't need to** = it isn't necessary:
We needn't buy any petrol yet. The tank's still half full.

Note
need not and **don't need to** are intransitive, so cannot be followed by a noun or pronoun object.
You need not wait
You don't need to wait.
(The first of these is more usual.)
Compare: *You don't need a coat on this afternoon.*

f **have to** expresses unavoidable necessity as distinct from personal obligation.
If you want to get about in Venice, you have to go by boat or walk.
As Jim's a policeman, he often has to work at night.

Notes
1 **must** and **have to** are often used interchangeably in conversation.
2 **I've got to go now** is common in spoken language.
3 NEGATIVE
I haven't got to go to work tomorrow.
This form often expresses an immediate or future action.
I don't have to work on Saturdays.
This may express a habitual action.
4 INTERROGATIVE
Have I got to answer all these questions?
Do I have to answer all these questions?
The meaning here is almost identical, the second example being slightly more formal.

Practice

Which of the following: should you do? shouldn't you do? must you do? mustn't you do? needn't you do?

1 lose your passport when on holiday
2 talk too much about yourself
3 sign your name at the end of a letter
4 always have your name and address on you
5 drive through a built-up area at a hundred kilometres an hour
6 hurry when you've still got plenty of time
7 speak with your mouth full
8 visit the dentist regularly
9 go swimming after a heavy meal
10 read intelligent newspapers
11 drive or cycle without lights after dark
12 memorise new English vocabulary
13 always speak English perfectly
14 have a ticket when you travel by train
15 cheat in an examination
16 eat too much sugar
17 read through a contract before you sign it
18 practise these forms any longer

All forms

a Give your own ideas about the following matters, using: **can/can't**
should/shouldn't (**ought to/oughtn't to**)
must/mustn't/needn't
have to/don't have to (**haven't got to**)

1 When can you think most clearly: in the morning, in the afternoon or in the evening?

2 How often should you clean your teeth?
3 Where must you stop when you're driving?
4 When do you have to stop when you're driving?

5 How long do most people have to work before they can get a retirement pension?
6 Which men needn't waste time every day shaving?
7 Should every young person get a grant (money from the State) to pay his or her expenses while at university?
8 Why can't most Europeans spend their annual holiday in Japan or New Zealand?
9 What should you say if you have to interrupt somebody?
10 What do most children have to do every weekday?
11 What kind of person should a nurse be?
12 How can a fat man lose weight?
13 What mustn't you forget to do before you leave a restaurant?
14 Suggest one reason why you shouldn't criticise other people?
15 When must you get up early in the morning?
16 When needn't you get up early in the morning?
17 What don't you need to do if you're a native-born English speaker?

b Which of the following: can you do? can't you do? should you do? shouldn't you do? must you do? mustn't you do? needn't you do? have you got to do? (do you have to do?) don't you have to do? (haven't you got to do?)

1 pay income tax
2 do the washing up
3 ski well
4 buy petrol if you run a car
5 do plenty of exercise every day
6 read small print in a bad light
7 spread false gossip about other people
8 spend some time in Britain to improve your English
9 own a television set
10 remember to return your library books
11 know how to type well
12 lose your temper
13 buy stamps for letters
14 clean your muddy shoes before wearing them again
15 show your passport whenever you deposit money in a bank
16 drive a car without insurance cover
17 learn some Dutch before visiting the Netherlands
18 have at least two hot meals every day
19 waste electricity and other fuel
20 do night work
21 travel to school or work by public transport
22 fill in a lot of forms
23 revise all you've learnt in this lesson

4 The present continuous

Uses

a To express an ACTION THAT IS HAPPENING NOW:
We are/We're learning English.
We are not/aren't doing maths.

Compare: *He lives/works in Manchester.* (This is his home town or normal place of work.)
with: *He is living/working in Manchester.* (for a certain time only)

b To express an ACTION THAT COVERS THE PRESENT TIME, though it need not be happening at this minute:
They're looking for somewhere to live.

c To indicate an ARRANGED FUTURE ACTION:
Compare: *I'm visiting great-grandmother tomorrow.*
with: *I'll visit great-grandmother tomorrow if I have time.*

Note
An arranged future is often a near future, but this is not always the case. A man of forty might say:
I'm retiring at fifty-five, and then I'm buying a home for myself in a warm, sunny country.

d With **always**, or a word of similar meaning, to express a HABITUAL ACTION, usually when some feeling, often one of annoyance, is involved.

Compare: *He always asks intelligent questions.*
with: *He's always asking silly questions.*

Practice

a Make statements, affirmative or negative, in answer to the following questions. Each answer should include a form of the present continuous. In cases where you are asked about an action you are not doing, give a negative answer. Suggest which of the uses explained above is involved in each case.

EXAMPLES
What are you looking at?
I'm looking at the question I'm answering. (now)

Why are you using your dictionary?
I'm not using my dictionary? (now)

What are you saving money for?
I'm saving to buy some hi-fi equipment. (an action covering the present time)

How soon are you having lunch?
I'm having it in an hour's time. (arranged future)

1 Where's your teacher standing or sitting?
2 Are you enjoying that glass of milk you're drinking?
3 Which student's answering this question?
4 What international subject are a lot of people discussing nowadays?
5 What are you doing after this lesson?
6 Mention something you're not doing tomorrow.
7 What novel are you writing now?
8 Are most of your fellow students wearing light-coloured or dark-coloured clothes?
9 Who is attracting a lot of attention in your country just now? What is he/she doing to attract it?
10 What are you doing next Saturday evening?

b What are these people doing: now? tomorrow? during the period which includes the present moment (though not necessarily at this moment)? What aren't they doing at these times?

EXAMPLES
Garrick Irving, the actor
Garrick is having a rest before this evening's performance.
He isn't attending a rehearsal.

He's performing twice tomorrow: at a matinée and in the evening.
He isn't going to a party after the evening performance.

He's writing an autobiography.
He isn't thinking of retiring yet.

1 Harry Hack, the politician
2 a coachload of holidaymakers touring Italy
3 Sue Smart, the air hostess
4 Evelyn Lamb, housewife and mother
5 a group of workers who are on strike

c The following are answers to questions. Each question has included a form of the present continuous. Suggest possible questions.

EXAMPLE
No, it isn't. The sun's shining.
Is it still raining?

1 Probably because he's hungry.
2 Next Saturday.
3 When I can afford it.
4 Because the sun's so bright.
5 At least two.
6 So that I can find out exactly where I am.
7 Sunbathing all day, I hope.
8 A week.
9 High-heeled suede ones.
10 Susan. She's always very helpful.

---

5 Verbs that rarely have a continuous form

Some of the following verbs may be used with a continuous form in expressing certain ideas, but normally the corresponding simple form is used. This applies to past, present and future time.

see	**know**	**think**	**want**	**belong**	**seem**
hear	**understand**	**believe**	**need**	**owe**	**appear**
smell	**wonder**	**realise**	**like**	**own**	**matter**
taste	**suppose**	**remember**	**dislike**	**contain**	
		forget	**refuse**		
		say			

There are also other less commonly used verbs, which include **hate, loathe, consist** (**of**) and **concern**.

General characteristics

In most cases, the verbs suggest no definite action. When a person *sees, knows, wants* or *owes* something, no clear action is happening. Compare **see/look at, know/learn, know/get to know** and **want/demand.**

Notice the distinctions between **learn** and **get to know**, and **know** and **get to know.**

I'm learning Thai now that I'm in Bangkok. I'm getting to know quite a lot of the local people.

I don't know any of my neighbours, but I'm getting to know some interesting people in my job.

Special cases

a **see** can have the meaning 'meet' in expressing a future arrangement.
I am seeing him tomorrow.

With a similar meaning, it can express an action covering the present period.
You're seeing a lot of him nowadays.

b Compare: *I think he's abroad just now.*
with: *I'm thinking about your suggestion.*

c Compare these uses of **smell**, **taste**, and **feel**:
This rose smells beautiful. (It has a beautiful smell.)
She is smelling the rose. (using her nose)

This soup tastes odd.
The chef is tasting the soup critically.

Some material feels soft and silky.
She is feeling the material to see if it feels soft.

d A few of the verbs listed may occasionally be used with a continuous form.
I'm wondering whether I ought to see a solicitor about it.
As time goes by, I'm realising more and more what a mistake I made.
As I get to know her better, I'm realising how kind she is.

In each case, the process is a gradual one.

e **appear**, with the meaning 'take part in a play or a film' may have a continuous form.
Dahlia Davenport is now appearing in the film version of the play.

f The verbs **see**, **hear**, **smell**, **taste**, and **understand** often follow **can**.
I can see a spelling mistake here.
Can you hear my radio in your flat?
I can't understand your writing. (See page 10, 1c.)

Practice

a Answer these questions, repeating in your answers the main verb or verbs of the question.

1 What can you see immediately in front of you?
2 Why are you looking at it?
3 At what times can you hear the news on the radio?
4 Are you listening to this evening's news on the radio or are you watching it on television?
5 What do some perfumes smell of?
6 Why is Muriel's dog smelling her shopping bag so excitedly?
7 Which of these tastes worst: sour milk, bad fish, burnt porridge or mouldy bread?
8 Is it Mr or Mrs Chaffinch who is tasting the bird's nest soup with some hesitation?
9 Which dialect in your own country can't you understand?
10 What do you think about during the five minutes after you wake up?
11 Are you now thinking only about these questions or about something more interesting? In the latter case, what are you thinking about?
12 Why do you sometimes refuse an invitation to a party?
13 Which of these do you like and which do you dislike?

tea with milk in it	fresh brown eggs
cream cakes	watching sport on television
pop or rock music	coca cola
brightly-coloured clothes	formal dinner parties
very hot weather	long country walks
noisy parties	curry
cats	playing badminton

14 What clubs, libraries or other groups do you belong to?
15 Which of the following does a successful person owe most to: ability, education, hard work, or luck?
16 Which of these do you own?
a motor-scooter
the clothes you're wearing
your home
a transistor radio
some paperback books
a pocket calculator
shares in a company
an aeroplane
17 What do these contain: a balloon, a safe, a box marked *fragile*?

b Finish these sentences.

1 I never see him driving a car. I suppose . . .
2 I can't find my key anywhere. I wonder . . .
3 I don't know exactly how far it is from New York to London but I believe . . .
4 When I make out a cheque I don't always remember . . .
5 I suggest we offer the job to Miss Smart. She seems . . .
6 If you're cheerful, healthy and have good friends it doesn't matter . . .

Short answers

The following questions are for revision of the tenses and verbs throughout this section. They contain examples of:
the present simple tense
the present continuous tense
to be as a main verb
has/have (**got**) as a main verb
can **should** **must** **have to**

Your answers to the questions should express your own opinions and ideas and should consist of a related short answer followed by a statement, either immediately or as a separate sentence. This statement should introduce one of the tenses or verbs listed above, though not necessarily the same one as that in the question. Answers can be affirmative or negative as you consider suitable.

Explain the particular use of the present simple or present continuous form which appears in the question. This is not necessary in the case of **has/have, can, should, must** or **have to.**

EXAMPLES
Are you smoking?
Yes I am. I always smoke when I'm studying.
or:
No, I'm not. I don't smoke.
(The present continuous tense refers to what is happening now.)

Must drivers always stop to allow people to use a pedestrian crossing?
Yes, they must. It is the pedestrians who have the right of way.
or:
No, they needn't, unless someone is about to step on to it.
or:
No, they mustn't, if there is a danger of a following car running into their own.

Note
Drivers don't *have* to stop at a pedestrian crossing as they do when somebody wants to get out.

1 Is it raining now?
2 Do you often use a typewriter?
3 Can you make a telephone call in French?
4 Must people in your country report any change of address to the local authority (or the police)?
5 Must they ask for permission to go abroad?
6 Do they have to wear very thick clothes to keep warm in winter?
7 Should all children have some kind of further education until they're eighteen?
8 Have most cars got six wheels? (Where are they?)
9 Are you having lunch with anybody tomorrow?
10 Do you have to use English very much in your daily life?
11 Have you got to cook a meal when you get home today?
12 Do you like dogs?
13 Is there a map on one of the walls of this room?
14 Should doctors always tell their patients the truth?
15 Are you studying or training for some kind of career?
16 Are politicians the most essential people to the community?
17 Must you wait until the traffic lights for pedestrians change to green before you cross a street?

18 Do you enjoy camping?
19 Are you spending next weekend at the seaside?
20 Do you pay income tax?
21 Are prices gradually rising in your country?
22 Do you have to get up early on weekdays?
23 Are you writing your autobiography?
24 Is this notice likely to be correct: 'Students cannot smoke in the college canteen'?

6 Passive forms and uses: present simple and continuous tenses

Formation of the passive

a PRESENT SIMPLE

present simple of the verb **to be**	past participle
I am	*paid.*
A book is	*written.*
We are	*told.*
Newspapers are	*printed.*

b PRESENT CONTINUOUS

present continuous of the verb **to be**	past participle
I am being	*interviewed.*
Are you being	*served?* (in a shop)
The Cup Final isn't being	*televised.*
Aren't the rooms being	*cleaned?*

Uses of the passive

a When the person doing the action is unknown, unimportant or obvious:
Pancakes are made from flour, eggs and milk.
The airport is being enlarged.
Letters are delivered twice a day.

b When the person or other agent doing the action is important, unexpected, or in some other way needs to be emphasised:
The Annual Flower Show is organised by our local police force.
The orchestra is being conducted by a girl of sixteen.

Compare: *His secretary is preparing the report for him.*
with: *The report is being prepared by a team of experts.*

A note on the use of the pronoun 'one'

a The passive can be used in the case of TRANSITIVE verbs, i.e. those that can take a direct object.

	SUBJECT	VERB	OBJECT
ACTIVE:	*They*	*organise*	*excursions every weekend.*

	NEW SUBJECT	PASSIVE FORM
PASSIVE:	*Excursions*	*are organised every weekend.*

In the case of a transitive verb, when the doer of the action is unknown or general, the passive construction is normal. Unlike in some other languages, the impersonal **one** is rarely used as a subject of a transitive verb.
English is spoken here. (not: *One speaks English here.)*
It is said that . . . (not: *One says that . . .*)

b In more formal English, **one** is sometimes used as a subject of a verb normally used INTRANSITIVELY, that is, without an object, as no passive form is possible.
If one spends too much time on one's own, one can please oneself about what one does but one may become rather selfish.

c The forms **you, we** and **they** are commonly used in everyday speech to express an impersonal action and can be used with both transitive and intransitive verbs and in active and passive constructions.
You can sleep nine or ten hours and still feel tired when you wake up.
They print a lot of rubbish in most women's magazines nowadays.
We aren't taught at school many of the things we really need to know.

Practice

Present simple

a Where do the following things happen?

EXAMPLES
the painting of pictures
Most pictures are painted in a studio or out of doors.
the growing of sugar
Sugar is grown in many tropical areas, including the West Indies.

1 the storing of perishable foods
2 the mining of coal (what region?)
3 the examination of passports
4 the performance of plays
5 the showing of films
6 the carrying out of scientific research

b When, or how often, do these things happen?

1 the giving of presents to friends and relations
2 the closing of shops on weekdays
3 the serving of dinner in most restaurants (between which times?)
4 the holding of the annual school examinations (what month?)
5 the reading of your gas or electricity meter

c How do these things happen?

EXAMPLE
the painting of pictures
Pictures are painted with a brush.

1 the writing of letters
2 the cutting of bread
3 the measurement of cloth (tape measure)
4 the cleaning of shoes
5 the driving of most trains in your country (the form of power used?)

d What do people use these things for?

EXAMPLE
a ping-pong ball
A ping-boll ball is used for playing table tennis with.

1 a saucepan
2 glasses (for the eyes)
3 a glass
4 a chair
5 a dictionary
6 string
7 shampoo
8 a camera

Present continuous

a Suggest ideas about where these things are happening at this moment or are arranged for some future time.

EXAMPLE
the marriage of Sabrina and Simon
Sabrina and Simon are being married at St Luke's Church.

1 the shooting of the film *Murder under the Midnight Sun*
2 the discussion of the new European trade agreement
3 the holding of the next meeting of the Town Council
4 the servicing of Barbara's car
5 the interrogation of the suspected spy

b At what time in the future might these things be happening? Suggest possibilities.

EXAMPLE
the development of new industries in the north-west
New industries are being developed in the north-west during the next five years.

1 the opening of a new supermarket in the town centre
2 the extension of the M80 motorway
3 the publication of Karen's latest novel
4 the broadcasting of Hilary's new play
5 the launching of the next spaceship to investigate the outer planets

With emphasis on the agent

Present simple:
Who does, or might be responsible for doing, the following things?

EXAMPLE
the making of appointments to see the doctor
Appointments to see the doctor are made by his receptionist, Miss Jones.

1 the treatment of people with emotional problems
2 the making of laws in your country
3 the care of hospital patients (care for)
4 the supervision of candidates doing an examination (invigilator)
5 the conducting of a well-known orchestra (which?)

Present continuous:
Who is, or might be, responsible for doing these things at the present time or in the arranged future?

EXAMPLE
singing the part of Madame Butterfly
The part of Madame Butterfly is being sung by Miss Bella Cantata. (an announcement from the stage)

6 directing *Galaxy Goddess* (a film now being made)
7 giving an important lecture on 'Relativity' tomorrow
8 feeding Mrs Spratt's cat while she's on holiday
9 answering this question
10 the meeting at the airport of the visiting American president (suggest a name)

---

7 Short answers expressing some personal reactions

Here are some short answers in which the speaker is expressing his or her reactions to the statement or questions he or she has just heard.

The responses may express UNDERSTANDING, CONFIRMATION, an OPINION, AGREEMENT or DISAGREEMENT.

Each short response consists of (a) a subject (often **I**) and (b) a present simple form.

Uses

a UNDERSTANDING
I see. — negative: *I'm afraid I don't (quite) understand.*

b CONFIRMATION
I know. — *I don't know.*

c AN OPINION

I hope so.		*I hope not.*
I'm afraid so.		*I'm afraid not.*
I think so.	similar in	*I don't think so.*
I believe so.	meaning	*I don't believe so.*

d AGREEMENT AND DISAGREEMENT
I agree. — *I disagree./I don't agree.*
I suppose so. (a weak or reluctant agreement)

Examples:

'Has Manfred got a university degree?'	*'I think so/I believe so. But I don't know if it's British or German.'*
'You realise we'll have to leave home at six tomorrow morning?'	*'Yes, I know. What an awful idea!'*
'Are you going to your cousin's wedding reception?'	*'I suppose so, though I'm not very keen, as I don't know any of the other guests.'*

Practice

a Respond to the following questions and statements with one (or more than one where this is possible) of the above forms. Then add a following comment or statement.

EXAMPLE
Is your father getting any better?
I'm afraid not. The most recent medical report was very depressing.

1 'Is London bigger than Tokyo?' 'No, . . .'
2 'Are you getting an increase in salary next month?' 'Well, . . .'
3 'Are you being considered for promotion soon?' 'No, . . .'
4 'Must you really read all those books for your exam?' 'Well, they're all included in the syllabus so . . .'
5 'Can I explain it like this? Our actual headquarters are in Bristol but it's our overseas department in York that handles most of our foreign trade.' 'Oh, . . .'
6 'My opinion is that we should raise prices and thus raise profits. What do you think?' 'No, . . .'
7 'I've heard that Douglas is retiring soon on account of his poor health.' 'Yes, . . .'
8 'Is it true that your firm's closing down shortly?' 'Yes, . . .'
9 'I think that too many schoolchildren learn too little about too much nowadays and too few of them know much about anything.' 'Yes, . . .'
10 'Is Tirana the capital of Albania?' 'Let me think. Yes, . . .'
11 'Are they offering you the use of a company car as part of the remuneration for the job they're offering you?' 'Well, . . .'
12 'Of course they could expect you to pay the insurance, road tax, garage rental and for servicing and petrol.' 'Oh, . . .'

b Ask one another questions or make statements that are of a type that can be followed by one of these forms and suggest suitable responses. Some possible subjects can be everyday and holiday arrangements, opinions about things happening in the world and in your own country, reasons for your likes and dislikes.

EXAMPLES
Are you spending your holiday in Scotland?
I hope so. It's such a beautiful country.
Do you understand everything I say?
I'm afraid not. But I understand most of it.

c Make statements which are likely to get one of these responses:
I agree. I disagree/I don't agree.
I see. I know.
Add suitable statements of your own.

EXAMPLES
'Daily exercise does you good.'
'I know. But I go everywhere by car and I'm still healthy.'

'Women are more intelligent than men.'
'Oh, I agree. But what good's my opinion? I'm only a woman.'

'You should turn the key twice to the right.'
'I see. And then the door should be securely locked.'

---

8 Responses expressing a similar situation to the one already stated

Examples

a AFFIRMATIVE
So am I. *So can we.* *So does mine.* *So must everybody.*
So is Elizabeth. *So can they.* *So do my parents.*

b NEGATIVE
Nor/Neither are you. *Nor/Neither can she.*
Nor/Neither have we. *Nor/Neither must anyone else.*
Nor/Neither should you.

Nor/Neither do Americans.
Nor/Neither does plastic.

Notes

1 Either **nor** or **neither** can be used in the negative form. Because each is negative, no other negative form is needed in the response.

2 Responses of this kind contain past, present and future verb forms. Present forms only are used in the practice below.

Examples of these forms in use

AFFIRMATIVE

'I'm tired.'	*'So am I. We both work too hard.'*
'Adam's got five hungry children to feed.'	*'So has his wife. And she has to do the cooking.'*
'My hair looks awful.'	*'So does mine. Sun and salt water don't do it any good.'*

NEGATIVE

'We aren't satisfied with our hotel room.'	*'Nor are we. Ours is much too small, dark and noisy.'*
'Politicians shouldn't talk so much.'	*'Neither should some of their less well-informed critics.'*
'Some employees don't work very hard.'	*'Nor do some bosses, but they get paid much more.'*
'My son never gets a bad report from school.'	*'Neither does mine. I don't allow him to.'*

Notes

1 Possible responses to **has/have got to** include:

'I've got to leave now.' *'So have I. I've got a bus to catch.'*

'Some doctors have to work twelve hours a day.'
'So do most housewives, without being paid for it.'

2 Responses of this kind can form part of the preceding statement:

Not only news is broadcast on the BBC World Service, but so are many other interesting programmes.

Dogs don't like cats, and nor do mice. But I do, when they behave themselves.

Practice

Add to these statements responses suggesting a similar situation, affirmative or negative as suitable. Follow each with some other remark as in the examples above.

1 I'm bored with this film.
2 India has got a very large population.
3 I really can't understand what he's talking about.
4 I must remember to buy some more coffee.
5 Our house hasn't got central heating.
6 The police shouldn't carry guns.
7 We stay in youth hostels when we're touring.
8 I've got to go to the library.
9 My son can play chess better than I can.
10 Teachers have to keep up to date with new ideas.
11 We're not interested in going to the club social tomorrow.
12 You should save more money.
13 Most children enjoy reading adventure stories and ...
14 My husband never gives me any help with the housework.
15 Our neighbours aren't very friendly.
16 Too much sugar in your diet isn't good for you.
17 Veronica doesn't know anything about bringing up children and ...
18 Elephants can't fly and ...
19 Telephone bills are sent out four times a year and ...
20 Rome is an ancient capital city and ...
21 You mustn't order other people about.
22 The cost of electricity isn't being subsidised by the Government ...
23 Children should be seen and not heard.
24 I'm tired of giving these responses.

Section B Past simple and past continuous tenses, used to

1 Past simple: active voice

Affirmative forms

a WEAK FORMATIONS
Examples:

hope → *hoped*	**wait** → *waited* /weɪtɪd/	**hop** → *hopped*
walk → *walked*	**add** → *added* /ædɪd/	**hurry** → *hurried*

b STRONG FORMATIONS
Examples:

eat → *ate*	**go** → *went*	**blow** → *blew*
drink → *drank*	**come** → *came*	**fly** → *flew*
speak → *spoke*	**see** → *saw*	**take** → *took*
am/is → *was*	**has/have** → *had*	**must** → *had to*

c **can** →
1 *could* =
a) had the ability to
b) had permission to

He could answer the questions in either French or German.
This could mean (a) that he knew both languages, or (b) that this was allowed.

2 *was able to* = had the ability to
He was able to speak both languages.

Uses

a The past simple expresses a STATE WHICH EXISTED or an ACTION WHICH IS NOW FINISHED. The emphasis is on the action itself, or on the surrounding circumstances at the time, and not on the present effect of the action, as often in the case of the present perfect.
Compare: *I saw you sunbathing on the beach yesterday.*
with: *I've seen you somewhere before.* (I have at this moment a vague recollection of you.)

Notes
1 The present perfect is normally used if the action happened in the same period as the present time (e.g. today). However, the past simple is commonly used if it is clear that the action is finished.
Compare: *I had my breakfast early today.*
with: *I've had too much breakfast today.* (I don't want any lunch.)
2 The finished past time is associated with the past simple and does not apply in the case of a SECOND CONDITIONAL (see Part 1, Section D13).
If you left within the next hour, you would be there by midnight.

b The actions expressed may have:
1 happened in isolation: *He drove to work yesterday.*
2 happened repeatedly: *He drove to work every day.*
3 lasted for a certain time: *He drove for three hours.*

Note
Where there is a strong emphasis on the DURATION of the action, the past continuous is commonly used.
Compare: *He drove for three hours yesterday.*
with: *He was driving for the whole of yesterday.*
In most cases, however, the past simple can effectively express duration.

Practice

Answer each of these questions in a complete sentence, choosing one of the suggested alternatives.

EXAMPLE
Did Dick have to pay a parking fine, or did he get to his car before the parking warden?
He had to pay a parking fine.
or: He got to his car before the parking warden.

1 Was Winston Churchill British or American?
2 Was there a lot of rain yesterday, or only a little, or was it quite dry?
3 Were there a few students absent last lesson or was everybody there?
4 Were you tired when you woke this morning or did you feel ready for anything?
5 Did you have a warm or a cold meal yesterday evening?
6 Could you stay up as long as you liked as a child or did you have to be in bed by a certain time each evening?
7 Did you have to help your parents at that time or could you do as you liked with your free time?
8 Were most of our great-great-grandparents able to spend holidays abroad or were they lucky to get away at all?
9 Did you sleep well or badly last night?
10 Did the earliest human beings eat raw or cooked meat?
11 Did you stay at home when you last had a cold or did you go to work or school as usual?
12 Did you drink more coffee or more tea yesterday?
13 Did Christopher Columbus think that the world was round or flat?
14 When you last sent a letter, did you write your address on the back of the envelope or at the top of the letter?
15 Did you stick the stamp in the right-hand or the left-hand corner of the envelope?

Short answers AFFIRMATIVE AND NEGATIVE FORMS

be	*'Were you here yesterday?'* *'Yes, I was./No, I wasn't.'*
have	*'Did we have a lesson then?'* *'Yes, we did./No, we didn't.'*
can	*'Could primitive people count?'* *'Yes, they could./No, they couldn't.'*
must (**have to**)	*'Did you have to work hard at school today?'* *'Yes, I did./No, I didn't.'*
talk (weak/regular verb)	*'Did you talk before you walked?'* *'Yes, I did./No, I didn't.'*
come (strong/irregular verb)	*'Did the dustmen come yesterday?'* *'Yes, they did./No, they didn't.'*

Practice

a Give suitable answers to these questions.

1 Was it a cold day yesterday?
2 Were you born on a Thursday?
3 Was there any interesting news on the radio yesterday evening?
4 Were there printed books in Ancient Greece?
5 Was I (the writer of this book) present at your last lesson?
6 Did we have lunch together the day before yesterday?
7 Were the police at your home the other day? (they)
8 Could you hear the answer to the last question?
9 Were you able to swim when you were five years old?
10 Did you have eggs for breakfast this morning?
11 Was your teacher in a bad temper in your last lesson?
12 Did people have to pay income tax in the Middle Ages?
13 Was your great-grandmother able to drive a car?
14 Did people ever grow food in what is now the Sahara Desert?
15 Did you have a bicycle while you were at school?
16 Did you have to go to the bank yesterday?
17 Were dinosaurs able to fly?
18 Did you feel depressed when you read this morning's papers?

b Answer each of these questions in two sentences. The first should be a negative short answer, the second an affirmative statement. The verb in the second sentence can be a different one from that in the first but it should have a past simple form. The words in brackets may suggest ideas but need not be used.

EXAMPLES
Were you in Scotland last week?
No, I wasn't. I was in China.
Did Sam catch any fish at the weekend?
No, he didn't. But he caught a very bad cold.
Did your solicitor give you any useful advice in his letter?
No, he didn't. He only sent me a bill.

1 Were there a lot of housewives on the early train? (office-workers)
2 Did you eat your picnic lunch in the rain?
3 Did early farmers have tractors? (horses)
4 Were eighteenth-century doctors able to carry out painless operations? (no anaesthetics)
5 Were there many spectators at yesterday's football match?
6 Could the early Romans build airports?
7 Did Rembrandt write a lot of poetry?
8 Did you drink cocoa with your lunch?
9 Did you go to the ice rink yesterday evening?
10 Did you have to pay duty on the chocolates you brought back from France? (perfume)
11 Did the early Romans speak Roman?
12 Did Jane Plain win the beauty contest?
13 Did you get a Rolls-Royce for your birthday present?
14 Were early sailors able to find their way with the help of a compass? (steer by the stars)
15 Did you feel pleased when you just missed the train?

Affirmative and negative statements

Which of the following did you do or didn't you do before or during a holiday (real or fictional). Follow your response with another statement (affirmative or negative) which adds to, explains, or comments on your response and includes a present or past simple verb form. In some cases the verbs **want**, **think**, **intend** and **hope** may prove useful. Some slight changes can be made in the words of the opening statement where necessary. The pronoun in each case can be **I** or **we**.

EXAMPLES
draw a lot of money out of my bank account
I didn't draw much money out of my bank account as I wanted to be sure of still having some money in it when I came back.
discuss your plans with friends
I discussed my plans with a few friends, as I hoped they could give me some useful advice.
have a meal in the plane
I didn't have a meal in the plane. I didn't even travel by plane.
travel with your family
I didn't travel with my family. I haven't got a family.

a Before the holiday:
1 start planning well in advance
2 decide to spend your holiday at the seaside
3 book accommodation in a luxury hotel

4 buy your tickets at a travel office
5 take out a holiday accident insurance
6 buy new clothes to take with you
7 ask a neighbour to look after your cat or dog
8 do your packing well before departure
9 carry a lot of foreign money in cash
10 put your passport in a safe but easily accessible place
11 leave home very early in the morning
12 have to carry your luggage as far as the station
13 take a taxi to the departure point
14 fly to Switzerland

b During the holiday:
1 get into conversation with somebody (anybody) interesting on the journey
2 have an enjoyable journey
3 arrive in the middle of the night
4 get a good first impression of the place
5 notice a considerable difference in the weather
6 stay with friends or relatives
7 spend the first day looking around
8 change cheques in the hotel
9 do a lot of shopping
10 prepare your own meals
11 speak the local language
12 lie on the beach sunbathing most of the time
13 take a lot of photographs
14 lose your way in a strange place
15 suffer from indigestion as a result of overeating
16 occasionally feel bored
17 find the local people friendly
18 come home a lot poorer than when you left

c Suggest other things that you did or didn't do while on holiday, using a past simple form in referring to each of them.

EXAMPLES
I went skiing every day though snow conditions weren't always ideal.
We went on an excursion through the Black Forest but it poured with rain all day.

Question forms

be	*(Why) was he/were you (annoyed)? was/were there? wasn't he (interested)? were/weren't you (hungry)?*
have	*(When) did you have (lunch)? (What) had you got (with you)? Didn't you have (enough time)? Hadn't you got (any money)?*
can	*Could you/Couldn't you (hear us)? (How) were they able to find you?*
must	*(How long) did they have to (wait)? Didn't you have to (pay)?*
should	*(How much) should I have (paid)? Shouldn't I have (said that)?*
walk (weak verb)	*(How far) did you and your friend walk? Didn't you walk home?*
choose (strong verb) (past affirmative: **chose**)	*(What colour dress) did your mother choose?*

Practice

The restaurant

a Marcus Merrimay and his wife Naomi had dinner in a restaurant the other day. Marcus arranged to meet Naomi after he left his office for the day.

Ask as many questions as you can think of about their visit to the restaurant. One person can ask a question and another person can answer it, using his/her own ideas. Notice that no details are given about where the restaurant is, its surroundings, what it is like or why they decided to go there. Use mainly past simple question forms, with an occasional present simple. The forms **I'd like** and **would you like** are also possible.

Use as many different opening interrogatives as you can think of, including the following:

what? which? who? where? when? how? why? what time? what colour? what kind of? what was/were . . . like? how long? how soon? how much? how many? how far? Also use verbal inversions such as: **was it/there? did they decide?** and so on.

Your questions can concern everything that happened from the time Marcus left his office to meet Naomi until the time they left the restaurant.

EXAMPLES
'Why did they go to this particular restaurant?'
'They often went there because they knew the food was always good.'
'Which table did they choose?'
'They chose one near the window so they could watch the passers-by.'

b Here is the menu that the waiter gave them. The price is fixed and they can choose one item from each course (meat together with vegetables for the main course).

MENU

starters
Mushroom Soup
Shrimp Cocktail
Fruit Juice

main course
Roast Beef and Yorkshire Pudding
Chicken Curry with Rice
Cold Chicken or Lamb with Salad
Roast/Fried/Creamed Potatoes
Peas/French Beans/Cauliflower/Brussels Sprouts

dessert
Apple Pie with Cream
Fruit Salad and Ice Cream
Cheese (Cheddar/Stilton/Camembert/Bel Paese) and Biscuits
Coffee

Ask questions and suggest answers about this menu. These could include:

1 what the Merrimays decided to have/not to have (why), chose, preferred, wanted to know more about, disliked etc.
2 their feelings about what they got
3 suggestions and recommendations from the waiter (including wine)
4 what some of the items were like, their contents, cooking and taste

c Ask questions about your personal choices from this menu and what you ordered, ate, drank, enjoyed, disliked in a recent visit to a restaurant or café. Each question and answer should include a past simple verbal form or, occasionally, a present simple form. Make use of as many of the interrogative openings in (**a**) as are suitable.

EXAMPLES
'What kind of salad was there with the cold chicken?'
'It consisted of chopped lettuce, tomato and cucumber.'
'How many different kinds of vegetable could they order?'
'They could order three kinds, including potatoes.'
'Did either Marcus or Naomi order cheese?'
'No. Naomi wanted fruit salad, and though Marcus considered ordering some Stilton, he finally decided to have apple pie.'

The holiday

Alec and Zita spent last year's holiday in Spain where they rented a villa. You are now considering staying in the same place and possibly even renting the same villa. You therefore want to find out all about the villa from Alec and Zita. Some of your queries will concern the following:

1 how they first heard about the villa and the arrangements they made to rent it
2 full details of the villa itself and its position and of other flats and villas available
3 price and conditions of renting as they were the previous year
4 local facilities including shops
5 ways of spending the time

Students can ask questions which other students answer, each question and answer including a past simple form. The class could keep a record of the information gained which is read out as a report later in the lesson or at the beginning of the following one. In addition to those in (**a**) above, the following opening interrogatives may be useful: **how big? how far? how long before? what price? what difficulties/problems?** etc.

EXAMPLES
'What was the minimum length of time you could rent it for?'
'The owners wanted to let it for the whole summer but we stayed only a month.'
'How long did it take to get to the nearest beach?'
'We could get to the nearest one in five minutes but it was rather crowded.'

2 May and might

Asking permission and making a request

a In everyday speech, **can** is often used for **may**. The following examples show the basic differences in meanings between the two words.

Can I have a room on the first floor? (POSSIBILITY – Is there a room available?)

May I have a room on the first floor, please? (a REQUEST)

May I have the dog with me in the room? (The speaker is asking PERMISSION.)

b **might** can be used instead of **may**. It usually suggests some hesitation in making the request and therefore gives an impression of greater politeness.

Compare: *May I use your telephone, please?*

with: *I wonder if I might use your telephone, please?* (Here the speaker is asking a special favour.)

In contrast, **might** can suggest sarcastic annoyance.

Might I ask why you're reading one of my letters?

Note

might replaces **may** in reported speech after a verb in the past.

He told me I might use his car.

Otherwise, **might** is not a past form of **may.**

In a few cases where a past form is necessary, this can be **was/were allowed to**:

Only residents may use the car park.

Only residents were allowed to use the car park.

Practice

a Which of the following are requests or offers? Which are asking permission to do something? Which ask whether something is allowed?

1 May I have your name and address, please? (from a policeman)
2 May I have your attention, please? (before an announcement)
3 May I go out to play now, Dad? I've done all my homework.
4 May I take my white cockatoo into England?
5 May I help you with your suitcase?
6 May I see you again tomorrow? (to a charming new acquaintance)
7 May I borrow your pen for a moment?
8 May I take photographs in the museum?
9 May I have the recipe for this delicious cake?
10 May I park here, do you know?
11 May I have my bill, please?
12 May we have a ten-minute break, now?

b Suggest what is said in the following situations, adding the information requested in brackets. Use **may** or **might** as suitable.

1 You want to leave something at the hotel desk for a short time. (what? for how long?)
2 You are suggesting giving someone a lift.
3 You want to speak to a certain person on the telephone. (who?)
4 In your hotel room you find a chambermaid trying to open one of your suitcases.
5 You have a through rail ticket from Dover to London: you want to know if it's possible to break your journey at Canterbury.
6 With some hesitation you're asking someone in a hotel whether it's possible to look at his road map which is lying on a table. (explain why)

c Which of the following can you do, may you do/are you allowed to do, may you not do/are you not allowed to do at a large and beautifully arranged zoo? Add a short remark or statement.

EXAMPLE

drop litter on the ground

You may not drop litter on the ground. Plenty of litter baskets are provided.

go for a ride on an elephant
You can go for a ride on an elephant if you buy a ticket.
record the voices of the animals and birds
You may record the voices of the animals and birds, though not many people do this.

1 pick the flowers in the gardens
2 throw stones at the monkeys
3 feed the lions and tigers
4 take photographs of the camels
5 ask the keepers questions
6 see animals from many different countries
7 frighten the deer
8 have a meal in the restaurant
9 climb on the cages
10 watch the monkeys for as long as you like
11 put your fingers through the bars
12 play with the tiger cubs
13 visit the zoo after dark
14 eat your sandwiches in the picnic area

d What are some of the things a motorist may not do? Here is some useful vocabulary:
exceed the speed limit (where, especially?)
overtake (unless . . .) **sound the horn** (where?)
wrong side of the road **park** (where?)
without a driving licence **red traffic lights**
be in charge of a car (under what age?)

Can you think of some other things a motorist *must* do?

e What were some of the things you were allowed to do when you were a child of ten? Choose among the following ideas and add some others of your own:

stay up until (when?) **choose** (what clothes?)
ride a bicycle **play** (where?)
go swimming (where?) **keep a pet** (what kind?)
use your father's typewriter (if . . .)

EXAMPLE
I was allowed to bring other children home to play with me.

f What were some of the things you were not allowed to do when you were a child of ten?

Choose among the following ideas, but add some others of your own: **play ball games** (where?)
stay out after (when?) **drink** (what?)
eat (what?) **make a noise** (when?)
leave your things about (where?) **smoke**
tell lies **play with** (what?)
speak rudely (to whom?)
stay away from school (when?)
spend your pocket money on (what?)

Possibility

Both **may** and **might** are used to express the possibility that something can happen. In the case of **might**, the possibility is usually less, though speech factors such as emphasis and intonation may reverse this.

AFFIRMATIVE
'Where can I buy a Japanese kimono?'
'You may find one in an Oxford Street store.' (this is possible)
'You might find one in the local shopping centre, though as you're probably the only person in town looking for one, I doubt it.' (possible but unlikely)

NEGATIVE
He may not come to tomorrow's meeting, as he's very busy. (his absence is quite possible)
He might not come to the meeting if he's exceptionally busy, but I don't think that's likely. (his absence is possible, but unlikely)

may/might have been
may/might have done
The ideas expressed may possibly already have happened.
'Did Ken come to the office yesterday?'
'He may have come, but I don't know as I wasn't here myself.'
'He may not have come: he had a terrible cold the day before.'
'He might have come, but I've got an idea he's in France just now.'

There may be an additional idea of reproach: the speaker has been disappointed by someone's failure to do something.

I didn't know you intended to bring your two visitors home to dinner: you might have warned/told me earlier.
I had to do all the washing up myself: you might have helped me.

Practice

a Add a statement which introduces **may/might have** (+ another verb) as a following sentence in each of these cases. The statement may have been made by the speaker or by somebody else present at the time, and may be in the affirmative or negative form.

EXAMPLES
I can't find my gloves anywhere.
I may have left them on the bus.
Roy's unusually late home tonight.
Do you think he might have had an accident?

1 That man who just passed us seems to know you.
2 I can't find the fish I left on the kitchen table.

3 I didn't see Mick on the bus this morning.
4 How very strange! My watch has stopped. (forget/wind)
5 Rosa wasn't at home when I telephoned yesterday.
6 You know it was my birthday yesterday.
7 I haven't seen the Winters' car outside their house for some time.
8 Phil was looking thoroughly miserable when I saw him on Friday.
9 You made such a noise when you came home last night that you woke us all up.
10 I hear that the Porters are buying a flat on the Costa Brava. (come into money = inherit it)

b Which of the following: must you do, may you do, would you like to do, wouldn't you like to do, don't you need to do, next weekend?

1 fly to Bermuda
2 go to the barber/hairdresser
3 do some shopping
4 go to the theatre
5 read a novel
6 buy some clothes
7 listen to records
8 have a discussion with some friends
9 go for a long walk
10 clean your shoes
11 go swimming
12 spend Sunday with relatives or friends
13 give a party
14 go to a football match
15 do some painting in your home
16 tidy your room
17 wash your car
18 write some letters
19 do overtime at work
20 learn some English
21 be invited out to dinner
22 get up early on Sunday
23 stay indoors the whole time
24 have to stay in bed with flu
25 have a very enjoyable time

3 Past continuous tense

Forms

a AFFIRMATIVE STATEMENT
I/He/She/It was standing.
We/You/They were listening.

b **must**
I/He/She/It was having to wait.
We/You/They were having to work.

c NEGATIVE STATEMENT
I/He/She/It was not (wasn't) drinking.
We/You/They were not (weren't) eating.

d AFFIRMATIVE QUESTION
Was I/he/she/it standing?
Were we/you/they moving?

General uses

The past continuous emphasises the DURATION of an action that HAPPENED IN THE PAST AND IS NOW FINISHED. Both the past simple and the past continuous tenses refer to finished states and actions.

Details of use

a The past continuous contrasts the length of time taken by two actions.

the longer action = PAST CONTINUOUS
the shorter action = PAST SIMPLE

He was sitting in the garden when an apple fell on to his head.

b It describes two actions which both lasted for some time at the same time.
He was sitting in the garden while she was doing the housework.

c It emphasises the duration of an action rather than the fact that it happened.
I was waiting for a bus for a whole hour yesterday.
You were speaking on the telephone for half an hour. It will cost us a fortune.

d It expresses the idea that a finished action continued through a point in the past.
At three o'clock yesterday, we were sunbathing on a beach in the Canary Islands. Now we're clearing snow from in front of our house in London.

e In descriptions, the past continuous suggests an existing state in the past, during which actions took place (past simple).
The sun was still shining, though the clouds were beginning to cross the sky. Crowds of people were strolling lazily along the streets or were sitting outside cafés where they were sipping coffee while (they were) observing the passers-by. Suddenly, it started to pour with rain, and everybody rushed for shelter.

f It is occasionally used to express an arranged future from a point in the past.
He hadn't time to talk to me as he was leaving in a few minutes.

Practice

a Here are some short answers to questions in the past continuous tense:
Yes, he was. No, I wasn't.
Yes, you were. No, they weren't.

Answer each of these questions with two sentences. The first should be a negative short answer, the second an affirmative statement. The second subject and verb can be different from the first, but the verb should have the past continuous form.

EXAMPLE
Were the guests laughing while your husband was telling his jokes?
No, they weren't. They were yawning.

1 Were you listening to the radio when I telephoned you?
2 Was it raining when you came in?
3 Were the two men actually fighting when you tried to separate them? (shout)
4 Was Elizabeth carrying out an experiment when you went into the laboratory?
5 Was Gary climbing a tree when he fell?
6 Were you feeling ill when you got up this morning?
7 Were the actors rehearsing while the visitors were going round the theatre?
8 Were you really watching a television film at the same time as you were doing your English homework?
9 Were you having to shout when you were talking to grandfather?
10 Was the doctor seeing another patient while you were sitting in the waiting-room?
11 Were you and your friends sitting in the café the whole of yesterday afternoon?
12 Were you still having breakfast at ten o'clock this morning?
13 Was Tracy still writing her essay at eleven o'clock in the evening?

b What were the following doing when the waiter dropped the plates?

EXAMPLE
the restaurant proprietor
The proprietor was checking his accounts.

1 the fat man who was sitting alone at a table
2 the chef
3 a couple who were just coming in
4 another waiter
5 the restaurant cat
6 three men who were waiting for their meal
7 the waiter himself

c What were the following doing while the television announcer was reading the news?

1 grandmother
2 grandfather
3 mother
4 the dog
5 Selina, aged eighteen
6 Robin, aged eight

d What were these people doing all yesterday morning?

1 Septimus, a secretary
2 Bartholomew, a barber
3 Cherry, a check-out assistant in a supermarket
4 Henrietta, a housewife
5 Katy, a kindergarten teacher
6 Snoopy, a news reporter

e Answer these questions in complete sentences, repeating part of the question.

EXAMPLE
Which dress were you wearing when the waiter spilled soup on you?
I was wearing my new white silk dress when he spilled soup on me.

1 What was Harry eating when he broke his tooth?
2 What town were you living in when you left school?
3 What was the Prime Minister doing when he heard the news of the disaster?
4 What was he doing at the time he spoke about it to the reporters?
5 Where was Eric Fauntleroy making a speech when he had his heart attack?
6 Who was driving the car when the accident happened?
7 Why weren't the lifts working when I got here this morning? (power failure)
8 How long were you actually working yesterday and how long were you doing other things?
9 What were you talking about while you were having breakfast this morning?
10 Where were you living this time last year?

Past simple and past continuous: contrasts

a Drake, who is a television news reader, had 'one of those days' yesterday: everything seemed to go wrong. Below there are 16 word groups. Eight of these suggest what he was doing at various times of the day and the other eight refer to things that went wrong while he was doing them. Pair suitable expressions to make sentences.

EXAMPLE
read the news/get hiccups
While he was reading the news, he got hiccups

have a cup of tea
cut his finger
slice bread
read the news
break the mainspring
get hiccups
a last-minute item comes in
scorch it
run out of petrol
hurry to finish reading the news in time
iron his shirt
drive along the motorway

drop the cup
wind his watch
sprain his ankle
run downstairs

b Which of these things did Sally do when she heard the time signal, and which was she doing at that moment?

1 check the time shown by her watch
2 stroke her cat
3 discuss the day's events with a friend
4 sit in an armchair
5 stop talking
6 enjoy a quiet doze
7 turn up the radio
8 say 'Oh, that's the six o'clock time signal.'
9 look at the radio
10 relax after a hard day's work
11 think about what to have for supper

Conjunctions Although they may be used with all tenses, the conjunctions **while**, **as** and **when** often appear in connection with the past simple and past continuous verbal forms. One meaning of each conjunction is associated with the other two (**a**), while each of them has a second meaning which has no association (**b**).

a **while** = during the time that
He learned German while he was living in Switzerland.

as = at the moment that
As the conductor raised his baton, a gunshot broke the silence.

when = just after
When she got home she made some tea.

b **while** with the meaning 'though' suggesting contrast
While he rarely tells a direct lie, he seldom tells the exact truth.

as = because
As she had few friends, she was able to read widely.

when = whenever
When she felt depressed, she went for a walk.

Practice

In finishing these sentences, include either a past simple or past continuous form.

1 While he was peeling the potatoes, . . .
2 He first met his wife while . . .

3 He often felt depressed while . . .
4 He slipped over on the door mat as . . .
5 As the church clock struck one, . . .
6 The policeman looked at me suspiciously as . . .
7 When the bus failed to stop, . . .
8 He decided to turn to the left when . . .
9 The unlucky bank robber was serving a prison sentence while his accomplice . . .
10 Mike was short, fat and cheerful while his brother . . .
11 While my mother saved every penny, my father . . .
12 Bill and Bunty weren't often able to go out in the evening as . . .
13 He always insists on shaking hands when . . .
14 When he had nothing else to do, . . .

THE UNLUCKY BANK ROBBER WAS SERVING A PRISON SENTENCE WHILE HIS ACCOMPLICE . . .

4 Passive forms: past simple and past continuous tenses

Past simple *People* **knew** *little about science in the Middle Ages.*

NEW SUBJECT IN THE PASSIVE	PAST SIMPLE OF THE VERB **to be**	PAST PARTICIPLE **know**
Little	*was*	*known*

PASSIVE SENTENCE
Little was known about science in the Middle Ages.

Past continuous *They* **were showing** *an old film on the television when I turned it on.*

NEW SUBJECT IN THE PASSIVE	PAST CONTINUOUS OF THE VERB **to be**	PAST PARTICIPLE **show**
An old film	*was being*	*shown*

PASSIVE SENTENCE
An old film was being shown on television when I turned it on.

Practice

a Using the passive form in your answer, explain when these things happened.

EXAMPLE
the earliest printing of books in Europe
Books were first printed in Europe about five hundred years ago.

1 the building of your local Town Hall
2 the assassination of President Kennedy
3 the invention of the motor car (towards the end of the last century)
4 the publication of this book (see the front pages)
5 the completion of the last exercise

b Using the passive form in your answer, explain how these things happened.

EXAMPLE
the preservation of meat before refrigeration was available
Meat was salted to preserve it before refrigeration was available.

1 the production of books before the invention of printing (copy – how?)
2 the illumination of homes before gas and electricity were available
3 the making of cloth before the Industrial Revolution (weave by hand)
4 the early production of flour from corn (grind/stones)
5 what people did to provide themselves with wood for their houses in early times

c Where did these things happen? Use a passive form in your answer.

EXAMPLE
the painting of the earliest pictures
The earliest pictures were painted on the walls of caves.

1 the keeping of small savings before banks existed (mattresses?)
2 the importing of silks, spices and tea into Europe in the eighteenth century (where from?)
3 the copying of books centuries ago (monastery)
4 the making of clothes before factories provided ready-made ones
5 the building of the Great Wall

d Who did these things? Use the passive form in your answer.

EXAMPLE
the invention of gunpowder
Gunpowder was probably invented by the Chinese.

1 the destruction of Rome some fifteen hundred years ago
2 the organisation of the earliest Olympic Games
3 the winning of the most recent World Cup football championship
4 the writing of *Hamlet*
5 the composition of *The Messiah* (Handel)

e George went for a walk in the town yesterday. He noticed many things happening. What was being done?

EXAMPLE
students were holding a noisy protest demonstration (where?)
A noisy protest demonstration was being held by students in the park.

1 the building of a new block of flats (where?)
2 the sweeping of the pavements (where?)
3 the questioning of a taxi-driver (by whom?)
4 the planting of flowers in the town hall gardens (by whom?)
5 the painting of the bus station (what colours?)

Suggest some other things that were being done.

---

5 Used to

Examples *I used to cycle long distances, but I don't now.*
I used to get up later than I do now.
I used not to be so/as lazy as I am now.

Use **used to** implies three things at the same time:

1 The state or action referred to NO LONGER HAPPENS.
In the few cases where it might still happen, this fact is in some way surprising, regrettable or a kind of challenge:
I used to work twelve hours a day as a young man, and now, at seventy-five, I still do.

2 The state or action LASTED FOR SOME TIME or HAPPENED REPEATEDLY.

3 It existed or happened A FAIRLY OR VERY LONG TIME AGO. You rarely hear:
I used to swim every day during my recent summer holiday.
but you may hear:
I used to swim every day when I lived in Jamaica.

Practice

Which of these things: used you to do, but do no longer? used you to do and still do? used you not to do? Add an extra statement.

EXAMPLE
play chess
I used to play chess, but I no longer have time for it.
enjoy music
I used not to enjoy music as a child, but I do now. Unfortunately I don't have much time to listen to it.
make mistakes in English
I used to make mistakes as a beginner, and I'm afraid I still do, though I don't make quite so many.
smoke cigarettes
I used not to/never used to smoke cigarettes in the past, and I still don't. I don't understand why people waste their money on them.

1 go jogging
2 be interested in sport
3 go fishing
4 go to dances
5 look forward to my birthday
6 have a dog
7 ride a motor-cycle
8 spend a lot of money
9 spend a lot of time with friends
10 go to the cinema occasionally
11 live with my parents
12 play tennis
13 like pop music
14 want to get older
15 do as I was told
16 hate studying
17 often lose my temper
18 talk a lot
19 be very energetic

Section C Perfect tenses

1 Perfect tense forms

	PAST	PRESENT	FUTURE
SIMPLE	*I had taken*	*I have taken*	*I shall have taken*
CONTINUOUS	*I had been taking*	*I have been taking*	*I shall have been taking*

2 General uses of all perfect tenses

All perfect tenses indicate an action which happened earlier, but either led up to or was in some way connected with:

1 a time or another action or state in the past (PAST PERFECT):
He had interviewed ten candidates before lunchtime yesterday/before he went to lunch yesterday.

2 the present time (PRESENT PERFECT):
He has already interviewed ten candidates and he isn't satisfied with any of them.

3 a time or another action or state in the future (FUTURE PERFECT):
He will have interviewed ten candidates before tomorrow/before he has lunch.

Note
Note the present tense **has** in a future time clause.

The past simple and present perfect tenses: comparative uses

PAST SIMPLE and PAST CONTINUOUS tense forms express states and actions which existed in the past and which are now finished.

PRESENT PERFECT tense forms express states and actions which existed or happened in the past but which are always in some way related to the present time. More descriptive names for this tense might be the PRESENT–PAST, or the PAST-IN-THE-PRESENT.

Specific uses of the present perfect

a A PERIOD OF TIME THAT INCLUDES THE PRESENT
A present perfect form is used to express states or actions which have existed or occurred in a period of time which includes the present (such as today, this week, or this century).
I have bought a new cooker this morning.
The firm has made a lot of money this year.
Have there been any earthquakes in your country this century?

Compare: *Have you been to the cinema this week?*
with: *Did you go to the cinema last week?*

Note
Compare: *He* **has gone** *to Rome.* (He is still there.)
with: *He* **has been** *to Rome.* (He went and has now come back.)

APPARENT EXCEPTIONS
The past simple may be used even when the action happened in a period of time including the present, when it is clear that the action has finished.
Have you heard the weather forecast today?
Did you hear the weather forecast today?
The first sentence suggests that comment or discussion will follow, or that the speaker missed the weather forecast and now wants information. The second merely asks whether a certain thing happened.
Have you had breakfast this morning?
What time did you have breakfast this morning?
It may still be morning in the second sentence, but past time is being emphasised.

b With certain ADVERBS and PREPOSITIONS, including **already, since, for, just, yet** (negative and interrogative), **ever** and **never**.

already, yet
'Have you arranged your holiday in Egypt yet?'
'Oh yes, I've already reserved a room in a hotel.'

since, for (from a past time until now)
'Haven't you had anything to eat since breakfast this morning?'
'No, I haven't. I haven't had anything to eat for eight hours.'
since: a point of time in the past until now
for: a period of time lasting until now

just
'Have you just arrived?'
Compare: *'No, I arrived five minutes ago.'*

c The present perfect is often used for an action which may or may not have happened in the past but which in any case may still happen (or happen again) in the future.
'Have you tried my home-made jam?'
'No, I haven't. But I'd like to.'

A question or negative answer may include the word **yet**:
'Haven't you seen the President yet?'
'No, I haven't seen anybody yet.'

Note
Note the contrasting use of **still** (see Part 1 Section C5):
I'm still waiting.

ever, never (up to this time)
'Have you ever visited Sydney?'
'No, I've never been there (yet), but I may go some day.'
Compare this with: *'Did you visit Sydney while you were in Australia?'*
Your opportunity to visit Sydney is related to a past occasion.

d THE APPARENT PAST WITH A PRESENT MEANING
'Have you forgotten to bring your book with you?'
'Well, no. Actually, I've lost it.'

Both the question and the answer have an additional meaning. A present form expresses this additional meaning in each case.
Question: *'Haven't you got your book with you?'*
Answer: *'No, I haven't got it with me. I can't find it.'*

Compare this with:
'Who opened the window?'
'Anne did.'
The questioner wants to know the name of the person who opened the window. But in the case of:
'Who has opened the window? It's freezing in here.'
the speaker is probably not at all interested in the person who opened the window. He/she is simply saying the room is too cold.

Forms of can, must, may

can → *has/have been able to*

must → *has/have had to*

may (**be allowed to**) → *has/have been allowed to*

Practice

Give suitable short answers to these questions, which are arranged in four groups. Then add a statement or question.

a) a period of time that includes the present:
1 Has it rained today?
2 Have you had to do overtime at work or study for a school exam this week?
3 Have you blown your nose during the past five minutes?
4 Has there been a change of government in your country during the past year?
5 Has the standard of living in your country risen during this century?
6 Have you been able to save much money during this month?
7 Have you seen much improvement in the housing situation (providing enough homes for people) during the past decade?

b) with certain time adverbs and prepositions:
8 Have you just yawned?
9 Have you already decided on your career?
10 Has the human race become wiser since the time of Aristotle?
11 Have you been in this room for the past hour?

c) an opportunity that may have happened or may still happen:
12 Have you had lunch yet?
13 Have you ever learned shorthand?
14 Have you made up your mind yet what to do next weekend?
15 Has there ever been a manned space flight to the planet Mars?
16 Have you never wished to be a millionaire?

d) the apparent past with a present meaning:
15 Have you spent the morning in the sun?
16 Have you been ill?
17 Have you seen my dog anywhere?
18 Has there been an accident?
19 Haven't we met before?

What is the speaker really saying in each of the last five questions?

Present perfect simple: affirmative and negative statements

a Which of these things: have you just done? have you already done this week? haven't you done since last Sunday? have you never done (haven't you ever done)?

1 read the instructions about how to answer
2 write several letters
3 have a meal in a restaurant
4 buy stamps
5 start speaking
6 spend a lot of money
7 write out a cheque
8 hear the sentences before this one
9 go to the cinema
10 lose your temper
11 lose something (not lose anything)

b Finish each of these sentences suitably. Use your own ideas if possible, or if not, use the verb in brackets.

1 I haven't visited Edinburgh yet but . . . (intend)
2 I've never owned a yacht . . . (would like)
3 I haven't made a will but one day . . .
4 Julius Augustus hasn't been elected president . . . (hope)
5 The party hasn't won an election yet . . . (grow in numbers)

c Explain the additional meaning suggested by these sentences.

EXAMPLES
Who has seen the blackboard duster?
(actual meaning: I want help in finding the blackboard duster.)
Have you seen this photograph?
(actual meaning: I want to show it to you.)
I've never heard of such a thing!
(actual meaning: I don't believe it.)

1 I've left my umbrella at home.
2 I've telephoned him three times. (get in touch with)
3 What have I done with my diary?
4 Have you had anything to eat?
5 I've explained that five times already!
6 Nobody has told me what to do.
7 We haven't had time for a moment's rest all day.
8 Have you seen that film at the Odeon?

---

3 The present perfect continuous

Like the present perfect simple, this tense refers to PAST ACTIONS RELATED TO THE PRESENT. Its special use is that it emphasises the LENGTH OF TIME an action has taken and is often used in answering the question **how long?** The action is STILL CONTINUING OF ONLY JUST FINISHED OR FINISHING.

Prices **have been** *gradually* **rising** *for several years. Will they ever stabilise or even go down?*
How nice to sit down! **I've been walking** *for five hours non-stop.*

Notes
1 Contrast the present perfect continuous with the present perfect simple:
A Force Ten gale has been blowing all night.
The gale has blown down several trees in the park.
2 Verbs which rarely have a present continuous form equally rarely have a past continuous, present perfect continuous or past continuous form.

Forms of can, must, may

With meaning of possibility:

can → *could have been (living)*
must → *must have been (working)*
may → *may/might have been (discussing)*

Practice

a Answer the various questions that follow, using a form of the present perfect continuous tense, together with your own ideas.

1 Mr Howard is putting away the lawn mower. What has he been doing?
2 Colin says he's too tired even to think. What has he been doing?

3 Janet has just arrived at London Airport from Australia. How long has she been travelling?
4 For the past hour I've been packing a suitcase. Why? (get ready)
5 Eileen has just stopped at a motorway service area because of the thick fog. How has she been driving?
6 Ken looks very sunburned. Where has he been spending his holiday?
7 How long has he been staying there?

b Which of these things have you been doing/ haven't you been doing for the past hour?

1 breathing
2 thinking
3 working
4 studying
5 sleeping
6 using grammar
7 sitting on a chair
8 smoking
9 wasting time
10 feeling tired
11 listening to your teacher and other students
12 longing for something to drink
13 teaching English
14 looking forward to the break
15 dreaming
16 spending money
17 speaking

c How long have you been doing these things?

1 learning English
2 earning your living
3 preparing for your career
4 speaking your own language
5 living at your present address
6 attending this course
7 using this book
8 doing this exercise

d Suggest what each of these people has probably been doing for the past hour.

EXAMPLE
Ashley is at a football match.
He has been watching the match.

1 Brenda is in the kitchen.
2 Clive is in the garden.
3 Daisy is in her office.
4 Elsie is at the ice-rink.
5 Freddie is on the golf course.
6 George is on the beach.
7 Hilary is in an art gallery.
8 Jock is in the emergency accident ward of a hospital.

---

4 Since, for

since From a certain point in the past until now:
since Tuesday *since the first of January*
since Christmas *since I last saw you*

for During a certain period of time until now:
for several hours *for ever*
for a long time

Examples *The committee has been discussing the new programme –*
since nine o'clock this morning.
since the meeting started.
for the past hour.
for far too long.

Notes
1 Remember not to use the present tense in this case before **since** or **for**.
2 In the case of the verb **to be** and other verbs with no continuous form the present perfect simple is used.
Marguerite has been able to read since she was three.

Practice

Continue each of the following statements in two different ways, adding in the first case a time expression with **since** and in the second a time expression with **for**.
In both cases use a present perfect continuous tense form. Ideas (which you need not use if you have ideas of your own) are suggested in brackets.

EXAMPLE
Pat is employed by the Safeshield Insurance Company.
He has been working there since he left school.
He has been working there for eighteen months.

Note
It is common in English to use the expression **eighteen months** in preference to **one and a half years.**

1 Fred is just completing the five-mile marathon. (run)
2 Our road is still closed to traffic. (men/lay pipes)
3 I still make mistakes in English . . .
4 The chairman is still making his opening speech.
5 At last she has finished her cardigan. (knit)
6 I'm quite exhausted. (travel)
7 Elvira is getting a little impatient as . . . (wait)

Using the present perfect simple and present perfect continuous tenses

Expand these word groups into questions and then answer these questions using your own ideas. Suggest a suitable subject where none is given.

EXAMPLE
How many/gloves/knit?
How many gloves has Sheila knitted?
She has knitted three pairs.
How long has she been knitting them?
She has been knitting them for five weeks. (or: since she was given the wool at Christmas.)

1 How many/letters/write?
2 How many/kilometres/drive?
3 How much/work/do? (first answer: NEGATIVE)
4 How far/the expedition/travel?
5 What countries/live?
(second question: How long/live/this one?)
6 Which subjects on the agenda/discuss?

The present perfect together with other tenses

Answer each of these questions in a complete sentence and with a suitable verb form. Use your own ideas in the answers.

1 Have you joined the English class this week, or did you join it at the start of the course?
2 Have you had dinner already, or are you having it this evening? (Some people have dinner in the middle of the day, others in the evening.)
3 Are you going to the cinema this week, or have you seen the film already?
4 Has it been raining most of the day, has the sun been shining, or has the weather been cloudy?
5 Have you bought a newspaper today, or don't you often read newspapers?
6 Have the buses been running normally today, or is yesterday's strike still continuing?
7 Have you made any plans for the weekend yet or are you waiting to see what the weather's like on Saturday?
8 Can you get compensation for your stolen property, or haven't you been keeping up the insurance?
9 Did you have dinner with Pat in the Bon Séjour Hotel, or isn't he staying there during this visit?
10 Have you really been eating for two hours, or have the waiters been even slower than usual?
11 Was Ronald Roundman really so enormous two years ago, or has he put on (or: been putting on) weight recently?

5 Yet, still

yet

yet is often, but not always, used with a perfect tense form. It suggests that a state or action has not yet started.

'Have you moved into your new house yet?'
'No, it isn't finished yet.'

yet is normally used in questions or after a negative.

still **still** is seldom used with the perfect form. It suggests that a state or action is still continuing.

'Are you still living in your rented flat?'
'Yes, we are. My whole family is living in three small rooms.'

still is less commonly used after a negative.

You're not still knitting that cardigan, are you? (expressing surprise, almost disbelief, at the prolonged continuation of the action)

It is usually replaced by **not any longer** or **no longer.**

We aren't living there any longer.
We're no longer living there.

Practice

Make sentences about these pictures, using **still** and **yet**. You may get some idea from the word(s) above the pictures. Then add a second sentence that follows naturally.

EXAMPLE
He's still sleeping. I wonder what he's dreaming about.
He hasn't woken up yet. What time did he go to bed last night?

sleep

1 land

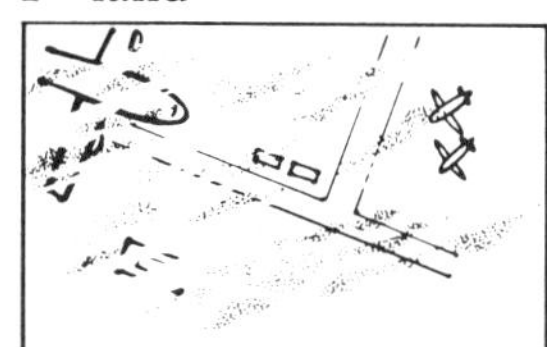

2 finish

3 station

4 speak

5 reach

6 wash

7 wait

8 chase

6 Past perfect: simple and continuous forms

Past perfect simple The past simple often expresses two or more states or actions which existed or happened one after the other in the past.

He **lifted** *the telephone receiver and* **dialled** *a number.*
He **waited** *for the pips before he* **inserted** *the coin.*
After he **finished** *speaking, he* **replaced** *the receiver.*

The PAST PERFECT form emphasises the fact that one or more actions had happened EVEN EARLIER than another action or actions.

He **had checked** *the number in the telephone directory* **before** *he* **dialled** *it, but even so he* **got** *the wrong number.*
It was only **after** *he* **had dialled** *the number that he* **remembered** *that his friend* **had changed** *his address some weeks before.*

Past perfect continuous This tense emphasises that one action had been happening EVEN EARLIER than another, and that the earlier action HAD LASTED FOR SOME TIME.

Although he **had been living** *in Athens for some years, he still* **spoke** *very little Greek.*

Notes

1 In REPORTED SPEECH the use of a past perfect form suggests that an action had happened before somebody reported it.

He told me he had telephoned me the day before.
I said I had been working in the garden all day.

2 Note this special use of the perfect form:

This was the first time I had heard this symphony.
This was the first time the orchestra had played it.

The perfect forms, which may be unexpected here, become clear when compared with:

I have never heard this symphony before.
The orchestra had never played it before.

Practice

a Answer each of these questions in a complete sentence, using the alternative you prefer.

EXAMPLE
Did standards of living begin improving after 1950, or had they already been improving before the war?
Standards of living had already been improving before the war.

1 Had you had a meal before you left home this morning, or did you just have a snack in a café?
2 Did Jill have difficulty in sleeping because she had seen a horror film on television, or because she was worrying about today's exam?
3 Did Annabel graduate after she had been studying at university for three years, or for four?
4 Did Pete grumble at you because you had made a mistake, or because he's in his usual bad temper today?
5 Did Harry ask for an explanation while the lecturer was still speaking, or after she had finished?
6 Did you feel tired yesterday because you had been working hard all day, or because you were still recovering from the effects of flu?
7 Did Sylvia work as a travel courier after she had left university, or while she was still studying?
8 Did Stephen say he had written his MA thesis, or that he was still writing it?
9 Did the choir sing a work they had performed before, or was this a new work for them?
10 Had you bought a ticket before getting on the train or did you have to pay the ticket-inspector when he appeared?

b Use a past perfect simple or continuous form to complete each of these sentences. Add a further sentence in each case.

EXAMPLE
Rochester Rovers were delighted because ...
Rochester Rovers were delighted because they had won the match. They got their highest score of the season.

1 Harry Harrison was worried because ...
2 Lucas still hadn't got a job although he ...
2 Evelyn adopted the kitten which she ...
4 Thomas Truebody retired at seventy-five after ...
5 Some years before he retired, he ...
6 He didn't buy the cottage until he ...
7 Columbus reached the West Indies after ...
8 My boss told me that I ...
9 I took the bad egg back to the shop where ...
10 This was the first time he ...

7 Passive forms: present perfect simple and past perfect simple

	ACTIVE	PASSIVE
PRESENT PERFECT	*They have extended the motorway.*	*The motorway has been extended.*
PAST PERFECT	*They had extended the motorway.*	*The motorway had been extended.*

Passive forms of the continuous present and past continuous tenses are so rarely used that they need not be practised.

Practice

a Aircastle, a new town some forty kilometres from Smogmarsh, is actually an expansion of an existing village of four hundred houses. Construction has been going on for the past ten years and a great deal has been achieved in that time. Some of the achievements are listed below. Say, in complete sentences, what these achievements are. As they will all be fairly recent, use the passive form of the present perfect tense to do so. Suitable verbs are suggested by some of the nouns included.

EXAMPLE
the creation of Aircastle, a new town some forty kilometres from Smogmarsh
Aircastle, a new town, has been created some forty kilometres from Smogmarsh.

1 the building (already) of houses and flats for twenty thousand people
2 the opening of four kindergartens, six schools and a technical college
3 the laying out of parks, sports grounds, recreation grounds and other open spaces
4 the starting of the building of a well-equipped three-hundred-bed hospital
5 the persuasion of several national industrial concerns to establish subsidiary factories
6 the construction of a dual-carriageway main road to the east of the town
7 the completion of an ultra-modern pedestrian-area shopping centre
8 the improvement of existing transport services in the area

b Before the creation of Aircastle was undertaken, very extensive plans had been made which took many years to complete. Some of these are listed below. In this case the plans had been made before the town was started so it will be necessary to use passive forms of the past perfect tense to express them. Explain what had happened. Rearrange the items in what you may consider a more suitable order.

EXAMPLE
the making (ten years earlier) of the decision to create a new town
The decision to create a new town had been made ten years earlier.

1 decision about the exact location of the town (first)
2 careful calculations about the ideal size of the town
3 the choice of a site within reach of Smogmarsh
4 the carrying out of a thorough geological survey
5 the estimate of the total cost of the project
6 a request to various well-known town-planners to submit their plans for the general lay-out
7 the construction of a new approach road from the motorway
8 wide publicising of the new project in newspapers and in other journals

8 Short questions referring back to what has just been said

These short questions express special interest, doubt or surprise about what has just been heard. The questioner may want a repetition of what has been said, but in most cases he accepts it and adds a comment or a question. Short questions can also express annoyance, and sometimes a determination to do something about the information received.

'Joan's getting married in the autumn.'
'Is she? But she has always said she never intends to get married.' (SURPRISE)

'The Turners don't live here now.'
'Don't they? They haven't told me they'd moved.' (DOUBT)

'I'm sorry, I can't pay you. I just haven't got the money.'
'Oh, haven't you? Then I suggest you go out and earn some.' (ANNOYANCE)

'You won't be able to eat all that.'
'Oh won't I. Just you watch!' (DETERMINATION)

Forms

'Does he come from Luxembourg?'	*'Yes he does.'*
'He comes from Luxembourg.'	*'Oh, does he?'*
'Did the exchange rate for the franc go down yesterday?'	*'Yes, it did.'*
'The exchange rate for the franc went down yesterday.'	*'Oh, did it? What a pity I didn't change my money earlier.'*

The short question uses the same verb tense as the statement it follows. A related auxiliary replaces the present or past simple form. Affirmative follows affirmative; negative follows negative.

'He lives here?'	*'Does he?'*
'I didn't see him.'	*'Didn't you?'*
'You haven't enough time.'	*'Haven't I?'*
'I must go now.'	*'Must you?'*

Practice

Suggest a suitable question form to follow each of these statements, and then add a further statement or question.

EXAMPLE
Jeremy handed in his resignation as club secretary yesterday.
Did he? Why did he do that?

1 The Hardings' house is up for sale.
2 We're spending Christmas in Morocco.
3 I'm changing my job in the New Year.
4 Ted's going into hospital tomorrow.
5 I'm so sorry. I must leave now.
6 You know, we should start our own riding stables.
7 Some people say they can concentrate best when they're standing on their heads.
8 Tim has won £20,000 on the football pools.
9 He's got three houses in England, a villa in the Bahamas, a chalet in Switzerland, a Rolls-Royce, a yacht and an aeroplane.
10 The company makes fabrics as well as high quality furniture.
11 I don't understand what you mean by that.
12 You can't force me to give you any money.
13 My watch doesn't keep very good time.
14 This letter isn't signed.
15 The Prime Minister called an urgent Cabinet meeting yesterday.
16 His latest book didn't get very good reviews.
17 I'd been working ten years for the company before I was dismissed.
18 I was driving very slowly and carefully when we crashed.

19 You've made a serious mistake you know, in refusing our generous offer.
20 I haven't been out all day.
21 Economists have been predicting a serious financial crisis for several months now.

9 So am I, nor/neither do I

These forms express shared ideas, or form responses expressing similar states, actions or opinions.

Affirmative

a The responses compared below may introduce nouns, pronouns or adjectives.

'I love the smell of roasting coffee.'	*'So do I.'* (PRONOUN)
'Too many cream cakes are fattening.'	*'So is too much macaroni.'* (NOUN)
'The twentieth century has been a time of revolutionary changes.'	*'So was the nineteenth.'* (ADJECTIVE – though a NOUN is understood here.)
'Hard work makes you tired – and so does doing nothing.'	(NOUN – a gerund)
'Our television broke down yesterday evening.'	*'How extraordinary! So did ours.'* (PRONOUN)

b In many cases the same verb tense appears in the statement and the response, though the verb in the response may be adapted in number to a different subject (see above – **are fattening/so is**). Sometimes, however, as in the third example above (**has been/so was**) the meaning of the response demands a different tense.

c In the case of the present simple and past simple tenses, the verb form in the statement is replaced by a suitable auxiliary form (**do, does, did**) in the response.

Practice

Give responses to these affirmative statements. In several cases, a new subject must be suggested. Then add an extra statement, remark or comment.

EXAMPLE
We're thinking of buying a villa on Capri.
So are we, though we don't know if we'll be able to afford it.

1 I'm in a hurry.
2 Britain is a beautiful country.
3 The Foreign Secretary has got a lot of responsibility.
4 Tax advisers can charge very high fees.
5 I must try to make my money go further.
6 Schoolchildren have been striking for a shorter working day.

SCHOOLCHILDREN HAVE BEEN STRIKING FOR A SHORTER WORKING DAY.

7 My husband seems to spend every evening entertaining visiting customers.
8 Australians visit Europe in their thousands.
9 I'm longing for the spring.
10 The teachers are demanding a pay rise next month.
11 I was awfully tired after last night's party.
12 Fred had the flu last week. (did)
13 We could see the Northern Lights last night.
14 I had to abandon my car during yesterday's snowstorm. (did)
15 The ancient Egyptians studied astronomy.
16 My boss made me work overtime yesterday.
17 I very much enjoyed last night's episode of *Stranded in Outer Space*.
18 I've joined the public library.
19 You should be more aware of other people's feelings.
20 We were listening to the six o'clock news when we heard about the new price rises.
21 We'd expected even higher ones.

Negative Here the question form is formed in the same way as the affirmative response, but instead of **so**, the opening word can be either **nor** or **neither**. Both forms are common.

'We don't often have time to read newspapers.'	*'Nor/Neither do we. But we hear the news on the radio.'*
'I'm never late.'	*'Nor/Neither am I – or at least, never very late.'*

'Factory workers in the last century had little time (rarely had time) for relaxation, and nor did country people, who spent all day working in the fields.'

Notes

1 Some adverbs have a negative effect. These include **never, rarely, seldom** and **hardly/scarcely ever** (see third example above).
2 The third example above also shows how the response can in fact be part of the sentence. This also applies in the case of **so**.

Practice

Suggest responses to or endings for these negative statements. In each case add an extra statement or question to what you suggest.

EXAMPLE
I can't read this writing.
Nor/neither can I. It looks like Greek or Russian to me.
Elsa didn't come to the meeting and . . .
nor did her husband. I don't think they are very interested in the project.

1 The buses aren't running today.
2 I haven't got a washing-machine.
3 I can't see our car where we left it.
4 You mustn't use the office telephone for personal calls.
5 My daughter isn't making much progress at school.
6 Teachers in England rarely start work before ten to nine.
7 We hardly ever invite friends home for a meal.
8 The first place we visited during our tour wasn't particularly interesting and . . .
9 I couldn't sleep for ages last night.
10 We didn't buy anything while we were in London.
11 I wasn't really listening to that very confusing lecture he gave.
12 I didn't understand what he was talking about and quite possibly . . .
13 I've never seen so many people in the shopping centre!
14 I hadn't realised there were going to be refreshments during the discussion.

Section D Future and conditional tenses

1 Expressing the future: future simple

Future simple forms

AFFIRMATIVE	NEGATIVE
I/we {*shall* / *will*} *come*	*I/we* {*shall* / *will*} *not come*
I'll/we'll come	*I/we* {*shan't* / *won't*} *come*
he/you/they will / *he'll/you'll/they'll* } *come*	*he/you/they* {*will not* / *won't*} *come*

There is a slight distinction in meaning between **shall** and **will**, but in speech the affirmative **'ll** form hides any difference and this is usually ignored in the negative.

The use of **shall** with **I/we** is usual in the question form.
Shall I/we come at eight o'clock?

Special cases: can, must may

a **can, must** and **may** (PERMISSION and POSSIBILITY) can all express the future unchanged.
We can discuss that tomorrow.
You must be ready to leave next Saturday.
You may go home an hour earlier tomorrow.
Inflation may be even more serious next year.

b The future forms of the three verbs are as follows:

can → *shall/will be able to*
The use of the future form may emphasise the idea that EXTERNAL FORCES will make the action possible or impossible.
You won't be able to travel tomorrow as there won't be any trains.

must → *shall/will have to*
The influence of external forces is emphasised here also.
I'll have to leave early in the morning to arrive before dark.

may (PERMISSION) → *shall/will be allowed to*
You won't be allowed to leave the country with that out-of-date passport.

may (POSSIBILITY) → no separate future form
The weather may be better tomorrow.

Using the future simple tense

In contrast to the arranged future expressed by the present continuous (see Part 1, Section A4), future simple forms express:

1 a WILLINGNESS/an UNWILLINGNESS to carry out a future action.
I'll do my best to come tomorrow.
He won't drive in snow or fog.

The interrogative **will you** (= are you willing to) is often used in a request.
Will you let me have it as soon as possible.
(As this is a request rather than a question, the question mark may be used, but is unnecessary.)

2 an OFFER or a SUGGESTION (question form).
Shall I leave my card with you?
Will you have a cup of tea?
Won't you stay to tea?

3 PROBABILITY, POSSIBILITY or UNCERTAINTY.
Very often a clause or other expression precedes or follows the main part of the sentence, and this weakens to some extent the certainty of what is being stated.
According to the weather forecast, it won't rain tomorrow. (But weather forecasts aren't always right.)
If there are any further difficulties, he will resign.
We shall inform you as soon as we have further details. (If the details aren't available, there will be no information.)

Note
As there is uncertainty about whether a condition will be fulfilled, a future form is normal in a result clause which forms part of a FIRST CONDITION.
If he decides to go, he'll let us know.

4 a STATEMENT OF INTENTION, DECISION or DETERMINATION or an ORDER.
In this case **shall** may sometimes be used with **you/he/she/it/they**, and **will** is common with **I/we**:
You shall pay for it. (I am determined you will do this.)
I will do it. (I am determined to do it.)

Examples:
I will attend to the matter immediately after lunch. (INTENTION)
All right. I'll take the job. (DECISION)
You will report to me at nine o'clock tomorrow morning. (COMMAND)
I will get even with him somehow or other. (DETERMINATION)

5 an ANNOUNCEMENT
The seven-thirty train to Penzance will leave from Platform 2.
The museum will be closed next week for repairs. (passive)

Practice

Using a future simple verb form, suggest what might be said in each of these situations. In each case, say whether the sentence is an example of **a**, **b**, **c**, **d**, or **e** above.

EXAMPLE
You are stating the departure time for tomorrow's coach excursion. (*where to?*)
The coach for tomorrow's excursion to Brighton will leave at half past eight punctually. (an announcement)

1 Toby's mother suggests that Toby is willing to drive you home. What does she say?

2 Someone intends to pour boiling water into a glass. What warning do you give? (Begin: That glass . . . if . . .)
3 An opinion poll suggests a victory for the Centre Party in the coming election. (According . . . win . . .)
4 You suddenly decide you want Morgan's opinion. What do you say? (Avoid **opinion** – **what he thinks**)
5 You're telling a friend that your father is unlikely to give you permission to join the climbing expedition. (use **let**)
6 Reference in a news bulletin to a speech to be made by the Prime Minister. (Where? When?)
7 Annabel's promise to her parents when she is leaving for a holiday in Austria. (send)
8 The time of tomorrow's committee meeting. (start)
9 The *Daily Doom*'s opinion about possible trends in unemployment during the coming year. (believes . . . there . . .)
10 A teacher hands back a careless and untidy piece of homework and tells the schoolboy what to do about it. (rewrite)

---

2 Present continuous and future continuous tenses

Future continuous forms

AFFIRMATIVE

I/we {shall / will} be coming

I'll/we'll be coming

he/you/they will be coming

he'll/you'll/they'll be coming

NEGATIVE

I/we {shall / will} not be coming

I/we {shan't / won't} be coming

he/you/they/will not be coming

he/you/they won't be coming

QUESTIONS

{shall / will} I/we be coming?

will he/you/they be coming?

Use

a The use of the PRESENT CONTINUOUS to express an ARRANGED FUTURE ACTION has been explained in Part 1, Section A4.

He is arriving in three hours' time.

The FUTURE CONTINUOUS can be used with exactly the same meaning – for an ARRANGED FUTURE ACTION.

He will be arriving in three hours' time.

There is no evident difference in the uses of the present continuous and future continuous in expressing the future with this meaning. Both forms are very often used to express the future.

b These tenses cannot be used in the case of:

1 verbs without continuous forms (see Part 1, Section A5).

We'll know the results tomorrow.

I'll believe you've got the money when I see it.

2 the verb **to be** as a main verb.

The taxi will be here at four o'clock.

The present continuous form of the passive (the future continuous form of the passive hardly exists) can, however, be used to express an arranged future.

The contract is being signed tomorrow.

Notes

1 An exception: the verb **see** with the meaning 'meet' is used in a continuous form to express an arranged future (see Part 1 Section A5).

I am seeing/will be seeing the director about it.

2 A time adverb (single word, phrase or clause) usually, but not always (see the example in Note 1), appears in connection with a continuous verb form used to express an arranged future. A time adverb is essential when there may be confusion between present and future meanings of the present continuous tense.

She is doing her shopping. (now)
She is doing her shopping tomorrow.

3 While the arranged future action expressed by these two continuous forms is quite often planned for the near future, this is not necessarily the case.

He says he is retiring as soon as he's fifty. He wants to have a chance of enjoying life before he gets too old. (He may be only thirty when he says this.)

4 For further uses of the future continuous see Part 1 Section D4.

Practice

Complete each of these sentences or suggest an additional one where suitable. Each word group you add should express a future meaning by the use of either a future simple or a present/future continuous form of the verb in brackets. If you use a continuous form, use two similar word groups, each introducing a continuous form. Add any information suggested by the other word or words in brackets.

EXAMPLES

You need not wash these test tubes. (ask) (when)
I'll ask the lab assistant to wash them when he comes back from lunch.

You'll have to write to Z and Y products ... (not call) (when?)
... as our representative isn't calling there tomorrow.
... as our representative won't be calling there tomorrow.

If you want to be sure of a warm winter holiday ... (have to) (where?)
If you want to be sure of a warm winter holiday, you'll have to spend it in the Canary Islands.

1 I can't telephone you this afternoon because ... (attend)
2 If you don't want that smoked salmon, I ... (eat)
3 Don't go out to post that letter in this cold weather. (post) (when?)
4 In my opinion the price of petrol ... (continue) (for how long?)
5 I've got an appointment with the hairdresser on Friday so ... (not be able to)
6 If the landlord doesn't repair this roof soon, I ... (not pay)

7 The increasing use of automation in industry ... (cause)
8 You certainly can't vote in an election now you're only eleven but you ... (may) (when?)
9 Plans for the new tunnel are now complete and they ... (start to construct) (when?)
10 Are you going to Sandy's wedding? He ... (get married) (when?)

11 This work is careless, untidy and full of mistakes. This evening you ... (do) ... and you (show) (when?)
12 According to the weather forecast for tomorrow there ... (be)
13 I promise ... (not forget) (to do what?)
14 Some of our staff are being transferred to Huddersfield. I only hope ... (not have to)
15 The road ahead is flooded. You ... (not be able to)
16 Can you tell me anything about Norway? I ... (spend)
17 Oh dear! I've left my glasses upstairs ... (fetch)
18 There's still plenty of cake left. (not have?)

3 Short answers

Present continuous/ future continuous

'Is Moira flying to Berlin?'	*'Yes, she is./No, she isn't.'*
'Will Moira be flying to Berlin?'	*'Yes, she will (be)./No, she won't (be).'*

Otherwise, the short answer follows the normal pattern.

Future simple

a In some cases, the normal pattern is used.

'Will there be extra buses for the football crowds?'	*'Yes, there will./No, there won't.'*
'Shall I have to pay duty on this watch?'	*'Yes, you will./No, you won't.'*

These are examples of ordinary questions and (in these two cases) have main verbs (**be, must**) which rarely, if ever, express arranged future action with a future continuous form.

b In most cases, however, future simple interrogative forms do not merely ask questions to which the answers might be simply 'yes' or 'no'. In such cases, the short answer has to be adapted to what is said.

'Will you telephone me in an hour's time (please).' (REQUEST)	*'Yes, by all means./I'm afraid I shan't be able to.'*
'Will you be able to finish this by five o'clock?' (partly a REQUEST, partly a QUESTION)	*'Yes, I'll try to./I'm sorry, I won't be able to.'*
'Will you have a cup of tea?' (OFFER)	*'Yes, please./No, thank you.'*
'Won't you sit down?' (SUGGESTION)	*'Oh, thank you./I'd rather not; I can't stay a moment.'*
'Shall I leave my card with you?' (SUGGESTION)	*'Yes, that's a good idea.'*
'Will there be snow tomorrow?' (nobody knows the answer)	*'Yes, I'm afraid so./I hope so./No, I don't think so.'*

Practice

Suggest suitable short answers to these questions, using your own ideas. Then suggest a sentence that might follow.

EXAMPLES
Will you be bringing your visitor home to dinner?
No, I won't. We'll be having dinner with the manager.

Will you give me your name, please?
Yes, of course. It's John Smith./But why do you want to know my name?

1 Will there be many price reductions in next week's sale?
2 Will it be cold again tomorrow, do you think?
3 Will my dog have to stay in quarantine when I return to England?
4 Will you need any sandwiches to take with you?
5 Will you be entertaining guests this evening?
6 Are you changing your address during the next month or so?
7 Will you be a little quieter, please?
8 Will you give Mr Drake a message for me, please?
9 Will you have to report at the police station tomorrow?
10 Shall I explain this exercise again?
11 Will you be at home next Sunday afternoon?
12 Will you be seeing your parents this evening?
13 Won't you come out for a twenty-kilometre walk with me?
14 Will you be taking part in the next Olympic Games?
15 Will you bring me my bill, please? (in a restaurant)

---

4 Continuous tenses covering points of time

a Besides expressing an arranged future action, the FUTURE CONTINUOUS tense may refer to an action that will happen before, during, and possibly after a certain point of time in the future.

At this time tomorrow, I **shall be sitting** *comfortably in an armchair before a blazing coal fire.*

Note
A rather less common use of this tense is to suggest that this action will last for a certain period of time.

I shall be sitting there for at least three hours.

b Other continuous tenses can also cover points of time: past and present as well as future.

What **was** *Mr Safe, the bank manager,* **doing** *at ten o'clock yesterday morning?*
At ten o'clock yesterday morning, Mr Safe **was discussing** *a possible loan with a customer.*

What **is** *he* **doing** *at this moment?*
At this moment he **is having** *a cup of tea.*

What **will** *he* **be doing** *at ten o'clock tomorrow morning?*
At ten o'clock tomorrow morning he **will be playing** *a round of golf with a colleague.*

Practice

a Explain what each of these people was doing/is doing/will be doing:
at eleven o'clock yesterday morning (Saturday)
now: eleven o'clock today (Sunday)
at eleven o'clock tomorrow morning (Monday)

Add any other information that is asked for.

EXAMPLE
Mr Barber, the surgeon:
yesterday *reading* The Lancet (where?)
now *attendance at a church service* (which church?)
tomorrow *performing an operation* (where?)

At eleven o'clock yesterday Mr Barber was reading *The Lancet* in his consulting-room. He is now attending a service in St Luke's Church. At eleven o'clock tomorrow morning he will be performing an operation in the Nightingale Hospital.

Note
In some cases you will have to supply a suitable verb, as in the second example.

1 **David Kemble, the actor**
yesterday: learning his lines for the part of Macbeth (where?)
now: writing the third chapter of his memoirs (where?)
tomorrow: rehearsing *Macbeth* (where?)

2 **Dorothy Drudge, the housewife**
yesterday: in a queue to pay in the supermarket
today: peeling potatoes (where?)
tomorrow: hoovering the carpet (where?)

3 **Hannah Hardlife, the teacher**
yesterday: correction of homework (whose?)
now: preparation of lessons (for whom?)
tomorrow: teaching English grammar (where?)

4 **Sid Scribble, the reporter**
yesterday: an interview with Lulu Lolly, the pop star (where?)
now: sleeping and dreaming (what about?)
tomorrow: watching a possibly violent demonstration (in favour of/against what?)

b Now suggest what each of these people was doing/is doing/will be doing at the three different times mentioned above.

1 yourself
2 Susie Small, the shop assistant
3 Miss Slick, the secretary
4 Mike Midas, the multi-millionaire

---

5 Present tense forms in future time clauses

a FUTURE TIME CLAUSES may begin with various CONJUNCTIONS including:

when	**immediately**	**before**	**after**
as soon as	**by the time (that)**	**while**	**(not) until**

They express a state or an action that is or is not expected in the future. In some languages other than English the tense of the main verb in the time clause is future. In English, however, the PRESENT TENSE form is used.

We shall let you know as soon as we **have** *any information.*
Father will deal with you when he **gets** *home.*
They won't be able to move until they **find** *a buyer for their home.*

b The time clause may come before (as in the first of the following examples) or after the main clause (as in the second example).

While we are having lunch we'll discuss the afternoon's programme.
He'll spend a week in Bournemouth after he has recovered from his illness.

Notes
1 In the second of the examples above, a present perfect form is used to refer to something which will finish in the future (compare Part 1, Section D6 below). This use of the present perfect is practised in the next exercise, but a present simple form can be used instead without change of meaning.
2 Not all clauses beginning with **when** are time clauses:
I don't know when he will arrive.
The clause **when he will arrive** is a noun clause, the object of **know**. It is not a time clause, so the future form is quite normal.

Practice

Answer each of these questions with a sentence containing a time clause beginning with one of these conjunctions: **when** **as soon as** **immediately** **by the time (that)** **before** **while** **after** **(not) until**

EXAMPLES
When do you intend to retire from work?
until:
I don't intend to retire from work until I'm ninety.
as soon as:
I intend to retire as soon as I can.
when:
I intend to retire when I'm tired of working.

When will the ship leave?
as soon as (PRESENT PERFECT):
The ship will leave as soon as loading has been completed. (PASSIVE VOICE)
(The present simple is also possible: *as soon as loading is completed.*)

1 When will you have lunch/dinner today? (when)
2 When will you get up tomorrow morning? (as soon as) (wake up)
3 When will Della go shopping? (after)
4 How soon will the sun appear? (when) (clouds/pass) (PRESENT PERFECT)
5 'How much longer must I wait for those letters I gave you to type, Miss Lamb?' Suggest Miss Lamb's answer. (immediately)
6 When do you hope to see your cousin in Rome? (while) (Italy)
7 When will June be doing her knitting this evening? (while)
8 When will the sales manager deal with his correspondence? (immediately)
9 When will Father be leaving hospital? (not until)
10 How long will Nigel and Norma continue saving every penny they earn? (until)
11 When will your son be leaving school? (as soon as)
12 When will you take your sea-sickness pills? (before)
13 When will Mr and Mrs Hope finish paying for the house they've just bought? (by the time)
14 When will you be reading tomorrow's newspaper? (while)

6 Future perfect: simple and continuous

Future perfect simple forms

I/we {shall / will} have eaten — *he/you/they will have eaten*

I'll/we'll have eaten — *he'll/you'll/they'll have eaten*

Future perfect continuous forms

I/we {shall / will} have been eating — *he/you/they will have been eating*

I'll/we'll have been eating — *he'll/you'll/they'll have been eating*

Uses

a Both tenses refer to actions which:
1 may have started in the past
2 may be existing or happening now
3 may start only in the future

But in all cases they will have finished by a certain time in the future, or they will continue until a certain time in the future.

b Both tenses are often followed by:
1 **by** (PREPOSITION)
2 **before** (PREPOSITION and CONJUNCTION)

Examples

We shall have saved all the money we need { *by next year.* / *in two years' time.* / *before we buy the house.*

By the end of this year we'll have been saving for our future home for ten years.

Will your parents have reached New Zealand by tomorrow?

How long will they have been travelling by then?

Practice

Future perfect simple

Paula has a lot to do today and she wants to finish everything before eight o'clock this evening. Her jobs include:

Telephoning her elderly mother; her bank; the local electrician's office about overcharging; her television rental company about a fault in the set; the railway enquiry office about a train; and the library to renew two books due back that day.
Writing letters to thank a friend for recent hospitality; to enquire about lost property; to answer a letter from a friend abroad; to congratulate a friend about getting an important job.
Typing out five pages of handwritten lecture notes.
Cleaning the kitchen and bathroom windows.
Washing the car.
Doing the weekend shopping (it is Friday).
Taking the week's washing to the launderette.
Ironing the newly-washed things.
Collecting a coat from the cleaner's.
Cooking lunch and dinner for herself.
Washing up after lunch and dinner.
Making her bed.
Mowing the lawn.
Cashing a cheque at her bank.

In fact by eight o'clock she'll have done only about half of these jobs: the others, she won't have done. Suggest those you think she *will have done* (by what time of the day?) and those she *won't have done.*

EXAMPLE
She'll have taken the week's washing to the launderette before lunch.
She won't have ironed it before the end of the day.

Future perfect continuous

SUBJECT	STARTING TIME	ACTION	TIME IN THE FUTURE
The Browns	*(8 a.m. yesterday morning)*	*travel*	*reach Vienna (8 p.m. this evening)*
Olive	*(May 1983)*	*work for her firm*	*be promoted (May 1988)*

The Browns will have been travelling for thirty-six hours before they reach Vienna.

Olive will have been working for her firm for five years before she is promoted.

Note the present tense in the time clauses.

Make similar sentences using this information.

	SUBJECT	STARTING TIME	ACTION	TIME IN THE FUTURE
1	Jim	January	save money	can buy a car (next December)
2	Matthew	two years ago	study (what?)	take his degree (next year)
3	The committee	2 p.m.	discuss (what?)	come to a decision (6 p.m.)
4	Ray	March of last year	collect material	start writing his book (November of this year)
5	Angus	1955	work	qualify for a full pension (1995)
6	Sarah	three years ago	live (where?)	apply for naturalisation (in two years' time)

7 Other ways of expressing future meaning

So far, various tense forms expressing future meaning have been explained. Here are some other ways of expressing future meaning.

going to + infinitive

This often expresses:

a INTENTION:
They are going to move to another flat next year.

Note
was going to may express a past intention. Often there is a strong suggestion that the intended action did not in fact happen.
'Did you take your car in for servicing last week?'
'Well, I was going to (take it in) but then I was asked to drive to Manchester that day.'

b PROBABILITY – which may be almost certainty:
According to the weather forecast, it's going to rain.

c IMMEDIATE FUTURE (with **just**):
The race is just going to start.

intend to/mean to + infinitive

The idea of INTENTION is even stronger in the case of either **intend to** or **mean to**, which are similar in meaning. If there is any difference between them, **mean to** could be slightly stronger than **intend to**.
I mean to/intend to find out who stole my bicycle, and get it back.

about to + infinitive

about to is similar in meaning to **just going to**, but suggests that the action will happen at once, or almost at once – in an even shorter time than that suggested by **just going to**.
Look out! That firework is about to explode.

bound to/sure to/ certain to + infinitive

bound to, **sure to** and **certain to** each suggest that something must exist or happen in the future.
He's bound to/sure to/certain to be furious when he realises that you just didn't bother to keep that appointment.

Practice

Suggest four sentences which could be used in each of the following circumstances. One should include **going to**. One should include **intend to** or **mean to**. One should include **about to**. The other should include **bound to** or **sure to** or **certain to**.

EXAMPLES
Percy has just given up his ticket at the barrier in Victoria Station. He is looking round in a bewildered way.
His friend Annabel was going to meet him but she isn't there.
He had some flowers with him that he had intended to give her.
As he was about to find a taxi, she came hurrying towards him.
She had said that she wasn't sure to come.

Dan has just taken a holiday brochure out of an envelope.
He is about to open the brochure.
He and Daisy are going to look through it.
They intend to discuss which island they will visit.
A holiday of this kind is bound to cost a lot of money.

Include negative forms whenever possible.

1 Ben has just sat down at a table in a restaurant which specialises in good but expensive food.
2 Fred is on his way to Glasgow, but has left things till the last minute. He is running at great speed along the street towards the station but has still two hundred metres to cover. All the train doors are shut and the guard has already signalled for the train to leave. (Use at least one negative form.)
3 Bert, who is carrying an outsize empty sack, has forced open the window of an empty house. Unseen by Bert, a police car is approaching. (burgle a house – a burglar) (Use at least one negative form.)
4 Nicholas is just walking towards an aeroplane. He is on his way to Greenland in midwinter.
5 Sally is wearing an outdoor coat and is carrying a basket. She is standing just inside her front door and is putting some coins into her pocket. Unknown to her, this pocket has a hole in it.
6 Ted is high up in an apple tree. He is stretching out his arm towards a large red apple. Unseen by him, the owner of the apple tree is approaching.

---

8 Passive forms of the future simple and future perfect simple

Future simple forms

ACTIVE	PASSIVE
they will do it tomorrow	*it will be done tomorrow*
they will not/won't do it tomorrow	*It will not/won't be done tomorrow*

Future perfect simple forms

ACTIVE	PASSIVE
they will have done it tomorrow	*it will have been done tomorrow*
they will not/won't have done it by tomorrow	*it will not/won't have been done by tomorrow*

Examples of use: active and passive forms

FUTURE SIMPLE
They will give no further information this evening.
No further information will be given this evening.

FUTURE PERFECT SIMPLE
They will have made the final decision by this time next week.
The final decision will have been made by this time next week.

Notes

1 Compare: *The final decision is being made on Monday.* (an ARRANGEMENT)
with: *The final decision will be made on Monday.* (an ANNOUNCEMENT)
and: *The final decision will have been made before Monday.* (Monday is the deadline.)

2 Passive infinitive after **going to:**
The prizes are going to be distributed by Lady Smith.

Practice

Future simple: passive forms

When/where/by whom will these things be done in the future? Suggest any other information being asked for.

EXAMPLE
The launching of a new passenger liner. (name? where? when?)
The new passenger liner *Atlantis* will be launched at Liverpool at two o'clock on Thursday afternoon.

1 the serving of tea (as a meal) (where?) (when?)
2 the publication of a biography (whose?) (when?)
3 the unveiling of a statue (whose?) (by whom?)
4 the holding of the next Olympic Games (where?) (when?)
5 the judging of the Dog Show (by whom?)

6 the reduction in price of many items in the sale (by how much?) (Express this as 'tomorrow's sale' or 'next week's sale'.)
7 the production of *Madame Butterfly* (where?)
8 the baking of the wedding cake (by whom?)

Future perfect simple: passive forms

Which of the following things will have been done by the end of the next seven days and which won't have been done by then?

EXAMPLES
your promotion at work
the emptying of your dustbin
I won't have been promoted at work by then.
My dustbin will have been emptied by then.

1 the cleaning of the windows of this room
2 the publication of the next issue of your favourite weekly magazine (give its name)
3 the payment of this month's salary (or your pocket money or allowance)
4 an increase in train fares
5 the posting of a letter you will write this evening
6 the return to the public library of a book which is overdue
7 the finding of a letter you mislaid yesterday
8 the celebration of your seventieth birthday

9 Conditionals: general notes

Types of conditionals

There are five types of conditional sentence. Each can be identified by the verb tenses or verb forms which suggest meaning. These five types express:

1 HABITUAL STATES AND ACTIONS (**if** = when, whenever).

2 A COMMAND (affirmative or negative) which must be obeyed if something is true or happens.

3 The result of POSSIBLE CIRCUMSTANCES (normally referred to as the FIRST CONDITIONAL).

4 The result of UNLIKELY OR UNREAL CIRCUMSTANCES (usually referred to as the SECOND CONDITIONAL).

5 What *might* have been the result of CIRCUMSTANCES THAT NO LONGER EXIST OR HAPPEN (usually referred to as the THIRD CONDITIONAL).

Examples

CONDITION	RESULT
1 *If he* **has** *a headache,*	*he* **takes** *an aspirin.*
(This always happens when he has a headache.)	
2 *If you* **have** *a headache,*	**take** *an aspirin.*
(You are being ordered or advised to do this, if the condition is true.)	
3 *If he* **has** *a headache,*	*he* **will take** *an aspirin.*
(He may have a headache.)	
4 *If he* **had** *a headache,*	*he* **would take** *an aspirin.*
(But I don't think he has got a headache.)	
5 *If he* **had had** *a headache,*	*he* **would have taken** *an aspirin.*
(He did not have a headache at the time, so he did not take an aspirin.)	

Order of the condition and result clauses

a Normally, the result clause follows the condition when it is the result that is being emphasised.
'What do you do if you don't have time for lunch?'
'If I'm really busy, I send out for sandwiches.'
In this case the RESULT clause answers the question and so is more important. It therefore finishes the sentence.

b The condition follows the result if it is the condition that is being emphasised.
'Do you often go to concerts?'
'Well, I go if the programme looks interesting.'
The answer to the question is now in the CONDITION, which is therefore more important and follows the result clause.

Conditional verb forms

SIMPLE AND CONTINUOUS CONDITIONAL FORMS
These appear in the SECOND CONDITIONAL.

	AFFIRMATIVE	NEGATIVE
SIMPLE	*he would take* *he'd take*	*he would not take* *he wouldn't take*
CONTINUOUS	*he would be taking* *he'd be taking*	*he would not be taking* *he wouldn't be taking*

PERFECT SIMPLE AND PERFECT CONTINUOUS CONDITIONAL FORMS
These appear in the THIRD CONDITIONAL.

	AFFIRMATIVE	NEGATIVE
PERFECT SIMPLE	*he would have taken* *he'd have taken*	*he would not have taken* *he wouldn't have taken*
PERFECT CONTINUOUS	*he would have been taking* *he'd have been taking*	*he would not have been taking* *he wouldn't have been taking*

Notes
1 **I** and **we** are followed by **should** or **would.**

should is more common after **I** and **we** in formal writing, especially in business letters:

I/We should be pleased to hear from you as soon as possible.

2 **could** is both the past simple and the conditional form of **can.**

He could read when he was only four.
I could telephone him if only I had his number.

would be able is also possible in conditional sentences.

I would be able to telephone him if only I had his number.

Conjunctions introducing conditions

a **if** is the most common.

b **unless** = if not (**if not** is also used).

He never does a minute's overtime unless he's paid for it.
He never does a minute's overtime if he isn't paid for it.

unless may emphasise the idea of a condition being made, although there is normally no practical difference in meaning between **unless** and **if not.**

He certainly won't give you permission unless you agree to work longer tomorrow.
He certainly won't give you permission if you don't ask for it.

c **provided that** and **providing** (with the same meaning) emphasise the force of the condition.

We'll lend you money provided that you can guarantee payment.

d **even if** suggests that a condition may have an unlikely result.

If he is ill, he doesn't go to work.
Even if he is ill, he goes to work.

She spends hours cooking dinner if she has guests.
She spends hours cooking dinner even if she's eating alone.

e **even if** and **even though** are similar in use but are slightly different in meaning.

Even if you've studied French for ten years (I don't know if you have) *you won't get an interpreter's job unless you speak it fluently.*
Even though you've studied French for ten years (I know you have) *you won't get an interpreter's job unless you speak it fluently.*

even if: The truth of the following statement is uncertain – this is a true condition.
even though: the following statement is known to be true.

Practice

Complete each of these sentences by adding at the beginning or end a suitable clause with its main verb in a present tense.

EXAMPLE
He has never been to France even though ...
He has never been to France even though he speaks French fluently.

1 I seldom get up before nine o'clock unless ...
2 He always stays in a first-class hotel even if ...
3 You need qualifications in shorthand and typing if ...
4 Even if ..., it's still dangerous to travel on icy roads.
5 Unless ..., you're running a serious risk of getting lung cancer.
6 If ..., I'll complain to the restaurant manager.
7 If ..., people go skating.

8 He often continues working till midnight even if . . .

9 He plays football every Saturday afternoon unless . . .

10 Conditionals expressing habitual states and actions

Forms

CONDITION	RESULT
ANY PRESENT TENSE FORM	ANY PRESENT TENSE FORM
If he **earns** *overtime pay,*	*he* **saves** *it.*
If it **isn't raining,**	*he* **goes** *for an hour's walk before breakfast.*
Even if it **is raining,**	*he* **goes** *for an hour's walk before breakfast.*

Use

a Both condition and result refer to states and actions that can happen on a number of occasions and may be everyday or frequent happenings.

if has almost the same meaning as **when** or **whenever.**
If he earns overtime pay, he saves it.
When he earns overtime pay, he saves it.

b There can sometimes be a difference in meaning between **if** and **when** or **whenever.**
If the sun shines, I go out for a walk. (My walk depends on the sun's shining.)
When(ever) the sun shines, I got out for a walk. (And possibly at other times too.)

Verb form In both condition and result clause, the verb has a PRESENT TENSE (present simple, continuous, perfect simple, or perfect continuous).

Practice

a What do you do in each of these situations? In each case, repeat the condition.

EXAMPLE
if the weather is warm enough
If the weather is warm enough, I sunbathe in the garden.

1 if you've got nothing important to do
2 if you're afraid of flying
3 if you make a spelling mistake in an important letter
4 if you're leaving your house or flat empty for several days
5 if you don't know someone's telephone number
6 if at the last minute you can't keep an appointment
7 if you haven't understood what someone has said
8 if you've been feeling tired and depressed for some time

b What don't you do in each of these situations? Repeat the condition in each case.

EXAMPLE
if you've spilt some coffee on the table cloth
If I've spilt some coffee on the table cloth, I use a damp cloth immediately to remove the stain.

1 if you're travelling in winter in an unheated compartment of a train
2 if you don't like the dessert on the restaurant menu

3 if you're short of money
4 if a certain kind of food doesn't agree with you
5 if you think a friend of yours is a hopeless cook
6 if you consider he/she is a dangerous driver
7 if you have no head for heights
8 if someone who owes you a lot of money asks for five pounds
9 if a friend tells you something in confidence (pass it on)
10 if you believe you're an unlucky person
11 if there's nothing interesting on television

11 Conditionals with an imperative

Forms

CONDITION	RESULT
ANY PRESENT TENSE FORM	AFFIRMATIVE OR NEGATIVE IMPERATIVE
If you **see** *Lorna*	**give** *her my regards.*
If he **is working**	**don't disturb him.**
If you've **made** *a mistake,*	**cross** *it out.*
If he **has been doing** *the job for ten years,*	**don't suggest** *you know how to do it better.*

Note
will may have the meaning 'be willing to', and in this case it may follow **if**.
If your bank will lend you the money, buy a flat now before prices rise.
If he won't help you, ask someone else to.

Practice

Tell me what to do or what not to do in each of these cases. Repeat the condition in each case.

EXAMPLES
if there's nobody at home when you reach my house
If there's nobody at home when you reach my house, ask the next-door neighbour for my door-key.
if I don't like garlic
If you don't like garlic, don't order that sauce.

1 if Mick says he doesn't know what to do with his money
2 if I need legal advice (solicitor)
3 if there is a knock at the door at midnight
4 if I'm having trouble with my eyes (eye specialist)
5 if my tooth's still aching tomorrow
6 if the new vacuum cleaner isn't working properly (ask)
7 if the sergeant gives an order (argue)
8 if the tap keeps dripping (call in a plumber/ put a washer on)
9 if the kettle's got a hole in it

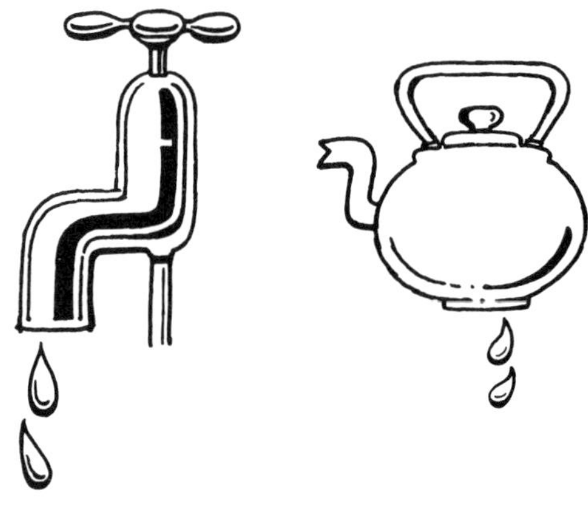

10 if I haven't got anything interesting to say

12 First conditional

Forms

CONDITION	RESULT
ANY PRESENT TENSE FORM	ANY FUTURE FORM
If he **gets** *the job,*	*he* **will have to** *move to Exeter.*
If he **doesn't get** *the job,*	*he* **will continue** *to draw unemployment benefit.*
RESULT	CONDITION
ANY FUTURE FORM	ANY PRESENT TENSE FORM
Martin **will have left** *his office by now*	*unless he* **is working** *late.*
Jane **won't be expecting** *me*	*if she* **hasn't received** *my telegram.*

Use This condition expresses a state or action that may happen or be true. It is possible that he will (or won't) get the job, that Martin is working late, or that Jane hasn't received the telegram. Accordingly, the result is also possible, though not certain.

Practice

a Suggest a result of each of these possible conditions, using either an affirmative or negative verb form.

EXAMPLES
if one of the twins buys a red, orange and pink blouse
If one of the twins buys a red, orange and pink blouse, the other will want one too.
even if you leave here at six in the morning
Even if you leave here at six in the morning, you won't be able to do the journey in one day.
if you want to take those three bottles of perfume into England
If you want to take those three bottles of perfume into England, you'll have to pay duty on them.

Practise using the verbs **will be able to**, **will have to** and **will be allowed to** where these are suitable:

1 if Jill's firm goes bankrupt
2 if the twins are put in different classes at school
3 if I've got time tomorrow
4 even if the moon is shining
5 unless you have a seat reservation for this special train (may not)
6 if petrol is rationed (motorists cannot)
7 unless they are satisfied with the quality (our customers)
8 if you fall into the river here (be drowned)
9 if you leave your car here (parking ticket)
10 even if I work till midnight
11 unless you've got an entry pass already (cannot)
12 if the doctor isn't satisfied with Myra's condition (must)

b Suggest possible conditions that will produce these results.

EXAMPLES
Father will be furious ...
Father will be furious if your next school report is unsatisfactory.
I'll never speak to you again ...
I'll never speak to you again unless you apologise.

1 The ice-cream will melt ...
2 The cat will steal that fish ...
3 I won't marry you (unless) ...
4 You'll have to pay more for your new car ...
5 Will you be able to go to university ...

6 Should we insure our luggage ...
7 I'll forgive you this time (provided) ...
8 Great grandmother won't wear those trousers (even if) ...
9 You won't be allowed across the frontier (unless) ...
10 Thousands of metal-workers will soon have lost their jobs ...
11 I'll be earning £12,000 a year ...
12 He refuses to give away a penny of his income (even though) ...
13 Will he be very upset ...

13 Second conditional

Forms

CONDITION	RESULT
PAST SIMPLE OR CONTINUOUS FORM	CONDITIONAL SIMPLE OR CONTINUOUS FORM
If we **had** *double glazing,* *If you* **were** *really* **concentrating,**	*this room* **wouldn't be** *so draughty.* *you* **wouldn't hear** *the noise outside.*

Note
Except in a REQUEST (explained on page 71), **would** never appears in a condition (after **if, even if, unless, provided** etc.).

Practice

Form short second conditions (incomplete sentences) with **you** as the subject in each case.

EXAMPLE
if/see (what?)
if you saw the picture ...

1 if/go (where?)
2 unless/be (ADJECTIVE?)
3 if/come (when?)
4 even if/take (what?)
5 provided/tell (whom?) (what?)
6 if only/know (what?)

Use The second conditional expresses a state or an action that is unlikely to happen or is unreal.

If all the world were paper ... what should we have to drink? (part of an old song)
If I were you, I shouldn't do it.

Other points

a **were, were to**
The use of **were** with a singular subject can be explained as the survival of the subjunctive form. It is still used quite commonly, especially when the condition is very unlikely or unreal.

If I were you ...
If mother were here, she'd be able to deal with it.
If it was fine tomorrow, we could have breakfast in the garden.
If it were fine now, we could sit in the garden.

were to sometimes expresses unlikelihood.

If I were to tell you all I knew, you'd be horrified.

b Conditional forms of **can, must** and **may**:

can	→ { *could* / *would be able to* }
must	→ *would have to*
may (PERMISSION)	→ *would be allowed to*
might (POSSIBILITY) / **should/ought to**	} → no change

If only I had more time, I **could/would be able to** *finish my novel.*
But even if I finished it, I **should have to** *find a publisher.*
If I visited the Forbidden City, **would** *I* **be allowed to** *take photographs?*
If I were allowed to do so, I **might** *ask for permission to go there.*

c REQUESTS
The conditional form is often used when making a request.
Note this apparent exception to the Note under 'Forms' above:
We would be pleased if you would reply as soon as possible.
would here is a past form of **will** = 'be willing to', so is not in fact a true conditional form. It follows the conditional **if** only when it is part of a request. (See page 70.)

Practice

a Sandy is on holiday in Spain right now. Explain what he will do if these quite possible things happen.

EXAMPLE
if he feels like exploring the surroundings
If he feels like exploring the surroundings, he'll hire a car.

1 if he needs to change some money
2 if he is staying in Granada (the Alhambra)
3 if he feels tired in the afternoon (siesta)
4 if he has some money left over on the last day

b The following situations are far less likely though not quite impossible (he is still in Spain so they could still happen). What would he do in these cases?

EXAMPLE
losing his passport
If he lost his passport, he would go to the nearest British Consul.

1 eating too much rich Spanish food
2 running out of money
3 dissatisfaction with his hotel
4 inability to pay his hotel bill
5 meeting an escaped bull
6 the offer of a job in Spain (if someone . . .)
7 continual wet weather

c In what situation would/wouldn't each of these things happen?

EXAMPLE
I'd be arrested . . .
I'd be arrested if I attacked a policeman.

1 I'd get an electric shock if . . .
2 I might be struck by lightning . . .
3 I could get a better-paid job . . .
4 I'd make a lot of new friends . . .
5 The factory wouldn't have to close down . . . (more orders)
6 I wouldn't be able to see an electron . . . (even if)
7 They wouldn't print that story . . .
8 I'm sure he'd give you his autograph . . .
9 There wouldn't be so many crimes . . .
10 We wouldn't be living in this horrible old house . . .

d Answer each of these questions with a condition followed by a result. Most of them are second conditionals.

EXAMPLE
What would you wear if you lived near the North Pole?
If I lived near the North Pole, I'd wear a fur hat, fur coat, fur gloves and long fur boots.

1 What would you say if you met a ghost?
2 Where would you probably be living if you spoke Norwegian?
3 How far would you travel each day if you were a migrating snail?
4 Who would be annoyed if you had a noisy party in your flat?
5 Which country would you prefer to live in if you had to leave your own?
6 What would you do with your money if you had too much of it?
7 How long would you have to study if you wanted to become a doctor?
8 What book would you like to have with you if you were shipwrecked on a desert island?

e What would you say if:
(Your answer should begin with **If**...)

1 you met (and recognised) an old school friend after ten years?
2 a public opinion poll questioner asked you your opinion of public opinion polls?
3 a man with a gun demanded your money?

f What would most people want to see if:

1 they were arranging a tour of Italy?
2 they could afford to visit the United States?
3 they were spending a day in Paris?
4 they were spending a holiday in England?
5 they were attending a conference in London?

g Ask each other these questions. Ask the same question to various people so as to get a number of different replies. Repeat the condition in each answer.

EXAMPLE
What would you do if a bad-tempered millionaire or millionairess asked you to marry him/her?
If a bad-tempered millionaire asked me to marry him I'd insist on sharing his money but not his home.
... I'd find out how to keep on the right side of him.
... I'd remind myself that money isn't everything and refuse.

What would you do if:

1 you won £100,000 in a lottery?
2 you met a little green man from outer space?
3 you had more free time?
4 when alone in the house, you heard a burglar moving about in the middle of the night?
5 just as the important guests arrived, you discovered that the meat you were cooking had got badly burnt?

h Suggest five different situations in each case in which:

EXAMPLE
you would give up your present job
I'd give up my present job if I disliked it intensely.
... I were sure of getting a better one.
... I inherited a large sum of money.
... I married a rich man/woman.

Use a different verb in each of the five sentences in each case.

1 you'd need to be a very capable person (use various verbs)
2 you'd move to a different house, flat or room
3 you'd complain to the manager in a hotel
4 you'd go without your dinner
5 you'd write a letter to a newspaper
6 you'd be very worried
7 you'd never believe your eyes
8 you'd turn off the radio

i Suggest what you would have to do in these cases.

EXAMPLE
if you wanted to insure your house
If I wanted to insure my house, I'd have to take out an insurance policy.

1 if you couldn't understand how to do one of these exercises
2 if you wanted to learn to drive a car
3 if you decided to qualify as an interpreter
4 if you had to catch a train at 6 a.m.
5 if you weren't able to find your way in a town

j What wouldn't you have to do:

1 if you had all the money you needed?
2 if you had enough bread, milk and butter?
3 if a deaf friend had a good hearing aid?
4 if you never felt tired?
5 if you knew the meaning of an English word already?

k What would you be able to do:

1 if you had eyes in the back of your head?
2 if you were a Swede?
3 if you were an eagle?
4 if you could foresee the future?
5 if you knew how to travel through time?

... IF YOU HAD EYES IN THE BACK OF YOUR HEAD ...

l What might you do:

1 if you had a wonderful idea for the plot of a detective story?
2 if you had a pen-friend in Bangkok?
3 if you were driven almost mad by your neighbour's radio?
4 if you were listening to somebody making an endless boring speech?
5 if you couldn't find anywhere to live?

---

14 Third conditional

Forms

CONDITION	RESULT
PAST PERFECT SIMPLE OR CONTINUOUS	CONDITIONAL PERFECT SIMPLE OR CONTINUOUS
If only you **had been** *more careful,*	*you* **wouldn't have broken** *it.*
(But it's too late now – the priceless	Ming vase is in pieces.)
If you **had been living** *a hundred years ago,*	*you* **would** *probably* **have been working** *twelve hours a day.*
If you **hadn't frightened** *the deer,*	*it* **wouldn't have run** *away.*

As in the SECOND CONDITIONAL, **would** does not appear in the condition (in this case it *never* appears).

Use It is impossible for the result in the third conditional to happen because it is too late – the opportunity no longer exists.

Forms of can, must, may etc.

		PAST PERFECT	CONDITIONAL PERFECT
can	→	*had been able to*	*would have been able to*
must	→	*had had to*	*would have had to*

	PAST PERFECT	CONDITIONAL PERFECT
may (PERMISSION) →	*had been allowed to*	*would have been allowed to*
may (POSSIBILITY) →	*might have* (*done*)	*might have* (*done*)
should	*should have* (*done*)	*should have* (*done*)
ought to	*ought to have* (*done*)	*ought to have* (*done*)

Note
The conditional **if I/he/we/you/they had done** occasionally appears as **had I/he/we/you/they done.**
If I had known earlier . . .
Had I known earlier . . .

Practice

a Shirley has just returned home after a satisfactory shopping expedition. If she had had difficulties, what would she have done or wouldn't she have done?

EXAMPLES
if there had been a long queue at the supermarket check-out
If there had been a long queue at the supermarket check-out, she would have left the shop and gone elsewhere
if the brussels sprouts hadn't looked fresh
If the brussels sprouts hadn't looked fresh, she wouldn't have bought any.

1 if the car park had been full
2 if she had almost run out of petrol on the way
3 if the prices in Sellwell Supermarket had been higher than those in Cheapbuy Supermarket
4 if she hadn't been able to find any English butter in Sellwell
5 if one of the assistants had been rude to her
6 if her purse had been stolen
7 if she had had to buy ten eggs when she wanted only six
8 if she hadn't been allowed to pay by cheque
9 if she had felt thirsty
10 if she had suddenly realised she had left the gas cooker in her kitchen on

b Last year, Sandy spent a long time considering how he would spend that year's holiday but was unable to come to a decision. A week before his (still unplanned) holiday, he went down with appendicitis and had to go to hospital to have his appendix removed. During his convalescence, he thought over all the plans which he would be unable to carry out and the conditions under which they might or might not have happened.

EXAMPLES
I wouldn't have had to speak a foreign language
If I had (I'd) gone to the United States, I wouldn't have had to speak a foreign language.
it might have rained the whole time
If I had (I'd) gone camping, it might have rained the whole time.

Suggest plans that would/wouldn't/might have had these results.

1 I could have sailed from port to port in the Mediterranean (have a yacht)
2 I might have climbed some high mountains (can/arrange)
3 I might have made some interesting new friends
4 I could have caught salmon in rivers (travel – where?)
5 I'd have had a lazy but interesting fortnight on the sea (join a cruise – to where?)
6 I'd have visited the Tower, the British Museum and lots of night clubs (stay with friends – where?)
7 it would have cost too much (decide/Australia)
8 I could have seen the Grand Canyon . . . (fly)
9 it would all have been a waste of money (enjoy myself)

15 Conditionals in general

Revision of forms

1 IF/WHEN CONDITIONAL (**if** = when/whenever)

If he **plays** *tennis, he always* **loses.**

CONDITION → ANY PRESENT TENSE
RESULT → ANY PRESENT TENSE

2 A COMMAND

If he **plays** *tennis with you,* **watch** *him.*

CONDITION → ANY PRESENT TENSE
RESULT → IMPERATIVE

3 FIRST CONDITIONAL (a possibility)

If he **plays** *tennis with Annie, he* **will lose.**

CONDITION → ANY PRESENT TENSE
RESULT → ANY FUTURE FORM

4 SECOND CONDITIONAL (unlikely, unreal)

If he **played** *tennis with Annie, he* **would lose.**

CONDITION → PAST SIMPLE OR CONTINUOUS
RESULT → CONDITIONAL SIMPLE OR CONTINUOUS

5 THIRD CONDITIONAL (impossible because the opportunity has passed)

If he **had played** *tennis with Annie, he* **would have lost.**

CONDITION → PAST PERFECT SIMPLE OR PAST PERFECT CONTINUOUS
RESULT → CONDITIONAL PERFECT SIMPLE OR CONDITIONAL PERFECT CONTINUOUS

Practice

a Complete the following sentences using one of the above constructions.

1 If water is heated to 100° Centigrade, . . .
2 If you've forgotten to bring your homework today, . . . (COMMAND)
3 If the police (plural) identify the terrorist, . . . (arrest)
4 If only I could remember his address, . . .
5 Even if I understood Einstein's theories myself, . . . (tense of **can**)
6 If you had gone skating on that thin ice, . . .
7 Unless you raise my salary, . . .
8 Even though tomorrow's a public holiday, . . . (tense of **must**)
9 If you hadn't helped me with the washing-up, . . .
10 If people ask me how old I am, . . .
11 Provided you give me at least a week's notice, . . .
12 Had you told me you were free this evening, . . .
13 If only we had a home of our own, . . . (tense of **can**)
14 If you think these mushrooms will make you ill, . . . (COMMAND)
15 Unless you pass the exam at your next attempt, . . . (tense of **may**)
16 Even if the fog lifted . . .
17 If he were really highly intelligent, . . .
18 If they had extinguished the fire quickly, . . . (damage)
19 If there were to be a revolution, . . .
20 If you want any more of these conditions, . . .

b In this case the results are given and the conditions have to be added.

1 He always makes a new will if . . .
2 Please don't be annoyed if . . .
3 We shall be able to go skiing tomorrow if . . .
4 We should all be much healthier if . . .
5 He wouldn't have tried to commit suicide if . . .
6 Don't hesitate to ask for my help if . . .
7 The new power station will come into operation next year provided . . .
8 I'd like to grow my own vegetables if . . .
9 You have to pay more income tax if . . .
10 He wouldn't have sent you those beautiful roses if . . .
11 The shop stewards have refused the new pay offer even though . . .
12 He wouldn't be so unpopular if only . . .
13 A bus doesn't stop at a request stop unless . . .
14 Would I risk getting a parking ticket if . . .
15 Would you have been allowed to stay in the station waiting-room all night if . . .

A BUS DOESN'T STOP AT A REQUEST STOP UNLESS . . .

16 He might have cancelled the appointment if . . .
17 She wouldn't have had to send a telegram if . . .

Section E Revision of tenses, reported speech

1 Revision

Practice

Short answers

Suggest suitable short answers to each of these questions, remembering that requests, offers, advice and similar forms involving **can/could, will/would** and **may/might** sometimes have their own form of short answer. Add an appropriate sentence that might follow.

EXAMPLES
Have you ever seen a ghost?
No, I haven't. I don't believe in ghosts.
Will there still be such cold weather as this in March?
Yes, there will. Or, at least, there usually is.
Will you turn your radio down a little, please.
Oh, I'm so sorry. I didn't realise I was disturbing you.

1 Do you usually go to the doctor when you have a cold?
2 Had you read today's newspaper before you left home this morning?
3 Could I have these photos processed by next Thursday, please?
4 Did you learn to play the piano as a child?
5 Are you afraid of walking alone after dark?
6 Should the police always carry guns?
7 Would it be dangerous to pat an unknown Alsatian dog?
8 Can you service your own car?
9 Were there many people in the streets when you came here today?
10 Do you usually have breakfast in the kitchen?
11 Will most people have to pay more income tax next year?
12 Would you join a demonstration in support of something you believe to be right?
13 Have you been vaccinated against smallpox?
14 May I take you out to dinner tonight?
15 Is your teacher sitting on the table?
16 Did you have to get dressed in a hurry this morning?
17 Must you help in doing the housework?
18 Have you got white hair?
19 Were you listening to records (or tapes) most of yesterday evening?
20 Have you been carrying out a difficult scientific experiment during the past hour?
21 Will you be advising the Prime Minister tomorrow?
22 Would you like a glass of Russian tea?
23 Are you going to sing to us at the end of the lesson?
24 Will astronauts have visited the planet Jupiter before the end of this century?
25 Would you volunteer to join a space expedition if you had the chance?

Revision of all tenses: active voice

EXAMPLES
John Brown (read) his newspaper.
PRESENT SIMPLE (**reads**): John Brown always reads his newspaper on the train.
PAST SIMPLE (**read**): He read two newspapers yesterday.
CONDITIONAL PERFECT (**would have read**): He would have read *The Times* if there had been a copy available on the bookstall.

The statement below should be dealt with in the same way. That is to say, it should be adapted to include each verb tense suggested by adding several additional words that show the meaning and use of the tense. The noun subject **Mark Clark** should be replaced in each case by **he**.

Mark Clark (**take**) photographs.

1 PRESENT SIMPLE (takes)
2 PRESENT CONTINUOUS (is taking) (now)

3 PRESENT CONTINUOUS (is taking) (*arranged future*)
4 PRESENT PERFECT (has taken)
5 PRESENT PERFECT CONTINUOUS (has been taking)
6 PAST SIMPLE (took)
7 PAST CONTINUOUS (was taking)
8 PAST PERFECT SIMPLE (had taken)
9 PAST PERFECT CONTINUOUS (had been taking)
10 FUTURE SIMPLE (will take)
11 FUTURE CONTINUOUS (will be taking)
12 FUTURE PERFECT (will have taken)
13 CONDITIONAL SIMPLE (would take)
14 CONDITIONAL PERFECT (would have taken)
15 should take
16 must take
17 must not take
18 need not take
19 used to take
20 is about to take
21 is going to take

Passive forms

a Suggest, in the passive voice of a suitable tense, the place in which the following exist or are happening. Use your imagination if the answer isn't obvious.

EXAMPLES
the last battle of the Napoleonic Wars
The last battle of the Napoleonic Wars was fought at Waterloo, near Brussels.
the next meeting of the General Assembly
The next meeting of the General Assembly will be held in New York.

1 the storage of goods (warehouse)
2 tomorrow's international football match (an arrangement – play)
3 the investigation of new sources of energy (throughout)
4 the showing of the new super space film tomorrow (an announcement)
5 the first invention of gunpowder
6 the cooking of food before gas and electric cookers were available
7 the siting of our new factory if it was decided to build one (to site = to choose a place for the building)

b Suggest in the passive voice of a suitable tense the time of each of these happenings. Use your imagination if the answer isn't obvious.

EXAMPLE
the current debate about subsidies for farmers
Subsidies for farmers are being debated now.

1 the present one-day closing of the museum every week
2 the sending of goods (to a customer) that are not quite ready yet
3 the recent performance of a well-known play (suggest which play and where)
4 the recent (and still continuing) development of silicon chips
5 your (arranged) promotion to a higher position in your work (what position?)
6 the probable construction of a very important building (what kind of building?) in your country

c Suggest in the passive voice of a suitable tense who carried out each of these actions. Use your imagination if the answer isn't obvious.

EXAMPLES
the vetoing of a recent UN resolution
The UN resolution was vetoed by one member of the Security Council.
the production of a current play
Peer Gynt is being produced by David Kemble.

1 the firm that manufactures most cars in your own or a neighbouring country
2 the conductor of the orchestra in tomorrow's (already arranged) concert
3 the organisers of the earliest Olympic Games
4 the carriage of goods overland throughout the latter part of the nineteenth century
5 the copying of books in Europe before the printing press was invented (what tense here?) (monks)
6 the doing of most work in the twenty-first century (perhaps) (robots)

7 who would represent the Prime Minister in the conference if he/she were unable to attend (deputy)

2 Reported speech: orders, requests and advice

Explanation DIRECT SPEECH: the actual words said or written
REPORTED or INDIRECT SPEECH: spoken or written words as they are reported

Examples

'*Write your full name (please).*'	*The clerk* **told** *me* **to write** *my full name.* *The clerk* **asked** *me* **to write** *my full name.* *The clerk* **advised** *me* **to write** *my full name.*
'*Don't write anything more (please).*'	*The clerk* **told** *me* **not to write** *anything more.* *The clerk* **asked me not to write** *anything more.* *The clerk* **advised** *me* **not to write** *anything more.*

Changes The imperative **write** appears in reported speech as **to write.**
don't write appears as **not to write.**

Note
He told me to come and see him.
There is no additional **to** before the second verb here.

Introductory verbs **tell** usually introduces an ORDER or COMMAND.

ask usually introduces a REQUEST.

advise suggests the giving of ADVICE.

Notes
1 **tell, ask** and **advise** introducing a reported speech form must be followed by the person being told or advised.
He told **me** *to write . . .*
He advised **the visitor** *to see . . .*
2 **suggest** cannot be used in reported speech of this type, as it is never followed by an infinitive.
Use either: *He suggested my writing my full name.*
or: *He suggested (that) I (should/ought to) write my full name.*
3 Other introductory verbs might be **recommend, appeal to** and **warn** (**not to**). All these are followed by a PERSON.

Practice

Using **told, asked** or **advised** according to which seems most suitable, suggest what reported command, request or advice might be given in the following circumstances (affirmative or negative).

EXAMPLES
What did the policeman ask Tim about the man who had attacked him?
He asked Tim to describe the man.

What instructions did the teacher give the class before he left them for a moment?
He told them not to make a noise.

1 What did mother want me to do for her while I was out shopping?
2 What two pieces of advice (affirmative and negative) did the doctor give his overweight patient?

3 What work did Mr Short give his secretary to do?
4 What did the passer-by say when I asked him the way to the Town Hall?
5 What did Mother say Bob had to do when she found his clothes lying about all over his room?
6 What two things (according to the chairman of the meeting) must the person do who kept standing up and shouting?
7 What appeal did the Prime Minister make to the trade unionists who were threatening industrial action?
8 What request did the parliamentary candidate make to the electors in his constituency?
9 What recommendation would you make to me about an interesting place I should visit if I came to your country?

---

3 Reported speech: pronoun and possessive adjective changes

PRONOUN and POSSESSIVE ADJECTIVE changes depend on the people involved.

Example:
Mr Box is speaking to Miss Cox. Here are his actual words:
'**You** *are to ask* **me** *for* **my** *permission before* **you** *use* **my** *typewriter to type* **your** *letters.*'

These words can be reported as follows, according to the person being addressed.

Miss Cox is speaking:
'**Mr Box** *has told* **me** *that* **I** *am to ask* **him** *for* **his** *permission before* **I** *use* **his** *typewriter to type* **my** *letters.*'

One of Miss Cox's colleagues is speaking:
'**Mr Box** *has told* **Miss Cox** *that* **she** *is to ask* **him** *for* **his** *permission before she uses* **his** *typewriter to type* **her** *letters.*'

Mr Box is reporting to one of his colleagues:
'**I** *have told* **Miss Cox** *that* **she** *is to ask* **me** for **my** *permission before* **she** *uses* **my** *typewriter to type* **her** *letters.*'

Note
No firm advice can be given about the inclusion or omission of **that** before the reported speech, as this depends on factors such as sound, rhythm and circumstances. It is not important.

Practice

a Sam has asked Joe if he can borrow Joe's bicycle and Joe passes this request on to his mother, who replies: 'You can lend him your bicycle if his parents telephone me to say that he has their permission to use it.'

1 Joe reports his mother's words to Sam. He begins: 'My mother says I can lend you . . .' Continue what he says. (What must Sam's parents do?)
2 Sam reports this to his parents. He begins: 'Joe says his mother has told him . . .' Continue what he says.
3 Sam's father (speaking for both parents) telephones Sam's mother. Before giving permission, he goes through what Sam has told him. He begins: 'Sam has told me you have said Joe . . .' Continue what he says.

b Today's *Daily Post* has the following headlines, each above a more detailed report of the incident referred to. The first sentence of each report gives the headline as a complete sentence.

EXAMPLE
PRISON RIOT IN GANGANGLIA
It is reported that there has been a prison riot in Ganganglia.

Suggest the first sentence of the report following each of these other headlines. Begin in each case with the words **It is reported that** and add whatever verb and other words that may be necessary.

1 SUMMIT CONFERENCE IN GENEVA NEXT WEEK
2 PREPARATIONS FOR NEW SPACE PROBE UNDER WAY
3 GRAIN SHORTAGE FORECAST FOR NEXT SPRING
4 COFFEE PRICES EXPECTED TO FALL SOON
5 PRIME MINISTER'S VISIT TO CANADA POSTPONED
6 M99 MOTORWAY TO BE EXTENDED NEXT YEAR
7 COLDEST SUMMER FOR EIGHTY YEARS

---

4 Reported speech: statements introduced by a verb in the past tense

The following statements are all introduced by a verb in a present tense.

'I'm very busy now.'	*He says he's very busy now.*
'We'll consider the matter tomorrow.'	*He has said they will consider the matter tomorrow.* (His statement is being reported the same day.)
'I can't help you.'	*It's no use asking him. He will say he can't help us.*

The verb tenses in the words reported do not change after an introductory present or future verb.

Verb tense changes

After an introductory verb in the past tense, such as **said**, **told**, **mentioned**, **explained** etc., the verbs in the direct speech move to their corresponding past forms. As a general rule (though not invariably) these changes are as follows:

PRESENT SIMPLE (*takes*)		PAST SIMPLE (*took*)
PRESENT CONTINUOUS (*am/is/are taking*)	→	PAST CONTINUOUS (*was/were taking*)
PRESENT PERFECT SIMPLE (*has/have taken*)	→	PAST PERFECT SIMPLE (*had taken*)
PRESENT PERFECT CONTINUOUS (*has/have been taking*)	→	PAST PERFECT CONTINUOUS (*had been taking*)
PAST SIMPLE (*took*)	→	PAST PERFECT SIMPLE (*had taken*)
PAST CONTINUOUS (*was/were taking*)	→	PAST PERFECT CONTINUOUS (*had been taking*)
PAST PERFECT SIMPLE AND CONTINUOUS	→	no change
FUTURE SIMPLE (*shall/will take*)	→	FUTURE SIMPLE IN THE PAST (*would take*)
FUTURE CONTINUOUS (*shall/will be taking*)	→	FUTURE CONTINUOUS IN THE PAST (*would be taking*)
FUTURE PERFECT SIMPLE (*shall/will have taken*)	→	FUTURE PERFECT SIMPLE IN THE PAST (*would have taken*)

FUTURE PERFECT CONTINUOUS (*shall/will have been taking*)	→	FUTURE PERFECT CONTINUOUS IN THE PAST (*would have been taking*)
CONDITIONAL FORMS WITH **would**	→	no change

Note
Future in the past forms (for reported speech) are the same as conditional forms, except that **would** only is used in the future in the past.

CONDITIONAL FORMS	*should/would take/be taking/have taken/have been taking*
FUTURE IN THE PAST FORMS	*would take/be taking/have taken/have been taking*

can, must, may etc.

can	*could, was able to, had been able to, would be able to, would have been able to*
must	*had to, had had to, would have to, would have had to*
may (PERMISSION)	*was allowed to, had been allowed to, would be allowed to, would have been allowed to*
might / **should** / **ought to**	no change
FIRST CONDITIONAL	the verbs change according to the above patterns
SECOND and THIRD CONDITIONALS	no change

Note
These verb tense changes need special attention from speakers of certain languages (German for example) in which they may not occur.

Practice

Mechanical practice of verb tense changes

Introduce each reported speech form with:
He said . . .

1 I'm surprised.
2 I can come later.
3 I must hurry.
4 It may rain.
5 You should get up earlier.
6 She plays the harp.
7 She doesn't play the mouth organ.
8 My shoes are hurting me.
9 We've lost a lot of money.
10 It has been raining all night.
11 The receipt was found.
12 I didn't pay the bill.
13 I had no money with me.
14 We were travelling the whole week.
15 I had finished before ten o'clock.
16 I'll be as quick as I can.
17 It would take a long time.
18 I must write to them in a fortnight's time.
19 If I don't get some peace and quiet, I'll go mad.
20 You wouldn't be happy if you married Jane.

Situational practice of verb tense changes

a Last week, Lolly Horrible, the pop star, gave an interview to a journalist who called on him in his luxury suite in the Topnotch Hotel. He made the statements given below, which were reproduced in reported speech form in the weekly magazine *Bombom*. Lolly's answers were reported separately in statements which began with such expressions as: **he said he explained he claimed he complained he told me he suggested he admitted**

Using these expressions, though not in the order in which they have been given, give the separate reported statements which appeared in *Bombom*.

EXAMPLE
'I don't suppose that many people will still be listening to my discs in a hundred years' time.'
He admitted that he didn't suppose many people would still be listening to his discs in a hundred years' time.

Note
There is no comma after the introductory verb: **said, admitted** etc.

1 I'm only a poor working boy but I've got big ideals.
2 I sing because I must.
3 My critics just don't understand me.
4 It's true I make big money and I spend big money.
5 But what I don't spend on myself I give to my poor old Mum and Dad.
6 I've just bought them a nice new Rolls-Royce.
7 You should remember I work hard for that money.
8 I'm living in a luxury hotel for publicity reasons but I really long for the simple life.
9 I was born in a Glasgow slum so I haven't done so badly.
10 My parents had eight children. I was the last.
11 I learned to play the guitar at a youth club.
12 I never learned to sing. I didn't need to.
13 I was discovered when I was singing with the group at some rich guy's party.
14 I hadn't been with the group for long then.
15 We've been top of the charts so often that I've lost count.
16 We've been together for two years: you must stick with your friends.
17 Though of course if I get a good offer, I may have second thoughts.
18 After all, when I'm really past everything – when I'm about thirty, I suppose – I'll start thinking about saving for my old age.
If I'm still alive to see thirty.

b Now report in a similar way an interview with one of these celebrities:

1 a well-known but somewhat conceited novelist
2 a famous tennis champion
3 the leader of a political party
4 a not-so-famous painter of pictures that the critics do not appreciate

---

5 Reported speech: non-verbal changes

When a statement or question is reported at a later time and/or in a different place, changes are necessary in order to avoid altering the original meaning.

'The meeting was held yesterday.'
Reported on the same day, the reported statement will be:
He said the meeting had been/was held yesterday.
Reported on a later day, it will be:
He said the meeting had been held the day before/the previous day.

These changes may vary according to the intended meaning in the direct speech (as in the case of pronouns and possessive adjectives already practised in Part 1, Section E3). It is important, therefore, to consider this meaning before making the changes.

Examples:

'I'm leaving **now**.'	*He said he was leaving* **at once/ immediately**.
'I'm too busy to see you **now**.'	*He said he was too busy to see me* **just then**.

Some of the most common changes			
	today	→	the same day, that day
	tomorrow	→	the next/following day
	next week/year	→	the following week/year
	yesterday	→	the day before, the previous day
	last month/century	→	the previous month/century

here	→	**there, in that place**
ago	→	**before** (*three weeks before*)
this/that/these/those	→	various possibilities including **the**, suitable possessive adjectives, **that, those** (depending on meaning)
PRONOUNS POSSESSIVE ADJECTIVES }		as explained in Part 1, Section E3

Note
Negative and verbal abbreviations (**isn't, can't, he'll** etc.) appear in full in written reported speech: **was not, could not, he would** etc.

Practice

Mechanical practice of non-verbal changes

Introduce each reported speech form with **He said . . .**

1 He visited Rome last year.
2 I'll be leaving tomorrow.
3 I can't do it now.
4 I've already read this article this morning.
5 It was pouring with rain all last night.
6 I was travelling all day yesterday.
7 I'll have finished with these books by next week.
8 You should have returned these notes to me two days ago.

Note
When practising reported speech changes, assume that you are reporting some time later.

Situational practice of non-verbal changes

a A little more than a year ago, Mr Ezekiah Solfaranian, the manager of a small shipping firm, interviewed a Miss Salome Browne for the post of junior clerk. She was not appointed, owing to lack of experience. The successful candidate has now given notice and, the post having been advertised, Miss Browne has applied for it again. Miss Candida Crabbe, Mr Solfaranian's secretary, still has a verbatim shorthand record of the earlier interview and, as Mr Solfaranian asks questions, she is able to give an adapted form of Miss Browne's answers in reported speech form. Here is her transcript of the original interview:

Mr S: May I have your full name, please?
Miss B: Miss Salome Sabrina Browne. That's Browne with an -e.
Mr S: So you aren't married yet?
Miss B: No, I'm not married now and don't intend to get married in the near future.
Mr S: Oh. Yes. Of course. How old are you?
Miss B: I'll be twenty years and three months the day after tomorrow!
Mr S: How long ago did you leave school?
Miss B: Four years ago.
Mr S: Did you pass any examinations at school?
Miss B: I've got four O-level passes, in English, History, Art and Maths.
Mr S: What have you been doing since you left school?
Miss B: I went to a School of Art for two years but that was a waste of time. Then I took my present job and have been working there until now.
Mr S: What kind of work are you doing?
Miss B: I'm working as a cashier in a supermarket. And sometimes I have to help out in the store.
Mr S: Why do you want to change your job?
Miss B: If I stay there I'll still be doing the same thing in five years' time. With four O-levels, I can do much better. So since September I've been attending a secretarial course in the evenings. I'd like to get experience in this field.
Mr B: Have you any certificates?
Miss B: I took the R.S.A. 1 typing exam last week and I'll be doing a shorthand exam next week. I don't know the typing exam results yet.
Mr B: How did you find out about this job?
Miss B: I saw the advert in the *Standard*.
Mr B: If we appointed you, would you be prepared to do overtime?
Miss B: Yes, I would.

Miss Crabbe reports Miss Browne's replies in answer to Mr Solfaranian's questions. She has to make some adaptations so that they make sense. Give Miss Crabbe's replies, each beginning with the opening words suggested.

EXAMPLE
Mr S: *What's her full name?*
Miss C: She said it was Miss Salome Sabrina Browne (etc.)

Mr S: Was she married?
Miss C: She stated very firmly ...
Mr S: How old was she?
Miss C: She told us ...
Mr S: When did she leave school?
Miss C: She informed us ...
Mr S: Did she pass any examinations at school?
Miss C: She claimed ...
Mr S: What had she been doing since she left school?
Miss C: She explained ...
Mr S: What kind of work was she doing?
Miss C: She said ...
Mr S: Why did she want to change her job?
Miss C: She had decided that ...
Mr S: Had she got any certificates?
Miss C: She claimed ...
Mr S: How did she find out about this job?
Miss C: She informed us ...
Mr S: Was she prepared to do overtime?
Miss C: She assured us ...

b One Friday morning Mr Almondtree was called away on account of his father's serious illness. In the afternoon he telephoned his secretary Estelle but she was keeping the minutes in a managerial meeting. He therefore dictated his instructions to a junior secretary, Maggie, who recorded them in shorthand. Mr Almondtree said that these instructions had to be passed on to Estelle as soon as she returned from the meeting. Here is a transcription of Maggie's notes:

Estelle is to write up the minutes of the meeting as soon as it finishes.
If she's busy, you can make photocopies for circulation as required.
One copy must be posted to me as soon as it's ready.
She'll have to cancel an appointment to meet Herr Wasserschutz in Berne early next week.
If she looks in the folder in the right-hand drawer, she'll find the notes I've been making for the new Washaway advertising campaign.
Mr Bright should know about these so he can carry on with them.
I hope she won't forget to send Sunny Cereal their account. I couldn't find it yesterday; it probably wasn't ready, or the Accounts Department may still be hanging on to it for some reason. They simply must have it ready by today – if they haven't forgotten it. This is really urgent.

In fact the managerial meeting lasted so long that Estelle did not return to the office but went straight home with a bad headache. So Maggie could not give her Mr Almondtree's instructions before Monday morning. When she did so, she expressed them in reported speech with suitable adaptations to this later date. She used many forms such as **he said, he suggested, he recommended, he insisted** etc.
What did Maggie say?

EXAMPLE
I'll probably be away for several days as my father will be having a major operation the day after tomorrow.
He told me he would probably be away for several days as his father would be having a major operation in two days' time.

c One student asks another about his/her recent present and future activities.

EXAMPLE
What did you do last weekend?

The questioner reports back the answers received (**He/She said that** ...) so that the rest of the class can hear them.

6 Reported questions beginning with an interrogative form

Examples	*'Where is it?'*	*He asked me where it was.*
	'When did you come?'	*She asked me when I had come.*

Changes a Pronoun, possessive adjective, verb tense and other changes have already been explained between pages 80 and 84.

b WORD ORDER

A question is reported in statement order. That is to say, the subject precedes the verb and there is no **do/does/did** auxiliary in the affirmative.

QUESTION ORDER	STATEMENT ORDER
'Where is it?'	*She asked me where it was.*
'What do you want?'	*She asked me what I wanted.*
'When will you come?'	*She asked me when I would come.*
'Why didn't they stop?'	*She asked me why they hadn't stopped.*

who? what? and **which?** as the subject of a verb are exceptions.

Compare:

'Who's there?'	*She asked me who was there.*
'Who is it?'	*She asked me who it was.*

and:

'Which bus stops here?'	*She asked me which bus stopped there.*
'What is it?'	*She asked me what it was.*

The subject of the verb in the second question of each pair is **it**, not **who?** or **what?**

Practice

a Change the following direct question forms into reported questions in two ways, starting first with **he has asked me** (no verb tense change) and then with **he asked** (with suitable tense changes).

EXAMPLE

Where do you live?

He has asked me where I live. (no verb tense change)

He asked me where I lived. (with suitable verb tense change)

1 Why is the door open?
2 Why aren't you at work?
3 What's your brother doing for a living nowadays?
4 What languages can you speak?
5 How often do you play bridge?
6 Why doesn't your secretary use a typewriter?
7 How long did you stay?
8 What were you writing?
9 What have you been doing?
10 Why didn't Rosa agree?
11 When will I hear from you?
12 Which club should I join?
13 Which is the best?
14 How soon should I pay membership fees?
15 Who started this company?
16 What dictionary would be the most useful for me?
17 What company had you been working for before you came here?

b Silas Salonen is a freelance journalist, who writes articles on various subjects of interest for newspapers and magazines. He travels a lot both in the British Isles and abroad to gather material. His wife, Melinda, knows what his job is but little else about exactly what he does.

One day while Silas is away from home, two strangers, a man and a woman, call at the house. The woman, a Miss Greta Grill, shows a police identity card but the man merely gives his name as Smith. They ask Melinda a lot of questions which she answers to the best of her ability.

When her husband returns a fortnight later, she tells him about this interrogation. Having an extremely good memory, she recalls word for word what was said. She also tells him her answers.

Naturally everything is expressed in reported speech form. Suggest what she actually said, using a variety of introductory expressions including:

asked (me) **wanted to know**
wanted information about
questioned me about **enquired** **said**
answered **replied** **told him** **informed him**
stated **explained**

EXAMPLES

Smith: *Where does he work?*

Melinda: *He's self-employed.*

Smith asked me where you worked and I told him you were self-employed.

Grill: *When did you last hear from him?*
Melinda: *Yesterday.*
Greta Grill asked me when I had last heard from you and I told her that I had heard the previous day.

Note
As there is no verb in Melinda's reply, the 'understood' verb is used in the reported reply.

Grill: What does your husband do for a living?
Melinda: He's a freelance journalist.
Smith: Where is he now?
Melinda: He's travelling.
Grill: Why is he travelling just now?
Melinda: He travels a lot to interview people and gather material.
Smith: Where would he be today?
Melinda: I don't know.
Grill: How can you get into touch with him if you need to?
Melinda: He sometimes telephones me in the evening.
Smith: When did he last telephone you?
Melinda: The day before yesterday.
Grill: What town was he telephoning from?
Melinda: He didn't tell me.
Smith: When did he say he'd telephone again?
Melinda: He said he might tomorrow.
Grill: Who may know where he is?
Melinda: I've no idea.
Smith: How long has he been away?
Melinda: He left three days ago.
Grill: And when will he be returning?
Melinda: He hasn't told me.
Grill: What visitors does he have here?
Melinda: None. We don't like visitors – of any kind.
Smith: Then who was the man who came here yesterday afternoon?
Melinda: He came to read the electricity meter. And now I'd like to ask you something.
Grill: What do you wish to know?
Melinda: Why are you here? Where do you come from? Who instructed you to come here? What will you be doing with the information you haven't discovered? And what right have you got to ask me all these highly impertinent questions?

---

7 Reported questions without an opening interrogative form

The following questions are in each case formed by reversing the order of the verb and its subject, or introducing an auxiliary before the subject.

Are you from Oman or Kuwait?
Did you see Yvonne yesterday?
Can you have my suit ready by tomorrow?

Explanation

a Changes in pronouns, verb tenses, word order and other words and phrases are the same as in reported questions already dealt with in Part 1, Section E6.

b The non-existent INTERROGATIVE FORM (**where? how soon?** etc.) is represented by **whether** or **if**.

'Are you from Oman or Kuwait?'	*He asked me if I was from Oman or Kuwait.*
'Did you see Yvonne yesterday?'	*He asked me if I had seen Yvonne yesterday.* *I asked Christine whether/if she had seen Yvonne the day before.*
'Can you have my suit ready by tomorrow?'	*Grant asked the tailor whether/if he could have his suit ready the following day.*

Practice

a Begin with **she asked me** or **she wanted to know.**

1 Is Mr Chanticleer in his office?
2 Can a horse sneeze?
3 Do you read your horoscope every day?
4 May I play my mouth organ?
5 Have you got a chauffeur?
6 Is the lift working?
7 Must you hum while you're reading?
8 Have you recovered from your bronchitis?
9 Was there a breakdown on the tube this morning?
10 Was Robinson working at the Embassy when he was in Thailand?
11 Were you employed by the British Council two years ago?
12 Had the new system been introduced by the time you left?
13 Should I come here again next week?
14 Will your research be completed by the end of this year?
15 Do you think there's any chance of a breakthrough in the cheaper development of solar energy?

b Herr Glockenspiel is the owner of a chain of retail stationery shops in Austria and gets a good deal of his stock from Steno Supplies Limited, a wholesale firm in London. During a two-day visit to London, Herr Glockenspiel rings the company manager, Mr Player, hoping to get an invitation to lunch or dinner and at the same time an opportunity to ask a number of questions.

Mr Player proves to be in Austria and will not be returning for two or three days. However, his secretary, Lavinia, writes down Herr Glockenspiel's questions and promises that her boss will send him the answers in writing. When Mr Player returns, Lavinia goes through the questions with him, presenting each, naturally, in reported speech form. Each of her reported questions begins with the verb in bold type. The words given are the ones that Herr Glockenspiel actually used so the **he** referred to is Mr Player.

EXAMPLE
asked
Will you find out from him if he considers that the new exchange rates are likely to affect his prices?
He asked me if I would find out from you whether you considered the new exchange rates were likely to affect your prices.

1 **asked**
Does he still stock the F42 files which he last supplied me with two years ago?
2 **wanted to know**
In that case, would he quote the present price for five gross?
3 **asked**
Can he let me have samples of any new children's stationery sets (notepaper and envelopes) that may now be on the market?
4 **wondered**
Does your firm market a light and inexpensive but really hard-wearing portable typewriter? If so, may I have a brochure and/or other details?
5 **enquired**
Will there be any discount if we order twenty gross packets of quarto-size Copyflair typewriting paper (top copies) at the same time?
6 **wondered**
Are prices of the Clearprint carbon paper the same as they were a month ago or have they gone up as he predicted at that time?
7 **wanted to know**
Will I need to send him confirmation in writing of these various enquiries?
8 **enquired**
Has he been having a good time in Austria and will he be coming to Vienna again soon? If he does, will he telephone me so that we can manage a visit to our usual café in Grinzing?

c The students in the class divide into pairs. One student in each pair asks the other a question beginning with an interrogative adverb, and gets an answer. The second student asks a question with no opening interrogative (inverted verb form) and is answered. Each student then reports back to the class what question he/she was asked (**He asked me . . .**), the partner following this with the answer he/she got (**She told me . . .**).

EXAMPLE
1: What's your favourite colour?
2: Orange. Do *you* have a favourite colour?
1: Yes, green.
2: (to class) She asked me what my favourite colour was.
1: He told me it was orange. Then he asked me whether *I* had a favourite colour.
2: She said she had – green.

Section F Infinitives and participles

1 Infinitives: short answers

General explanation

Certain statements, questions and commands may contain a verb or other part of speech which is followed by an infinitive, with or without **to**, e.g. **is able to do, can do.**

Short answers given in response to statements or questions may consist only of:

POSSIBLE INTRODUCTORY WORD OR PHRASE	SUBJECT	MAIN VERB	to
Yes.	*I*	*intend*	*to.*

The infinitive word is not repeated.

Examples

'Could you / *'Would you be able to* } **find out** *what's wrong with this lamp?'*	*'Well, I'll try* **to.**' (find out)
'Do be careful **not to break** *any of those glasses.'*	*'All right, I'll try* **not to.**' (break any)
'Could you **work** *this projector for me?'*	*'I'm sorry. I don't know* **how to.**' (work it)

Practice

Complete each of the unfinished sentences below adapting suitably the most appropriate of the various expressions suggested above each group and adding **to.** The verb may be either affirmative or negative according to meaning.
Then add another remark or question which might follow naturally.

EXAMPLES

want to refuse to

'Did Graham agree to pay half towards your expenses?' 'No, I'm afraid not. He ...
He refused to. He said he didn't see why he should.'

advise me to tell me to

'Do you think it was a good idea to apologise?'
'Personally, I don't. But my lawyer ...
But my lawyer advised me to. He said they could claim damages.'

a need to would like to ('d like to)
be able to intend to remember to refuse to

1 'Are you really going to drive a thousand kilometres in one day?'
'Yes, I certainly ...
2 'Did you manage to find the document I wanted?'
'No, I'm sorry. I ...
3 'Will you have to look for a new job now?'
'No, as a matter of fact I ...
4 'You will send me a postcard during your tour, won't you.'
'Well, if ...
5 'Will you agree to be transferred to the new department in Leeds?'
'No, I won't. I absolutely ...

6 'Would you be able to join our excursion to the sea?'
'Oh, yes. I . . .

b know how to learn how to want to have to seem to/appear to expect to start to

1 'Surely that river doesn't really run uphill.'
'That should be impossible but from here, it . . . (2 possibilities)
2 'Will you really finish your thesis this year?'
'Oh, yes. It's almost finished already so I certainly . . .
3 'Will you need to hire skis for your skiing holiday?'
'No. I've got some already so I . . . (negative)
4 'Can your baby talk yet?'
'No, not really. But he's . . .
5 'Do you make your dresses yourself?'
'My goodness, no. I . . . (negative)
6 'But if you went to dressmaking classes, you could . . .
7 'Are you really going to join that cruise round the world?'
'Well, needless to say, we . . .

c try (**not**) **to ought** (**not**) **to pretend** (**not**) **to hope** (**not**) **to prefer** (**not**) **to**

Note
In the case of these five verbs, the **not** usually precedes the **to** of the infinitive.

1 'Does he really work for the Secret Service?'
'I very much doubt it, but, as you know, he . . .

2 'I don't think you can qualify in only two years.'
'Perhaps not. But I can . . .
3 'He's always reading, though with his poor sight, he . . . (negative)
4 'Would you like to come swimming with us?'
'Well, it's pretty cold, isn't it. I'd really . . . (negative)
5 'Do you think you'll get that scholarship for study in the States?'
'Well, naturally I . . .

d advise (**someone**) (**not**) **to tell** (**someone**) (**not**) **to ask** (**someone**) (**not**) **to recommend** (**someone**) (**not**) **to**

Note
These verbs are always followed by a personal object. In this group the verbs and sentence openings which they are to follow are in the same order.

1 'Did Ron take part in the cross-country run last Saturday?'
'No, he didn't. His doctor . . .
2 'Did you use a dictionary when you were writing this essay?'
'No, I didn't. You . . .
3 It's not Barry's fault I didn't check the time of the train. He certainly . . .
4 'Is it really good for you to do all this daily exercise?'
'Well, it was the doctor who . . .

e A few passives: **be allowed to be persuaded to be paid to**

1 'We didn't really want to go on the day excursion but we were . . .
2 'We'd have liked to take some photos of the harbour but we . . . (negative)
3 'We wouldn't have stayed in the so-called luxury hotel even if we'd (negative) been . . .

f Other forms: **afraid** (**not**) **to used** (**not**) **to about to going to**

1 'He wanted me to go gliding with him, but I'm . . .
2 'Do you find English grammar particuarly difficult?'
'Well, I don't now, though I . . .
3 'Have you typed that urgent letter for me yet, Miss Dally?'
'It's quite all right Mr Treadmill. I'm just . . .
4 I've never ridden a camel and at my age I'm not . . .

2 Infinitives following certain main verbs

General explanation

When a main verb is followed immediately or almost immediately by another verb, the second verb may have one of these forms:

INFINITIVE	*He tried* **to find** *another job.*
PARTICIPLE	*I could hear him* **snoring.**
GERUND	*He enjoys* **working** *in his garden.*
FINITE FORM IN A CLAUSE	*I thought he* **looked** *worried.*

As there are few guidelines to help a non-English speaker to decide which is the form used, it is necessary to give particular attention to and to memorise individual verbs and the form that normally follows them. It is a good idea to memorise some sentences introducing various verbs.

Rather less common verbs which may be followed by an infinitive

I **wish** *to express my congratulations on your success.*
I **regret** *to inform you that we must cancel our order.*
You **deserve** *to be sent to prison.*
Enrico Bellavoce has **consented** *to sing at the charity performance.*
He **resolved** *to become a multi-millionaire.*
He (was) **determined** *to stop at nothing.*
She **endeavoured** *to sing a top A.*
He **struggled** *to swim against the strong current.*
I **hesitated** *to criticise so important a person.*
(Compare: *He hesitated before stepping into the busy road.*)
He **paused** *to consider carefully what he would say next.*
He **claimed** *to be the lost heir to the fortune.*
They **conspired** *to take over the government.*
He **demanded** *to be given the information.*
He **swore** *to have revenge on his enemies.*
She **prepared** *to leave at once.*
We **aimed** *to complete the journey in two hours.*
The firm **guaranteed** *to supply the goods within ten days.*

Notes

1 **know/show/describe/explain/understand** how to do something
learn/teach to do or how to do something.
The child **learned to dress** *himself.*
A model must **learn how to dress** *suitably on all occasions.*
She **taught** *her children* **to say** *'please' and 'thank you'.*
She **taught** *her children* **how to lay** *the table properly.*

2 **happened to see** = saw by chance
I happened to meet him while I was out shopping.

Practice

You have already used some main verb + infinitive forms in the first practice in this section. The following material introduces some more.
A number of situations are explained. Suggest what might be said or what might happen in each of them, introducing the verb above each, followed by a suitable infinitive. Suggestions about additional information to be included together with other advice are given in brackets.

EXAMPLE
manage
You want something (what?) to be sent to you very quickly (how soon?) (Begin: **Could you**)
Could you manage to send me my brown walking-shoes today?

1 **arrange**
You're telling a friend you're going to attend a holiday course. (where?)

2 **tend**
You're describing the normal January weather in your area which is surprisingly different from what it's like this year.

3 **afford**
You'd like to have a holiday but you haven't got enough money (why not?)

4 **begin**
You're explaining how you are a week after a serious operation when you no longer feel quite so bad as you did.

5 **decide**
Nathaniel Nutting is telling his secretary that he will not be visiting a customer. (name? in what place?) (include the verb **cancel**)

6 **I'd love**
Sylvia is saying she'd be very interested in seeing Paris but she can't. (why not?)

7 **attempt**
Gareth was unsuccessful in beating the record for the fifty-kilometre cycle race. (why did he fail?)

8 **fail/manage**
He couldn't break the record but at least he finished first.

9 **threaten**
Maurice is speaking about his landlord, who has talked about eviction if Maurice doesn't . . . (do what?) (turn out)

10 **offer**
What did the shopkeeper do when he saw it would be impossible for me to carry home all the goods I had bought? (deliver – when?)

11 **long**
Describe Fiona's feelings now she has left home in Northern Scotland for the first time and is working in London. (suggest why she feels like this)

12 **agree**
How much did you say you would pay the house decorator for painting your house?

13 **get ready**
Explain what most working people are doing at around six, seven or eight o'clock on a weekday morning.

14 **promise**
What hesitant answer did Penny give when one of her boy friends asked her to marry him? (Begin: **She . . .**)

15 **mean** (= intend)
Fraser has made some kind of a good resolution.

16 **prefer**
Phoebe is telling the receptionist what kind of room she would like to have in the hotel.

17 **continue**
Fifty-year-old Grace is answering when someone has asked her when she intends to retire. (how long?)

18 **volunteer**
What job did Andy say he'd be willing to do when he and his friends had found a place to camp for the night?

---

3 Verb + noun or pronoun object + infinitive

Examples

a TYPE A
He **wanted to tell** *you the news.*
He **wanted me to tell** *you the news.*

The verb is used with or without an object, before a following infinitive.

Note
Never: *He wanted that I . . .*

b TYPE B
He **told me** (*not*) **to tell** *you the news.*

The verb must have an indirect object whenever an infinitive follows.

Practice

Type A

Answer each of these questions in a complete sentence, introducing the words in bold type. An indirect object can be included where suitable.

1 Which form of entertainment did the visiting diplomats **ask to go** to in the evening: a concert, the opera or a night club?
2 Why did the Parliamentary candidate **ask the electors to vote** for him?
3 How can people **help to keep** town streets tidier?
4 What might **help you achieve** a better English pronunciation? (English pronunciation tapes)
5 Blake is studying in a medical school. What's he **training to become**?
6 What is something you can **train a dog to do**?
7 How much do you usually **pay to go** to the cinema?
8 What might you **pay a car mechanic to do**?
9 What would you not **like to find** in the next letter you receive?
10 What would you **like your boss to say** when you next ask for a rise in salary?
11 What do the demonstrators **want the government to do**?

Type B

In this case the main verb must be followed by a noun/pronoun object before an infinitive. Complete these sentences by replacing the line by a suitable pronoun object, by then adding an infinitive form and finally completing the sentence with an answer to the question in brackets.

EXAMPLE
The doctor **advised** _____ ... (*what advice did he give?*)
The doctor advised his patient to have an immediate operation.

1 The dentist **told** _____ ... (what instructions did he give?)
2 The sergeant **ordered** _____ ... (what order did he give?)
3 Advertisers **urge** _____ ... (what action do they urge?)
4 My wife **reminded** _____ ... (what action must be remembered?)
5 A wheel-chair **enables** (object here = a handicapped person) (what can he/she do in a wheel-chair?)
6 The mother **coaxed** _____ ... (what did she want to happen?)
7 The American President **invited** _____ ... (what kind of invitation did he give?)
8 The stockbroker **advised** _____ ... (what advice did he give?)
9 The sunny weather **tempted** _____ ... (to do what?)
10 The head teacher has **forbidden** _____ ... (what must not happen?)
11 The Hotspur Rovers football team has **challenged** _____ ... (to do what?)
12 The sights and sounds of the countryside **inspired** _____ ... (what action resulted?)
13 The chairman of the meeting **requested** _____ ... (what request did he make?)

4 The infinitive without to: make, let, had better, would rather

make, let

a Compare:
The nurse **made** *the patient* **take** *the horrible medicine.*
The nurse **forced/compelled** *the patient* **to take** *the horrible medicine.*

b Compare:
The cat **let** *me* **stroke** *her.*
The attendant did not **allow** *us* **to eat** *sandwiches in the museum.*

Notes
1 **allow** may suggest more formality than **let.**
2 **allow,** not **let,** is used with the passive form.
3 **let us** (**let's**) is often used in making a suggestion.
Let's sit down for a while.

4 **not allowed** and **forbidden** are rarely used in notices.
Normally: NO SMOKING NO PARKING NO ENTRY

Practice

Finish these sentences.

1 The teacher tried to make the lively class . . .
2 I wish I could make my dog . . .
3 The armed bandits forced their terrified victims . . .
4 The ticket-collector made the passenger . . .
5 The tyrant king compelled the citizens . . .
6 As there was so much extra work to do, my boss made me . . .
7 A sudden feeling of helpless terror compelled me . . .
8 You must be dying of thirst. Please let me . . .
9 I feel like a change. Let's . . .
10 The emigration officer wouldn't allow the man without a passport . . .
11 The angry dog wouldn't let the postman . . .
12 Visitors to this area are not allowed . . .
13 Try not to be so noisy. You'll make the baby . . .
14 If we go on a conducted tour of the opera house, shall we be allowed . . . ?

---

had better, would rather

You'd **better** *save that money – you may need it later.* (ADVICE)
But I'd **rather** *spend it now.* (= I'd prefer to)
We'd **better** *not eat that fish – it doesn't smell too good.*
I'd **rather** *not have anything to do with them – I don't trust them.*

Practice

Suggest what might be said in each of these situations using an affirmative or negative form of either **had better** or **would rather** (**'d better** or **'d rather**) followed by a suitable infinitive and other ideas which answer the questions in brackets.

EXAMPLES
You're short of milk. (*where will you buy it?*)
I'd better get some more milk at the dairy.
You advise someone against delaying his decision to accept a job.
You'd better not leave it much longer. They may offer it to someone else.
You don't want to sit in the sun. (*why not?*)
I'd rather sit in the shade/I'd rather not sit in the sun. It's much too hot today.
Which do you prefer: earning money or spending it? (*why?*)
I'd rather earn money than spend it. Then I've got more to spend.

Note
I'd sooner (**do**) is exactly the same as **I'd rather** (**do**).

1 You've been asked whether you'd like tea or coffee. (with or without milk/cream?)
2 You're advising someone to hurry. (for what reason?)
3 Terence is asked whether his wife wants to work or stay at home. He gives a reason for her preference.
4 Mr and Mrs Conway are discussing the time they should leave home the following morning. Mrs Conway speaks and gives a reason for the decision.
5 You're thinking you really should get up. (why?)
6 You're advising someone against driving that evening. (why?)
7 You don't really want to play tennis. (why not?)

8 Which would you prefer: do an examination or visit the dentist?
9 A farmer is advising you against letting your dog chase his sheep. He says what will happen if the dog does. (Begin: **Your dog . . .**)
10 Which is more enjoyable: going to a boring party or reading an interesting book? (why?) (Use **than** in your answer.)

---

5 Alternative forms of need + infinitive

need has alternative negative and interrogative forms.

	FIRST FORM	SECOND FORM
Negative statements	*I/we/you/they don't* / *he/she/it doesn't* } *need to go*	*I/he/we/you/they need not go*
Interrogative	*do/I/we/you/they* / *does he/she/it* } *need to go?*	*need I/he/we/you/they go?*

Use of alternative forms

a Note that before a noun or pronoun object only the FIRST FORM is possible.
I don't need a coat today.
Do you need extra money?
This is transitive **need**, which is never followed directly by the infinitive.

b Before an infinitive both forms are possible.
You don't need to / *You need not* } *pay for your ticket.*
Do you need to leave home so early?
Need you make that horrible noise?
Some impatience could be expressed by the use of **need you.**

Past forms

There is a difference in meaning between:
You **needn't have** *bought another pair of shoes – you've got ten pairs already.*
and:
Fortunately, I **didn't need** *to work during the hottest part of the day.*

need not have done – something you actually did
didn't need to do – something you didn't in fact do

Practice

a Which of these things do you need when you write (not type) and send off a letter? Which of these things don't you need?

EXAMPLE
carbon paper
at least ten minutes' time
I need at least ten minutes' time to write a letter.
I don't need carbon paper.

1 notepaper
2 a paint brush
3 a ball of string
4 an envelope
5 a ball-point or other pen (or pencil)
6 brown wrapping paper
7 a stamp
8 a pocket calculator

b Which of these things do you need to do (need you do) when you change money in a bank into another currency? Which of these things don't you need to do (needn't you do)?
(The alternatives in brackets are also possible.)

EXAMPLE
have some money to change
have an account in the bank
I need to have some money to change.
I need not have an account in the bank.

Notes
1 **I don't need to have** is also possible, but practise the **need not** form here.
2 If you are not quite certain about what you need, don't worry. You can guess.

1 give your age
2 sign your name on a slip of paper
3 show your passport
4 hand over the money to be changed
5 give your home address
6 telephone beforehand to make an appointment
7 have your own pen with you

c Stephanie, who lives in London, arranged a weekend in Paris in August and made an all-in payment for her flight to Paris, hotel, meals and excursions. While she was getting ready for her trip, she did several things she needn't have done and when she travelled, she took several things she needn't have taken. What were they? Explain why she need not have done/taken each of them. Ignore the things that she needed.

EXAMPLE
make sure her passport was up to date
arrive at the airport three hours before take-off
She need not have arrived at the airport three hours before take-off.

1 wear a fur coat
2 revise her Italian
3 have her hair set
4 arrange to have her letters forwarded
5 cancel the delivery of newspapers for a week
6 take her car insurance certificate
7 be inoculated against typhoid
8 buy food to eat on the journey
9 ask her neighbour to feed her cat
10 find out the address of the British Embassy in Paris
11 buy tinned food to take with her

d Sabrina is a widow with two children. Monday was the first day of her annual holiday from the factory near Acton where she usually works and she arranged to take the children for a picnic later in the morning. As it was a holiday she didn't need to do some of the following things (and so she didn't do them). Which things didn't she need to do?

EXAMPLE
check in at her factory
wash up the breakfast things
She didn't need to check in at her factory.

1 get up at six o'clock
2 prepare a lot of food to eat out of doors
3 get breakfast ready
4 have lunch in the works canteen
5 put a new film in her camera
6 put the picnic things in the car
7 catch the 8.15 train to Paddington
8 fill a thermos flask with iced lemonade
9 telephone the factory to apologise for her absence
10 put sun-tan lotion on her face and arms
11 take the tube from Paddington to Acton

Unfortunately just as they got to the picnic spot it started to pour with rain and they had to return home. So there were several of the things listed above she need not have done. What were they?

6 The infinitive used after a main verb in the passive voice

In Part 1, Section F3 you practised the construction:
VERB + NOUN OR PRONOUN OBJECT + INFINITIVE

The verb in this case can take a passive form with the noun or pronoun object becoming its subject.
The doctor advised Hugh to have an immediate operation.
Hugh **was advised** *by his doctor* **to have** *an immediate operation.*

In many cases, the AGENT (**by his doctor**) is not mentioned:
They asked me to sell refreshments at the charity bazaar.
I was **asked to sell** *refreshments at the charity bazaar.*

Practice

Finish these sentences with an infinitive and any additional words needed. An agent can be given but this is not necessary in most cases.

1 The students were reminded not . . .
2 The visiting scientist was invited . . .
3 The hungry child was tempted . . .
4 During a trial a jury is forbidden . . .
5 Passengers are requested not . . .
6 Housewives with time to spare were asked . . .
7 Old people should be helped . . .
8 Children have to be trained . . .
9 A suitable family may be paid . . . (an orphan child) (to foster)
10 The overworked businessman was advised . . .
11 The nervous child was encouraged . . .

7 The infinitive expressing purpose

I'll ring directory enquiries **to find out** *his number.*
The speaker's PURPOSE in ringing is expressed by the infinitive – with **to**, but no other preposition (such as **for**) before it.

Note
There is a slight difference in meaning between the expressions **go/come and do something** and **go/come to do something.**
He went out and bought some peppermints. (Two things happened one after the other.)
He went out to buy some peppermints. (This was his purpose in going out.)
The purpose may exist in the first example, but is much more definite in the second.

so as, in order

a **so as** and **in order** must precede an infinitive of purpose when the infinitive form is negative.
She said nothing about what had happened **so as not to cause** *trouble.*

This construction is not very common. The use of the verb **avoid** with an affirmative is more normal.
She said nothing **so as to avoid** *causing trouble.*

b They are also used to emphasise the idea of PURPOSE.
Compare: *He climbed to the top of the hill to see the view.*
with: *He climbed to the top of the hill in order to see the view.*

Note
There is no difference in meaning or use between **so as** and **in order**.

so that + clause

There is very little difference between the constructions **so as to/in order to** + INFINITIVE and **so that** + CLAUSE. In the following examples, **so that** + CLAUSE avoids the complex construction **so as to be able to.**
He's climbing to the top of the hill **so that he can** *see the view.*
He went to bed early **so that he could** *get a good night's rest.*
He set his alarm for six o'clock **so that he should** *be sure of waking early.*

There is very little difference in meaning between the INFINITIVE and the CLAUSE constructions.

Note
in order that may be used instead of **so that** with the same meaning, but is much less common.

Practice

Finish each of these sentences suitably with a construction expressing purpose.

1 He is saving money . . .
2 He went to the post office . . .
3 The detectives took the murder suspect to the police station . . .
4 I wrote down his name and address at once so as . . .
5 He has gone into hospital . . .
6 He took a large torch with him so as . . .
7 You could telephone the station . . .
8 He always leaves his office some time after the rush hour in order . . .
9 The watchmaker examined my watch through a magnifying glass so that . . .
10 After driving for three hours he stopped at a roadside café . . .
11 The staff of our firm are allowed to leave two hours earlier on Fridays so that . . .
12 My cat usually returns at seven o'clock punctually every evening . . .
13 He always drives slowly and carefully in order not . . .
14 Linda took a basket with her so that . . .

8 Noun + infinitive

Very many nouns may be followed by an infinitive, which is then used adjectivally, and often expresses purpose.

He gave me a **form to fill in.** (PURPOSE)
I haven't got a **pen** (or **anything**) **to write** *this letter* **with.**

Notes
1 The infinitive or its object may be followed by a PREPOSITION.
2 The pronouns **somebody, anybody, nobody, something, anything, nothing, somewhere, anywhere** and **nowhere** may be followed by an infinitive.
nobody to talk to *something to read* *somewhere to live*
Adverbs may be used in the same way.
I don't know anybody to ask.
somewhere/anywhere/nowhere to live

Practice

Complete these sentences with a suitable infinitive, which in some cases may be followed by a preposition.

1 He's got an important letter . . .
2 I haven't any smart shoes . . .
3 They're looking for a comfortable house . . .
4 He's hurrying because he's got a bus . . .
5 He went to the public library to get a book . . .
6 Excuse me a moment. I've got a telephone call . . .
7 Is he a good boss . . .

In the following sentences the noun is separated from the infinitive by other words.

8 Is there a kindergarten in the village . . . (send)
9 He's looking for a good school for his children . . .
10 There are very many interesting buildings in this town . . .

In the rest of these sentences add an infinitive and at least four more words.

11 The Social Committee is making plans . . .

12 I need some soap powder . . .
13 He bought some rare plants . . .
14 Could you lend me a few records . . .
15 He's looking for a really good camera . . .
16 Isn't there anybody at Reception . . .

Notes
1 Some exceptions:
have difficulty in doing **the advantage of living** **profit from making** **success in inventing**
2 Nouns normally accompanied by a preposition are followed by a gerund (see Part I, Section G7).

In the following cases the infinitive you suggest will be following a pronoun or adverb. Add several more words in each case.

17 We'd love to have a grand piano, but we haven't got anywhere . . .
18 With four lively children she wishes she could find someone . . .
19 Now that he's retired he says he's got nothing . . .
20 Old Jeremiah has plenty of money, and as a bachelor, he's got no one . . .

9 Adjective + infinitive

SUBJECT	VERB **to be**	ADJECTIVE	NOUN/ PRONOUN	INFINITIVE
This example	*is*	*easy*		*to understand.*
It	*shouldn't be*	*difficult*	*for you*	*to find the way.*
It	*is*	*advisable*	*for a dog*	*to be trained.*

Note
The third example shows a passive form of the infinitive.

QUESTION

Is it	*normal*	*for him*	*to be so talkative ?*

Notes
1 There is a slight difference in meaning between these constructions: *sure to come/to be there* (an arrangement that can be relied on) *sure of having a good time* (a strong personal feeling).
2 The adjectives **busy** and **worth** are followed by GERUND forms.

Practice

Finish each of these sentences with an infinitive and additional words where necessary. The adjective in each case is printed in bold type.

1 It's important for **elderly** people . . .
2 Is it really **necessary** for you . . .?
3 This train is **sure** . . .
4 On a bitterly cold day like this, it really isn't **sensible** . . .
5 Do you think you're **likely** . . .?
6 Would it be **true** . . .?
7 It's obvious you've got the flu. Wouldn't it have been **better** for you . . .?
8 If you want to be sure of getting on with a new mother-in-law, it's **advisable** . . .
9 On a thoroughly wet day it's so **unpleasant** . . . (have to)
10 In most countries it's **usual** for a passenger in a taxi . . . (a tip)
11 As you're staying only for two days, it shouldn't have been **necessary** for you . . .
11 In a small country village it's quite **uncommon** . . .

Notes
1 See 3 above. There is a difference between the

meanings of these two constructions:
sure to come/to be there (an arrangement that can be relied on)

and: **sure of having a good time/of getting a good meal** (a strong personal feeling).

2 The adjectives **busy** and **worth** are followed by gerund forms (see Part 1, Section G7).

---

10 Too and enough + infinitive

too + ADJECTIVE or ADVERB and **enough** before a NOUN or after an ADJECTIVE or ADVERB are sometimes followed by an infinitive (without **for**).

You're **too stupid to do** *anything but stand about.*
This house is **too big** *for one person* **to look after** *alone.*
The rabbit ran **too quickly to be overtaken** *by the fox.*
He really hasn't got **enough experience to have written a** *worthwhile book.*
You're not **old enough to have been working** *for twenty years.*
He didn't speak **clearly enough to be heard** *by everybody.*

Practice

Complete these sentences with an infinitive and additional words.

1 He's got too few qualifications ...
2 It really isn't warm enough today for grandfather ...
3 I'm sorry. I'm too tired ...
4 I haven't got enough money ...
5 Mrs Gabble dictated this morning's letters too quickly for me ...
6 And he was too irritable and impatient ...
7 There aren't enough hotels for all the expected visitors ...
8 The Arctic explorers took enough food with them ...
9 This writing is too small for me ... (be able)
10 I didn't meet her often enough ...
11 A grand piano would be too large and heavy ...
12 His style of writing is too abstract and obscure for his books ...

---

11 Infinitive forms

	SIMPLE	CONTINUOUS	PERFECT	PERFECT CONTINUOUS
ACTIVE	*(to) make*	*(to) be making*	*(to) have made*	*(to) have been making*
PASSIVE	*(to) be made*		*(to) have been made*	
must (ACTIVE ONLY)	*(to) have to*	*(to) be having to*	*(to) have had to*	*(to) have been having to*
can (ACTIVE ONLY)	*(to) be able to*		*(to) have been able to*	

may	use forms of *be allowed to*

Examples *I should like* **to make** *an announcement.*
He seems **to be stopping** *every third person.*
You must **have made** *a mistake.*
You ought not **to have been working** *so long.*
He's arranged **to be taken** *to the airport by a hired car.*
These immense monuments are said **to have been put up** *by Stone Age people.*
I saw him **give** *a signal to an accomplice.*
Did you let that child **be kidnapped** *without doing anything to save him?*

Practice

Answer these questions, introducing into each of your replies one of the infinitive forms shown above and adding other words.

1 What are eggs used to make?
2 What does the sun appear to be doing throughout the day?
3 What's one important thing you hope to have done by the end of this week?
4 How long are human beings believed to have been living in towns?
5 What does that coin seem to be made of?
6 What's one important world problem you expect to have been solved by the end of this century?
7 What should you do when you see a house on fire and there is nobody else about?
8 What should you be giving all your attention to now?
9 What might you have had to do for a living if you'd been living two hundred years ago?
10 What's one thing scientists would like to be able to discover and develop during the next twenty years?
11 What might you have been doing if today had been a holiday?
12 Suggest one important happening or subject that might have been filmed if there had been film-cameras in Ancient Greece?

---

12 Infinitives used after is/was, can/could, may/might, must/need, should/ought to

is, was *He* **is to see** *me at once.* (A very firm order.)
The motorway **is to be completed** *by 1989.* (A very firm arrangement.)
I **was to see** *him yesterday.* (But I didn't.)
It **was to have been completed** *by 1979.* (But it wasn't.)

can, could *You* **can/could discuss** *that with him tomorrow.* (This is possible.)
You **could have discussed** *that with him yesterday.* (But you didn't.)
He **couldn't have recognised** *you after so many years.* (The speaker believes this impossible, but there is some indication that it is actually true.)

may, might *I* **may/might discuss** *this with him tomorrow.* (This is possible).
I **might have left** *my gloves in the restaurant.* (This is possible.)
He **may/might have telephoned** *while we were out.* (Possible, but unlikely.)
You **might have told me.** (But you didn't and I'm upset.)
He **mightn't have got** *your message yet.* (A possible explanation.)

should, ought to

You **should do** *it at once.* (I advise you to do it.)
The new television series **should be** *popular.* (This is likely.)
You **should have seen** *a doctor at once.* (But you didn't.)
He **should have arrived** *by now.* (Probably, but we're not sure.)
You **shouldn't have mentioned** *it to him.* (But you did.)

ought to may replace **should**.

Note
should has two meanings: DUTY and PROBABILITY.

Note on the above

Whether **could have, may have, might have** and **should have** (**done**) suggest failure to happen or possibility of having happened depends on context.

need not/didn't need

I **need not have** *gone.* (But I went.)
I **didn't need** *to go.* (And I didn't go.)

must/must have, can't have/ couldn't have (contrasts)

He **must be reading** *your letter now.*
He **must have read** *your letter by now.*
(Both of these suggest near certainty, given the facts.)

He **can't have read** *your letter yet.*
You **couldn't have carried** *that by yourself.*
(Both of these actions are impossible, given the circumstances.)

Practice

Using one of the forms in bold type, suggest what might be said/what might have been said in each of these situations. Supply the information referred to in the brackets.

is to/are to

1 A dog-owner is addressing his lively dog before taking him for a walk.
2 You are announcing the date an election will be held.

was to

3 They expected the film star Greta Dietrich to launch the new cruise ship but she didn't. (why not?)

can/could (Say the sentence twice, once with **can**, the second time with **could**.)

4 A suggestion to someone about how to reach London from Edinburgh by train early in the morning (use: **overnight**).

could have/couldn't have

5 A possible explanation of why there's no reply when you telephone a small firm at half past five in the afternoon.
6 Why you're worried by the non-arrival of a close relative who's coming home by car on a foggy evening.
7 A sudden realisation of why the fruit you've stewed tastes sour.

may/might/may not/might not

8 A possible reason for Robin's refusal to learn to drive a car.
9 An unlikely explanation of why your neighbour is digging a long deep trench (a long hole) in his garden.
10 A few possible reasons why a student fails to respond when the teacher asks him a question.
11 A possible reason why the police are calling at the house next door.
12 A possible reason why someone has suddenly cancelled her intended holiday.

may have/might have/mightn't have

13 A suggestion about the reason why Peter speaks such good colloquial Spanish.
14 A possible though unlikely reason for the disappearance of some cheese.
15 An expression of annoyance when you discover that someone has eaten all the ice-cream that was bought for the two of you.
16 A possible reason for somebody's failure to answer an urgent letter.

should/shouldn't

17 Advice to someone who usually gets sea-sick on a long sea journey.
18 Advice about what not to do when living in a hot country.
19 The probability that one of the firm's products will sell well. (what product?)
20 The probability that something won't cost you much (what and why not?)

should have/shouldn't have

21 You think it's time somebody has made a decision so you're going to telephone her. (a decision about what?)
22 You can't find something that's usually in the top drawer of your desk. (what?)
23 You eventually find it somewhere quite unexpected. (where?)

must

24 You suggest that somebody is mistaken. (what about?)

must have/couldn't have

25 In the early morning you find that everywhere is white with snow.
26 Someone arriving at your Glasgow house late in the evening says that he left Australia the evening before.

didn't need to/needn't have

27 You didn't take much money with you when you went shopping. (why not?)
28 You sent a telegram to book a room in a hotel in Florence but you find the hotel half empty when you get there.

13 Passive infinitives

The two forms (shown in the table in Part 1, Section F11) are:

SIMPLE *(to) be made*
PERFECT *(to) have been made*

Examples of usage

These blinds seem to be made of some kind of plastic.
I left instructions for the matter to be investigated immediately.
This church is said to have been first built in the sixth century.
This letter should have been posted yesterday.

Practice

Finish each of these sentences by adding a passive infinitive (simple or perfect form) of the verb in bold type, together with other words supplying answers to the following questions.

1 A new airport is ... (**build** – when? why? = infinitive of purpose)
2 The wounded man is reported ... (**shoot** – by whom?)
3 This cheque is invalid as it ought ... (**sign** – where?)
4 These famous words are known ... (**write** – by whom?)
5 New supplies of oil are expected ... (**discover** – where?)
6 He asked for any telephone messages ... (**record** – when?)
7 This envelope, which should have been sealed, appears ... (**open** – suggested reason?)
8 It's usual for fresh grapefruit ... (**eat** – how?)
9 This picture is believed ... (**paint** – by whom?)
10 The junior clerk hopes ... (**promote** – how soon?)
11 It's essential for the baby ... (**feed** – how often?)
12 Your car ought ... (**not park** – where?)

14 Verbs followed by an infinitive or a participle with a resultant meaning change

Verbs associated with three of the five senses, SIGHT, HEARING and FEELING (usually expressed as TOUCH) can be followed by either an infinitive or a participle.

see/watch/observe/notice someone { *jump* / *jumping* }

hear/listen to someone { *shout* / *shouting* }

feel something { *move* / *moving* }

The verb **smell** is normally followed only by a participle, not an infinitive.

Meaning differences

She watched me **write** *my surname.*
She watched me **writing** *my letter.*

I heard Mavis Thrush **sing** *a top C.*
I heard Massimo Tenore **singing** *in his bath.*

I felt the child on my lap **shiver** *when his father shouted at him.*
I felt the child on my lap **shivering** *with the cold.*

The INFINITIVE suggests a momentary and/or completed action.

The PRESENT PARTICIPLE suggests a continuing action. It expresses an interest in the doing of the action rather than its completion.
She watched us throwing the ball backwards and forwards.
I could hear him coughing/hammering/giving orders.
I noticed him tapping the table with his pencil while he was thinking.
He could see the fog creeping up from the sea.
I can smell something cooking. (A smell usually lingers for some time, so a continuous action is almost certainly being referred to.)

Notes

1 A common mistake is the use of **to** with the infinitive:
We saw him stop.
I heard him say my name.

2 The PRESENT PARTICIPLE may:
a) form part of a continuous verb tense.
he is coming, they have been coming
b) be used as an adjective.
the coming week, coming events.

The GERUND (noun) and PRESENT PARTICIPLE (adjective) are identical in form, but different in function. This difference may have some effect on usage after certain verbs.
I don't approve of his **coming** *so often.* (GERUND) (**his** is adjectival before the noun **coming.**)
I didn't see him **coming.** (PARTICIPLE) (**him** is a pronoun associated with the participle/adjective **coming.**)

Practice

Complete the following sentences with a number of words which include an infinitive or a participle related to the verb in bold type. The form you use will depend on the meaning you wish to convey.

1 On this wonderful spring morning I could hear ... **sing** (where?)
2 The store detective reported to the manager that he had seen ... **steal** (what?)
3 During an earthquake one can feel ... **shake**
4 While Amanda was upstairs she smelt ... **burn** (so what did she do?)
5 I think I know where your season ticket is. I saw it ... **lie** (where?)
6 A keen ornithologist may spend a lot of time observing ... **build** (where?)
7 Did you hear ... **explode** (where?)
8 Mick was doing a jigsaw puzzle while his mother stood watching ... **fit**
9 For over an hour the concert audience sat completely silent and motionless listening to ... **play** (what?)

Section G Gerunds, clauses after certain verbs, make and do, have something done

1 The gerund as subject of a verb

Definition of the gerund

a The gerund is a NOUN consisting of an INFINITIVE form + **ing**. In some cases a spelling adjustment is necessary.

singing *riding* *swimming* *lying*

As a noun it may be SUBJECT, OBJECT or COMPLEMENT of a verb, or it may follow a PREPOSITION.

Gliding *is* **flying** *without engine power.* (SUBJECT and COMPLEMENT)
A cat dislikes **getting** *wet.* (OBJECT)
Accidents are usually caused by careless **driving.** (following a PREPOSITION)

b The above characteristics are all those of a NOUN. The gerund may also have certain VERBAL characteristics.

1 It may take an OBJECT.
Spending money *is easier than* **earning money.**

2 It can be modified by an ADVERB.
He attracted attention by **shouting loudly.**

3 A gerundial form of **be** and **have** followed by an appropriate past participle can express a PASSIVE or PAST idea.
Dogs usually enjoy **being bathed.** (PASSIVE)
Having driven *alone across the Sahara Desert is something to boast about.* (PERFECT FORM)

To the learner of English, the most important aspects of the gerund are its uses (a) as SUBJECT of a verb, (b) as OBJECT of certain verbs, and (c) after PREPOSITIONS.

Infinitive or gerund as subject of the verb

In many languages the infinitive form may appear as the subject of the verb. This is grammatically possible in English:

To make a speech *for five hours non-stop demands a strong voice, determination, stamina and a chained audience.*

However, the gerund is far more commonly used for this purpose.

Doing nothing *isn't always restful.*
Singing *may be more enjoyable for the performer than the audience.*

Note
The use of **it** as subject followed by a suitable verb (often **to be**) is more common than the use of an infinitive subject.

It is important to sign a letter legibly. (not: *To sign a letter legibly is important.*)
It needs a lot of patience to train a dog in obedience. (unnatural: *To train a dog in obedience needs a lot of patience.*)

Practice

a Suggest a suitable gerund subject (which may consist of more than one word) for each of these sentences.

EXAMPLE
... can be extremely tiring.
Visiting art galleries and museums can be extremely tiring.

1 ... is an enjoyable form of exercise.
2 ... is faster than other forms of travel.
3 ... requires considerable skill.
4 ... may waste a lot of time.
5 ... may sound pleasant but be boring.
6 ... costs a lot of money.
7 ... needs skill, intelligence and concentration.
8 ... is one of the main problems of the future.
9 ... takes up far too much of my time.
10 ... can get you into trouble with the law.

b Use each of these gerund forms as subject of the sentence. Vary the verbs that follow them.

EXAMPLE
doing crossword puzzles
Doing crossword puzzles can become a time-wasting addiction.

1 cycling
2 stamp-collecting
3 using a dictionary intelligently
4 reading an English book
5 driving carelessly
6 downhill skiing
7 smoking a pipe
8 rock-climbing
9 prolonged travelling
10 getting something for nothing

2 The gerund as object of a verb

Many verbs can be followed by an infinitive form. Fewer, but still a fair number, can be followed by a gerund. Some verbs can be followed by either infinitive or gerund without a meaning change (see Part 1, Section G3) or with a meaning change (see Part 1, Section G4).

The following are the most common verbs which can be followed by a GERUND, but not by an infinitive.

suggest	**finish**	**deny**	**miss**
enjoy	**spend time** (e.g **a week**)	**consider**	**risk**
mind	**waste time/money**	**excuse**	**escape**
can't help	**postpone**	**forgive**	**grudge**
keep	**delay**	**avoid**	**can't bear**
			can't stand

Notes

1 As a noun, the gerund can be preceded by a possessive adjective.
He suggested **our visiting** *the cathedral.*
Do you mind **my smoking**?
Please forgive **our interrupting** *you.*

2 **deny doing** and **deny having done** have, with rare exceptions, similar meaning.
He denied publishing/having published the libellous article.

3 **go swimming** – **swimming** is not here the object of the verb **go**. Other examples are **go skiing** and **go riding**.

4 Verbs expressing positions of the body are often followed by the gerund
stand waiting *sit reading* *lie thinking.*
Compare: They stood to sing the National Anthem. (PURPOSE)

Practice

What would you say in each of these situations? In your response, use a form of the verb in brackets followed by a suitable gerund.

EXAMPLE
You are describing how you nearly had an accident. (escape)
I narrowly escaped having an accident while cycling in the dark.

1 You are discussing a suitable Christmas present for your great grandfather. (suggest)
2 You are describing what you like to do on your holiday. (enjoy)
3 You are asking somebody to post a letter for you. (mind)
4 You are advising someone not to travel in London during the rush hour. (avoid)
5 A father is criticising his son for wasting his time. (spend far too much time . . . and far too little . . .)
6 Explain how you can waste a lot of time. (waste time)
7 You are explaining why it wasn't your fault you were late. (couldn't help . . . because . . .)
8 Explain why somebody annoys you. (keep)
9 You are surprised at how long a meal lasted. (finish – eat)
10 Describe how Alec spends Sunday morning. (sit)
11 Mr Maybloom is feeling a little better this morning so he won't make his will yet. (postpone)
12 Parliament refuses to ratify the treaty until there are more guarantees. (delay)
13 Explain that Trevor has said he didn't steal the money. (deny)
14 You went without lunch yesterday. Why? (miss)
15 Ask politely what country somebody comes from. (excuse my . . .)
16 How you felt about the taxi-driver who had been very unpleasant and unhelpful. (give him a tip) (grudge)
17 Your reply to somebody who has asked you what kind of car you want next. (consider – PRESENT CONTINUOUS TENSE)
18 What happened when Barnaby's car swerved off the road into a deep lake. (escape being)

3 Verbs followed by either an infinitive or a gerund with very little meaning difference

These verbs include:

I **like** *to skate.*	*I* **like** *skating.*
I **love** *to dance.*	*I* **love** *dancing.*
He **began** *to argue.*	*He* **began** *arguing.*
He **started** *to cry.*	*He* **started** *crying.*
They **continued** *to talk.*	*They* **continued** *talking.*
He **recommended** *(my) selling the house.*	*He* **recommended** *me to sell the house.*

Notes

1 The GERUND is more common than the INFINITIVE after **like** and **love**.
2 The GERUND rarely follows **begin**, **start** or **continue** when they are used in a continuous form.
He is beginning to improve.
He was starting to cry.
3 In the case of the verbs **dislike**, **hate** and **dread**, a following GERUND form is far more common than an INFINITIVE.
He dislikes/hates/dreads meeting strangers.

Practice

Some of these questions include a gerund form, others an infinitive. When suggesting answers to the questions, reverse the form used: a gerund in place of an infinitive and vice versa.

EXAMPLE
When would you recommend my visiting Greece?
I'd recommend you to visit Greece in the spring.

1 Why do you think a lot of people like spending their holidays near the sea or a lake?
2 Why do old people love to speak about the past?
3 What could human beings start to do after fire had been discovered?
4 How long will you continue attending this course?
5 What area would you recommend my visiting if I spent a holiday in your country?

4 Verbs followed by an infinitive or by a gerund with a meaning change

remember, forget

remember / **forget** — **doing** something which has in fact already been done.
One has (or has not) the memory of doing it still in one's mind.
remember / **forget** — **to do** something one ought to do.

'Please **remember to post** *this letter.'* (8 a.m.)
'Did you **remember to post** *it?'* (6 p.m.)
'I don't remember. I posted some business letters, but I can't **remember posting** *yours.'*

I mustn't **forget to telephone** *Estelle.*
I've never **forgotten meeting** *her for the first time twenty-five years ago.*

need

need to do — *I* **need to change** *some more money.*
need doing — *My hair* **needs cutting.** (with PASSIVE implication)

try

I **tried to reach** *a book on the top shelf, but I couldn't.*
I **tried standing** *on a dictionary to reach it, but I still couldn't manage it.*
You **try doing** something that is quite easy to do, to help you when you are **trying to do** something more difficult.

stop

stop doing what you are already doing.
stop to do something different.
Sebastian **stopped reading** *his newspaper* **to turn on** *the television.*

used

(pronunciation ju:st/)
Compare: *I* **used to get up** *early but I don't do this now.*
with: *I am* **used to getting up** *early, so I don't mind doing it.*

regret

I **regret to inform** *you that we cannot offer you the post.* (This is a formally polite way of giving bad news.)
I now **regret having** *said such unkind things.*

prefer When two things are being compared, **prefer** is used with the GERUND.
I **prefer going** *for a walk to lying on the beach.* (two possibilities: GERUND)
I **prefer to stay** *indoors when it's cold.* (one possibility: INFINITIVE)
I'd **prefer**/*I would* **prefer to live** *away from London.*

leave *I* **left** *Bert* **working** *in the garden.* (He was working already.)
I **left** *Bert* **to work** *in the garden. At least, that is what he said he was going to do.* (He intended to work.)

Practice

Finish each of these sentences suitably, using the verb in bold type and supplying the information referred to by the question in brackets.

1 I must remember . . . (**ask** what?)
2 He says he doesn't remember . . . (**promise** what?)
3 Did you forget . . . (**buy** what? when?)
4 He will never forget . . . (**see** what terrible thing?)
5 You must always remember . . . (**say** what? when?)
6 I tried in vain . . . (**find** what? why couldn't you?)
7 If I'm not there in the morning, try . . . (**telephone** when?)
8 If I don't stop . . . (**smoke** – what will happen?)
9 When an inventor is really absorbed in a new project he won't stop (**concentrate**) . . . even . . . (add several more words)
10 When I was young, I used . . . (**enjoy** what?)
11 Greenlanders are used to . . . (**work** in what conditions?)
12 I've often regretted . . . (**spend** so much – what on? why?)
13 We regret . . . (**announce** what?)
14 I prefer . . . (**discuss** what?) to (**talk about** what?)
15 When shopping, I prefer . . . **pay** (how? – by cheque, credit card or in cash?)
16 I'd prefer not . . . (**have** what? when?)
17 I left my dog . . . (**sleep** where?)
18 I left my husband to . . . (**do** what? but what actually happened?)

5 The gerund after prepositions and conjunctions

Like other nouns, a gerund often follows a preposition. It is used in all cases where an action or state is being referred to. The only two exceptions are **except** and **but** (see below).

Examples *by using for making on hearing of losing while sitting when speaking*
He got a sore throat **from talking** *too much.*
He is used **to going** *without food.*

Exceptions *He did everything he could to annoy me* **except sing**.
They did nothing **but grumble**.

Prepositional phrases Here are some examples of prepositional phrases followed by a gerund:

on account of living *in the middle of playing* *after finishing*
by means of saving *in addition to wearing* *since arriving*
in spite of trying *with reference to hiring* *besides owning*
in the event of losing *before starting* *apart from having*

Practice

Finish each of these sentences with a suitable gerund form and additional words.

1 He made his large fortune by . . .
2 He hasn't done a day's work since . . .
3 Learning English in the classroom is quite different from . . .
4 Stephen felt rather ill after . . .
5 He was given a reward for . . .
6 He thought over the matter very carefully before . . .
7 She runs a café besides . . .
8 He became famous as a result of . . .
9 He screamed in terror on . . .
10 He does odd jobs for people in addition to . . .
11 He gives me no help at all apart from . . .
12 He learned Arabic while . . .

6 The gerund after verbs followed by prepositions or adverbial particles

After verbs A gerund may follow a PREPOSITION which itself follows a VERB or ADJECTIVE.

about *see/think/learn/grumble about having*
for *apologise/blame someone/compensate* (*someone*)*/punish someone for losing*
use/pay (*someone*)*/reward someone for doing*
from *prevent someone from escaping*
save someone from drowning
in *succeed in winning*
persist in contradicting
we believe in eating
on *go/keep/insist/decide on asking* (**keep** can be used without **on**)
depend/rely on finding
congratulate on winning
of *think of selling*
accuse of stealing
to *look forward to meeting*
object to being sold
with *put up with working long hours*
like *feel like having a coffee*
against *warn against driving dangerously*

Note

1 **depend on/rely on** + GERUND:
The future prospects of the firm **depend on** *our* **finding** *new customers.*
depend on/rely on somebody + INFINITIVE:
A blind man may **depend/rely on his dog to guide** *him safely.* (**rely on** often suggests personal trust as well as need.)

Examples *I must* **see about doing** *the washing up.*
He's **talking about redecorating** *his bungalow.*
I'm just **thinking about doing** *some housework.*
He **blamed** *my dog* **for spoiling** *his rose-bed.*

Practice

a When responding to these questions, include the verb shown, followed by a suitable preposition and gerund. Suggest answers to any additional questions.

EXAMPLE
grumble
What do many law-abiding citizens object to doing?
They grumble about having to pay high income tax, value added tax (VAT) and rates.

1 **apologise**
What did Brian say when he turned up half an hour late? What excuse did he give?
2 **succeed**
How much money did you collect for the refugees? What was it used for?
3 **accuse**
Why aren't Ricky and Vicky on speaking terms?
3 **feel**
Describe Miss Marter's feelings when her boss gave her four long letters to type during her lunch hour. What did she actually do?
5 **pay**
How does a solicitor earn money? (Begin: His clients . . .)
6 **use**
What use do you make of a paper clip?

7 **prevent**
What do the angry farmers hope to achieve by blocking the main road with their tractors?
8 **insist**
Why were the textile-workers on strike for two months? Were they successful?
9 **reward**
What happened when Ginger took the lost dog back to its owner?
10 **punish**
Why is Micky sitting in the classroom while the other boys are out playing football? (Use a passive form.)
11 **go**
How long did Mr Brook's speech last yesterday? What was he talking about?
12 **warn**
What's the purpose of the road sign 'steep hill'?
13 **congratulate**
What was the Managing Director saying to the Sales Manager?
14 **look forward**
What are your feelings as you walk home on a bitterly cold and wet winter evening?

b Each of these verbs may be followed by some kind of preposition or adverbial particle before a gerund. Suggest a suitable subject for each verb in cases where no subject is suggested. Add the normally-used preposition or adverbial particle.

Choose at least two of the following actions which could relate suitably to the verb (used with an affirmative or negative meaning), adapting the verb so as to form a grammatical sentence. Add other words where suitable.

EXAMPLES
blame depend object
get a theatre seat at the last moment
be shouted at break the window
pay a pound for a cup of coffee
be able to find somewhere to stay late at night
cause the accident

You can't **blame** me **for breaking** the window. I wasn't even there.
Webster **blamed** the other driver **for causing** the accident.
You can't **depend** on **getting** a theatre seat at the last moment.
You shouldn't **depend** on **being able** to find somewhere to stay if you don't arrive until midnight.

I strongly **object to being** shouted at.
The tourist **objected to paying** a pound for a cup of coffee.

Verbs to use:
think apologise prevent succeed accuse grumble

1 have to do so much overtime
2 forget his wife's birthday
3 win the first prize
4 tell lies
5 thick fog (SUBJECT) . . . see
6 not earn enough to make ends meet
7 commit the recent murder
8 build an extra room on to his house
9 climb Mount Everest
10 tread on his toe
11 laryngitis (SUBJECT) . . . speak
12 invest my money in oil shares

insist look forward warn put up feel

13 celebrate Christmas with his family
14 be bitten by mosquitoes
15 always get exactly what he wanted
16 trust tall, dark, good-looking strangers
17 see their son-in-law and daughter in Australia again
18 eat only nuts, fruit and vegetables
19 spend hours travelling to work
20 tell that slave-driver, my boss (what?)
21 leave chilly England to live on a sunlit tropical island

After adjectives followed by prepositions	about	*enthusiastic/angry/depressed about having to work long hours*
	at	*good at repairing*
	for	*responsible for supervising*
	of	*afraid/ashamed/tired of making (mistakes)*
		proud/capable/sure of passing (an exam)
		fond of listening
	on	*keen on playing*
	to	*opposed/used to working*
	with	*bored/fed up with learning*

Examples *He isn't* **enthusiastic about teaching** *Greek to the Sixth Form.*
With a pocket calculator handy, he's no longer **afraid of making** *mistakes in arithmetic.*

Practice

Answer each of the following questions with a sentence which includes one of the listed adjectives together with a suitable preposition and gerund. At least one of the answers will be negative.

depressed incapable good responsible keen tired afraid used ashamed

EXAMPLE
Why's Nathaniel so miserable?
He's **depressed about having** quarrelled with his girl-friend.

1 What are the main duties of a cashier?
2 Why is Dillan so polite and quiet today? He certainly wasn't yesterday. (lose one's temper)
3 Why's Lucy running to the railway station?
4 Why has Daniel refused to go and watch the cricket match?
5 Why does Sabrina always carry the map when they go on a cross-country ramble (= walk)? (map-reading)
6 Why doesn't Duncan want to take his car abroad with him? (on the right)
7 Why has Jeremy insisted on eating in a restaurant today?
8 Why does Des always wear glasses, even when he's swimming?

7 Other expressions followed by a gerund

Noun + preposition + gerund

the **difficulty of finding** *enough time to do everything*
the **problem of feeding** *the world's population*
the **value of learning** *self-control*
the **necessity of/for earning** *a living*
the **effects of polluting** *the atmosphere*
an **interest in stamp-collecting**
a **way of improving** *industrial techniques*

Many other examples could be given.

Adjectives with no following preposition

a **busy sewing**
worth seeing

b Certain other adjectives can be followed either by a GERUND or by an INFINITIVE, with similar meaning:

It's **useless/pointless** {**planting** / **to plant**} *roses in this kind of soil.*

It's **hopeless** {**trying** *to* / **to try** *and*} *grow carnations here.*

Note
Notice these constructions:
It's **no use planting** *dahlias either.*
It's **no good hoping** *that they'll grow.*
There's **no harm in trying** *some chrysanthemums though.* (Note the preposition here.)

how about

how about is often used with a GERUND to make a suggestion.
How about going on an excursion tomorrow?
How about our buying a tent and going camping?

what about is sometimes used in this way, but is more often used to ask a question.
What about the matches to light a fire with? We haven't brought any.

Practice

Suggest an ending to each of these sentences which includes a suitable form of the verb in bold type together with other words.

1 Can you imagine the difficulty of . . . **look for**
2 Nobody can fully foresee the results of . . . **destroy**
3 Far too few people show any interest in . . . **give**
4 Arguing endlessly with people isn't necessarily the best way of . . . **persuade** (several more words here)
5 I don't think you've considered sufficiently the cost of . . . **heat**
6 Young parents don't always realise the importance of . . . **teach**
7 What's your opinion of . . . **invest**
8 The two waitresses in the crowded restaurant were busy . . . **take** . . . and . . . **carry**
9 A book that's really worth . . . **read**
10 Well, that's at least got the garden tidy. How about . . .? (suggest your own verb)

8 Verbs followed by a clause

A CLAUSE is a group of words containing:

SUBJECT + RELATED VERB + (probably) OTHER WORDS

Many verbs may under certain circumstances be followed by a clause. These fall into three main categories.

Verbs that can be followed by a clause

Only a noun/pronoun or a clause object are possible in these cases. This category includes:

realise	**ensure**	**estimate**	**doubt**	**guess**
convince	**be convinced**	**emphasise**	**imagine**	**suspect**

and verbs which denote the giving of or asking for information, such as **say**, **state** and **reply**.

We suddenly realised it was getting late.
He convinced me that he was telling the truth.
He asked me whether/if I was coming/how I felt.

Notes
1 Certain verbs such as **forecast**, **imagine**, and the verbal phrase **have no idea** are normally followed by a clause, though a gerund is also possible in some cases:
Everybody forecasts his winning the race.
Can you imagine my winning a beauty contest?
2 **estimate** and **imagine** can be followed by an infinitive.
I estimated/imagined him to be about sixteen.

Verbs followed by either an infinitive or a clause

a Some verbs can be followed by either an infinitive or a clause, but must be followed by a clause when the subject of each verb is different.
They've decided to move to London. (INFINITIVE)
They've decided that they'll move to London. (CLAUSE)
They've decided that there are more opportunities there. (CLAUSE – The subjects of **decided** and **are** are different.)

Other verbs include:

hope	**arrange**	**would rather**	**swear**
expect	**claim**	**agree**	**propose**

Note
There is no **to** before an infinitive following **would rather**.
He would rather leave now.
He would rather you left now.

b The fact that either an infinitive or a clause may be used when the subject of the main and the following verb is the same usually makes little or no difference to the meaning.

I expected to meet him/(that) I'd meet him today.
He hoped to be able to come/(that) he'd be able to come.
They pretended to be VIPs (Very Important Persons)/(that) they were VIPs.
He guaranteed to send it/(that) he would send it promptly.
He reminded me to go/(that) I had to go at four.

c In the following cases there is a change of meaning. This is usually related to a change in meaning of the main verb.

I **wish** *to speak now.*	*I* **know** *how to do it.*
I **wish** *I could speak now.*	*I* **know** *(that) I can do it.*

Verbs that may be followed by either a gerund or a clause

Some of the verbs in these examples are followed by a preposition before the gerund.

He **suggested** *(our) going home.*
He **suggested** *(that) we (should) go home/(that) we went home.*

He **recommended** *my buying it/that I should buy it.*
He **denied** *seeing/having seen the accident/(that) he had seen the accident.*
He **reported** *finding/having found the money/(that) he had found the money.*
He **insisted** *on (their) buying it/(that)he/they should buy it.*

Practice

Heidi, an eighteen-year-old Swiss girl, has arranged an au-pair job with an English family in a small country town and although she knows very little about them, she has her own impressions of what might await her. Using each of these sentence openings, followed by a suitable clause, say what you think these impressions might be. Ideas are suggested in brackets (with verbal infinitives) but if you have some ideas of your own, so much the better. Practise occasional negative forms.

EXAMPLES
It seemed unlikely . . . (other Swiss girls – where?)
It seemed unlikely there would be any other Swiss girls in the same town.
She was aware . . . (spoilt children)
She was aware that she might have to look after spoilt children.

1 She imagined that . . . (large house)
2 She hoped . . . (meet her – where?)
3 She expected . . . (stay – how long?)
4 She realised . . . (work hard)
5 She knew the family . . . (speak German)
6 She was convinced . . . (best way of)
7 She wondered if . . . (have the opportunity)
8 She guessed . . . (a lot to do)
9 She had an idea . . . (have a very exciting time)
10 Her English friend suggested . . . (bring what with her?)
11 She had already insisted that . . . (a room to herself)
12 The family had guaranteed that . . . (attend English classes – where?)
13 She had agreed . . . (work – how long each week?)
14 It had already been arranged that . . . (be paid – how much?)
15 She would rather the family . . . (live – where?)
16 She had already discovered that . . . (beautiful area)

9 Revision: various constructions involving infinitives, gerunds and clauses

Practice

a Give your opinions or ideas on the following three subjects. Select from the verbs listed below in each case, together with an infinitive, gerund or clause as appropriate to the verb. Practise both affirmative and negative forms. An example follows the first subject.

1 Explain why you would prefer to live:
in or near a large or fairly large town
in a small quiet town or village
should like ('**d like**) **object**
should rather ('**d rather**) **enjoy like**
spend a lot of time be interested feel like
enough
I shouldn't like to live in the centre of a town: I'd rather live in the suburbs.

2 Explain why you'd prefer to work for/in:
a large company, organisation or school or
a small company, organisation or school
realise suppose think want help (**me**)
expect encourage hope try decide
doubt decide tend succeed profit
so as by while mind

3 As a travel office clerk you are advising an English-speaking customer who is planning to tour an area of your country in his/her own car. Suggest some interesting places to visit and give some advice about finding accommodation and making the most of the tour.
advise suggest recommend enjoy
avoid help arrange seem manage
persuade dislike feel like don't mind
had better ('**d better**) **prefer worth**
tired (**of**) **delighted** (**with**) **interested**
too little time

b Max, aged seventeen, is determined to spend a year in England and has at last persuaded his father to pay for an English course in a language school in London and to allow him just enough money to live on. As his father knows, however, that Max is really more interested in what seems the exciting experience of living in a large cosmopolitan city than attending language courses, he gives his son a lot of serious advice, though he hasn't got very much hope that the boy will pay a lot of attention to it. (Max's father speaks English as well as you do, and often uses it when speaking to his son to give the boy practice in understanding.) He begins each sentence with one of the following openings (though occasionally preceding it with a suitable word or phase). He always follows the opening with some kind of verbal form: infinitive, gerund or clause. Some ideas which he expresses are suggested below the sentence openings though (as Father) you may have some of your own to suggest.

Suggest some of the advice that Max's father gives.

EXAMPLE
Don't forget . . .
Don't forget to keep in touch with us at home by letter or telephone whatever happens.

Sentence openings:
I want you . . . I recommend you . . .
You must promise me . . .
I hope you don't decide . . .
Don't let other people encourage . . .
It's very important . . . I suggest . . . I doubt . . .
Don't be afraid . . . I hope you manage . . .
Be careful not . . . You should avoid . . .
It isn't worth . . . Don't be too . . .
You'd better . . . Remember . . .
I hope you will succeed . . . If you happen . . .
There is, of course, the difficulty . . .

Some possible ideas to follow the opening with (suitably adapted):
(not) carry too much money about with you
make a lot of friends
(not) lose your passport
see as much as possible
keep out of trouble
attend classes regularly
write home at least once a week
behave sensibly
use your commonsense
get on well with your teachers
find somewhere pleasant to live
soon settle down
improve your English enormously
waste your money on non-essentials
make the most of every minute of your time
believe all you're told

---

10 The verbs do and make

do, make + object Mistakes often arise from the confusion of these two verbs, partly because it is impossible to define an exact meaning difference between them. Broadly speaking:

one **does** an ACTION
one **makes** or creates a NEW THING

but this definition does not always apply, so each example of usage has to be learned and practised separately.

There are far too many **do** and **make** expressions to include here, but a good dictionary for learners of English will list most of them.

The following are among the most common and the most important to know.

do *work* (*homework, housework* etc.)
a job (*an exercise, a test, an exam* etc.)
lessons
the washing up
the shopping (also: *go shopping*)
one's hair
any (*no*) *good/harm*
(*someone*) *good/harm*
a good turn/a favour
a lot (*to help*)

make *something* (*a cake, coffee, a dress* etc.)
the beds
a noise/a fuss/trouble/a mess
an appointment/an agreement/an arrangement/progress/ an improvement/a mistake/a (*typing*) *error*
a copy *money* *changes* *sense* *fun of*
a will *a profit* *friends with* *a difference* *allowances for*

Practice

In replying to each of these questions and suggestions, make use of one of the above expressions, suitably adapted in tense and form. Try to decide without looking at the list, referring to it only as a check.

1 What do you use your comb for?
2 When does a teacher suggest your correcting something you've said in English?
3 Why are a lot of housewives away from their homes at around ten o'clock in the morning?
4 What's a coffee percolator used for?
5 Why do some people take vitamin tablets and tonics?
6 What does a shy housewife often have difficulty in doing when she and her family move to a new area?
7 What do you usually have to do before you visit an important person or your dentist?
8 What are children usually asked not to do when one of the family is ill?
9 Why hasn't the teacher got any correcting to do at home this week?
10 Why do doctors advise against smoking too much?
11 Why is Enid's teacher able to give her a better report this term?
12 What provision does an older person make for the distribution of his/her property?
13 How do children spend most of their time at school?
14 What does a sensitive person hate other people doing?
15 What does a new and energetic manager usually want to do when he/she first takes over a job?
16 What do company directors always want to do?
17 What does a teacher make the students do occasionally in order to find out what they know?
18 What should a schoolteacher remember to do mentally in the case of a child who makes little progress owing to ill health?
19 What do secretaries normally do when typing important letters?
20 Mother has tidied the sitting-room ready for the evening's guests. When the children want to play in it, what does she beg them not to do?
21 If there isn't a dishwasher, what job has to be carried out after every meal?

22 What effect are private lessons having on Ben's schoolwork?
23 What might you say if you received a message that seemed to have no meaning?
24 'Will you do me a favour?' Say this in another way.

Phrasal forms and other expressions with do and make

do
do something for a living (to earn money for everyday necessities)
I could do with (a long cool drink). (You'd like to have it.)
That's done. (finished)
That's done it. (started trouble or spoilt something)
This meat is overdone/underdone. (too much or too little cooked)
These shoes are done for. (worn out)
Will this do? Yes, it'll do nicely. (be quite suitable)
do away with (get rid of)
do without (manage without having something)
do up a house (redecorate it)
Nothing doing. (a refusal to co-operate)
have something/nothing to do
have something to do with (be related to or connected with)

make
make up one's mind (decide)
make sure (confirm)
make the most of (use or enjoy as much as possible)
three and five make eight
make up for (compensate for)
We'll make it. (manage to do something such as catching a train)
What do you make the time? (often asked when one doubts one's own watch)
make do (with) (use something else when the most suitable thing isn't available)

Many phrasal forms of **do** and **make** appear in the sections on prepositions (Part 3).

Practice

Using a suitable one of the expressions given above, suggest what might be said in each of these situations. The verb should be adapted to its context.

EXAMPLES

You have been asked what job Julian Richmond does.

Oh, he doesn't have to do anything for a living. His father's an oil millionaire.

You've been asked why you always carry a map when you go for a walk in the surrounding countryside.

Just to make sure I don't get lost. The ground's very marshy in some parts.

1 When a friend asks if you've got a cigarette lighter you produce some matches. What question do you ask?
2 What reply does your friend give?
3 Your fridge has broken down, so what do you say to Mick who insists on having ice cubes in his lemonade?
4 Mandy has been overworking and looks tired out. She says she wants a holiday and explains why this is impossible.
5 You've just discovered a pullover full of moth holes. What do you say about its condition and what you must do with it. (Begin: This pullover . . .)
6 What has happened to steam trains in many European countries?

7 When she opens her flat door, Penelope has paint on her hair, her face and her hands. She apologises and explains. What does she say?

8 After three days of rain while you're on holiday, you at last wake up to a beautiful sunny day – but will the fine weather last? What do you say you are determined to do?
9 You are stating your opinion that there is no connection between astrology and science.
10 Say this in another way: 12 minus 8 = 4.
11 You're checking with someone that it really is half past five.
12 What might you say to a waiter when you don't yet know which item on the menu you want to order?
13 As a social welfare officer you are trying to explain why some young people steal cars and get into other kinds of trouble.
14 Explain to a waiter why you can't eat the vegetables he's brought you.
15 Turn down someone's suggestion that you join a certain political party.
16 As a worker who has just lost his job, explain why you aren't satisfied with the redundancy payment.
17 On her way to the cinema, Lana can't quite remember whether she turned the gas out, and insists on going back to check. What does she say to her husband?
18 Brown believes that Pestdeath spray may kill the greenfly on his roses, but White, who has tried it, doesn't agree. What does White say?

---

11 Having things done

If you are unwilling or unable to do a job yourself, you may arrange for another person to do it for you.

For example, Annette never washes and sets her hair herself.
She goes to the hairdresser to **have her hair washed and set.**
Annette does not do the job herself – she asks someone to do it for her.

She **has** {**her hair** / **it**} **washed/set/cut/permed/styled/done for her.**

get is sometimes used instead of **have**, with little difference in meaning, though it may suggest more activity or intention on the part of the subject.
Compare: *I must* **get** *my hair* **cut/shampooed.**
and: *My dog must* **have** *his hair/coat* **cut/shampooed.**
get gives the impression that the dog himself must make the arrangement.

Examples *have a suit made/altered/pressed*
have shoes mended/repaired
have a coat shortened/lengthened/cleaned
have one's photograph taken
have photographs developed/printed/processed
have a house built/demolished/redecorated/valued
have an extra key cut

have furniture delivered
have a letter photocopied/forwarded/filed
have a book typed/printed/published/reviewed
have a tooth extracted/filled
have one's eyes tested
have one's voice trained
have one's homework corrected/marked
have a picture framed
have one's car serviced/washed
have tyre pressure/oil/brakes checked
have one's fortune told
have one's portrait painted
have one's fingerprints taken

Verb forms The verbs **have** or **get** need to be adapted to (a) their SUBJECT, (b) the TIME OF THE ACTION, and (c) OTHER WORDS IN THE SENTENCE.

I am **having** *my watch repaired.* (PRESENT CONTINUOUS)
She **has had** *her glasses changed.* (PRESENT PERFECT)
He is going **to have** *his voice recorded.* (INFINITIVE)
I saw him **having** *his name and address taken by a traffic warden.* (PARTICIPLE)
My cat enjoys **having** *her coat brushed.* (GERUND)

Practice

Finish each of these sentences or suggest an additional one introducing one of the short examples above together with any other information asked for. The form will have to be adapted suitably and the noun object may be different.

EXAMPLES
Owen visited the fortune-teller at the fair. He wanted ...
to have his fortune told.
The police suspect Bob Brakin of burglary. He's at the police station now where ...
he's having his fingerprints taken.
The Earl of Chesterfield, in scarlet robes, was standing motionless on a platform, ... (GERUND)
having his portrait painted.

1 It's a bit risky having only one door key. Why don't you ...?
2 Hector's got an appointment with the dentist tomorrow. Poor chap! ... (arranged future)
3 Heather's very short-sighted and so she believes in ... (GERUND)
4 I was so tired of orange wallpaper and brown paint in my sitting-room that ...
5 I'm afraid I can't carry all these vegetables myself. Would it be possible ...?
6 You should have hung those trousers up, not folded them. Now you'll need ...
7 I've written some English exercises, Miss Chalker. May I ...?
8 Before you set out on such a long car journey, I advise you ...
9 She's just completed her first novel and she now has the problem ...
10 I've got to send away two copies of each of these certificates. How much would it cost ...?
11 When they're away on holiday they make arrangements with the Post Office ...
12 'What's that terrible screaming noise?' 'Oh, that's Ruby practising. She ...'
13 I've just finished taking photos with my first roll of colour film. Now where can ...?
14 Before the insurance company will give me cover against theft and burglary, they insist ...
15 It's time I took this skirt to the cleaners ...
16 That's a superb portrait enlargement of your baby. Why ...?
17 The car seems to be running all right but before we go to Norway, I think we ...

Part 2

Contents Non-verbal parts of speech

Section F Adverbs

Section G Word order

Section A Nouns

1 Countables and uncountables

Nouns used countably

Nouns used COUNTABLY refer to objects and ideas of which there can be one or more examples of the same kind. They can therefore:
1 be preceded by **a** or **one**
2 have a plural form

one suitcase *a suitcase* *three suitcases* *several suitcases*
Compare: *luggage*

a fact	*facts*	
a report	*reports*	Compare: *information*
a detail	*details*	

Nouns used uncountably

Nouns used UNCOUNTABLY refer to ideas which are apparently (a) indivisible and generalised so that isolated examples cannot exist, and (b) formless so that they cannot be separated and counted.

air *sunshine* *darkness* *steel* *electricity*
water *Nature* *concrete* *wool* *nuclear power*
weather
abstract nouns including *knowledge, progress, strength*

1 As an isolated example cannot exist, these nouns cannot be preceded by **a/an** or **one.**
2 As the idea expressed cannot be counted, they can have no plural form.

A plural idea may be suggested by the addition of another appropriate noun.

a glass of water	*glasses of water*
a type of weather	*types of weather*
a ball of wool	*balls of wool*
an item/a piece of information	*items/pieces of information*

A certain amount, or none, can be referred to by expressions such as (**a**) **little, some/any, a lot of** and **no.**
a little knowledge *a lot of progress* *some air* *no strength*

Though note that similar expressions referring to number, including (**a**) **few, many, several** and **various** cannot be used before uncountables.

Varying uses and meanings of countables and uncountables

A few of many possible examples are suggested.

a Nouns used uncountably and countably with different meanings:

UNCOUNTABLE	COUNTABLE
paper (material)	*a paper* (newspaper or document)
glass (material)	*a glass* (for drinking)
	glasses (for the eyes)

UNCOUNTABLE	COUNTABLE
iron (material)	*an iron* (for ironing)
wood (material)	*a wood* (a group of trees)
space (in the universe)	*a space* (between two objects)
speech (the power of speech)	*a speech* (a formal public address)
cold (in temperature)	*a cold* (a form of illness)
youth (a time of life)	*a youth* (a young man)
life (being alive)	*a life* (of an individual)

b Nouns used uncountably and countably with different but related meanings:
In each case the uncountable form suggests an abstract or general idea, the countable form a single concrete example.

light	*a light*	*crime*	*a crime*
danger	*a danger*	*law*	*a law*
duty	*a duty*	*thought*	*a thought*
pain	*a pain*		

life could be included here, though there is a slight difference in conception.

Other pairs that are slightly different are:

UNCOUNTABLE	COUNTABLE
hair (of the head)	*a hair* (a single one)
gas (used for heating)	*a gas* (of any kind)
salt (used with food)	*a salt* (a chemical compound)

c Differing words used uncountably or countably to express a related idea:

UNCOUNTABLE	COUNTABLE
work	*a job, an occupation*
bread	*a loaf, a roll*
meat	*a joint*
machinery	*a machine*
shopping	*a purchase*
clothing	*a garment*
fruit	*an apple, an orange* etc.
poetry	*a poem*
poultry	*a chicken*
money, cash	*a banknote, a coin*

Practice

While you are staying in a hotel, you wish to have the following objects, services and information. Use each of the nouns listed in a complete sentence beginning with the words **I'd like**. The sentences may have differing constructions: **I'd like something, I'd like to do something** and **I'd like somebody to do something.**

Add one or more additional sentences, statements or questions, which refer to the other objects and ideas given in each case.

Each noun before the colon should be used in a plural form if it is countable. If it is uncountable only a singular form is possible, but in most cases it can then be preceded by **some**.

EXAMPLES
newspaper: The International Times/The Daily Shocker
I'd like two newspapers, please. Have you got *The International Times* and *The Daily Shocker*?

notepaper: hotel-headed white paper with envelopes to match
I'd like some notepaper, please. May I have some hotel-headed white paper with envelopes to match?
luggage (a porter to carry down): two suitcases/ two travelling bags/several large parcels
I'd like a porter to carry down some luggage, please. I've got two suitcases, two travelling bags and several large parcels.

1 information: sightseeing tour arrangements/ today's cinema programme
2 advice: how to operate the room television/ where to find a reliable dry-cleaning service
3 enquiry (make): times of meals/postage rates for letters and cards to your own country
4 coach tour (ask): places you can visit/where to book
5 sports facility: local provisions for golf/ tennis/riding/boating
6 furniture: a writing table/an extra chair
7 money (change): (you've got) Swedish krone/ German marks/Singapore dollars
8 damage (report): a broken balcony chair and a blocked washbasin outlet
9 sports equipment (where you can hire): you are interested in both skiing and skating
10 help: in closing a window and also opening a cupboard, both of them stuck
11 shopping: you want to leave at the reception desk two parcels, a plastic bag and a string bag full of purchases
12 coffee: for three people
13 fruit: you want to know if there are any oranges available
14 sightseeing (do): various places in and around the town you can visit
15 work (carried out in your room): a light bulb to be replaced, a dripping tap attended to and a jammed window blind mended

16 bread: what exactly do you need?
17 cutlery: two knives/two forks/a soup spoon/ a dessert spoon
18 iced water: with three tumblers
19 stationery: notepaper/one or two foolscap envelopes/two air letters
20 accommodation (ask about): rooms for a group of people travelling together/arriving when?
21 laundry (to be done for you): a cotton dress/ two blouses/handkerchiefs need washing

---

2 Singular or plural

As already stated, nouns used uncountably have no plural form, and are therefore followed by a verb in the singular.

His hair **is** *brown.*
The money **was** *stolen.*
All my shopping **is** *in two large carrier bags.*

They are also referred to by a singular related pronoun.

The money was stolen. **It** *had been left on the table.*

Uncountables ending in -s

A few nouns that appear to be plural are in fact uncountables. These include **news**, **mathematics** (**maths**), **physics**, **economics**.

The news about the riots is in today's papers. It's on the front page in most of them.

Nouns with identical singular and plural forms

The very few of these that exist include **sheep**, **deer**, **salmon**, **trout**, **fish** (**fishes** is possible)

The sheep {*is* / *are*} *grazing on the hillside.*

Plural forms that are singular after 'a pair'

These include **trousers, pyjamas, slacks, scissors, pliers.**

This pair of scissors needs } *sharpening.*
These scissors need }

Nouns with only a plural form

These include:

belongings	**the police**	**surroundings**	**goods**	**negotiations**	**glasses** (for the eyes)
earnings	**the clergy**	**premises**	**contents**	**manners** (polite behaviour)	**thanks**
savings		**headquarters**	**remains** (what is left)	**odds** (chances)	**cattle**
riches					

His savings are in the Post Office.
The police are making intensive investigations.
I'm afraid the odds are against you succeeding.

Note
people (singular: **person**) is plural unless a race or nation of people is being referred to.

Thousands of people are demonstrating against the building of an additional airport runway.

but: *a people/peoples of Central Asia*

Practice

a Complete the sentences beginning with the words below. The following verb should be **is, are, has** or **have**, either alone or as part of the present continuous or passive form. Ideas for completing the sentences are suggested but you can use your own ideas if you prefer.

EXAMPLE
Unfortunately the surroundings of this beautiful town ... (what are they like?)
Unfortunately the surroundings of this beautiful town are spoiled by unplanned and ugly industrial development.

1 The police ... (question local residents/what about?)
2 The news ... (when broadcast?/what wavelength?)
3 The headquarters of the company ... (where?)
4 The model's own clothes ... (how do they compare with the ones she shows?)
5 The scissors you're using ... (say something about them)
6 A pair of scissors ... (lying in what unexpected place?)
7 Her earnings as a company director ... (how much annually?)
8 An untidy boy's belongings ... (where?)
9 Mathematics ... (how important as a school subject?)
10 Angora rabbit wool ... (special characteristics?)
11 People who live in cold countries often ... (what colour hair?)
12 Cattle ... (reared for what purpose?)
13 Their children's manners ... (very good or terrible? with what result for the parents?)
14 Goods made in this factory ... (exported where?)
15 The negotiations between management and unions ... (likely to last how long?)
16 Do you like people who ... (a characteristic of some people)

b Go through the above sentences again (adding different endings if you wish) replacing the noun subject of the verb you suggest with a suitable pronoun.

EXAMPLE
Unfortunately the surroundings of this beautiful town ...
Unfortunately they are ugly, dirty and depressing.

3 Possessive and related forms

Nouns referring to living beings

Possession is usually indicated by the use of an apostrophe (-'s with a singular form, -s' with a plural form).

the doctor's car *doctor's fees*
a waitress's tips

Note
Exceptions: **men's, women's, children's, people's**
children's games

Nouns referring to inanimate objects

A phrase incorporating **of** is normal.
the hands of the clock *the heel of a shoe*

In many cases, however, a second noun is used adjectivally before the first.
a picture frame *bicycle wheels* *rose petals*

Little guidance can be given as to the choice of form, which almost entirely depends on common usage. In many cases both are possible, as with **the door of the house** and **the house door**. In most cases the form normally used can be learned only as part of general vocabulary.

Practice

a Each item referred to by a word in List B forms part of or belongs to one referred to in List A, though the items in each list are arranged in a different order. Some of the words in List A have a possessive form with an apostrophe (**'s** or **s'**): others follow **of/of the** after the noun from List B. Pair the words suitably and then use each phrase in a sentence.

EXAMPLES
A *old people* *a reporter* *a town*
B *a notebook* *a home* *a name*
an old people's home a reporter's notebook
the name of a town
My grandparents are now living in an old people's home.
A lot of strange things are written in a reporter's notebook.
Do you remember the name of the town in Germany where they make those famous sausages?

LIST A
this book Mount Everest a cat a spider
the taxpayer our house my Aunt Agatha
the millionaire England the committee
people the Company Director
LIST B
canary private yacht windows title
history whiskers cost Chairman
secretary web height hard-earned money
everyday lives

b Explain the difference in meaning between the ideas expressed in these pairs and then use each word or word group in a sentence.

1 a cup of tea/a teacup
a box of matches/a matchbox
a jug of milk/a milkjug
a reel of cotton/a cotton reel
2 the painting of a wall/a wall painting
the building of a town/a town building
3 a sheet of paper/a paper sheet
the neck of a bottle/a bottleneck
4 the body of a student/a student body
the collection of stamps/a stamp collection
the organisation of charities/a charity organisation
a number of telephones/telephone numbers

Section B The articles: a (an), the

1 Forms and pronunciations

Articles are associated with NOUNS, and sometimes PRONOUNS and ADJECTIVES USED AS PRONOUNS.

the one here *a few*
the rich *a thousand*

The indefinite article

a before a consonant sound:

a Londoner *a European* *a uniform*

an before a vowel sound:

an Austrian *an Egyptian* *an Indian* *an Outer Mongolian*
an uninvited Martian

The definite article

the is pronounced:
/ðə/ before a consonant sound:
/ðə/ *world* /ðə/ *universe* /ðə/ *one and only you*

/ðɪ/ before a vowel sound:
/ðɪ/ *ocean* /ðɪ/ *earth* /ðɪ/ *other planets*

---

2 The main uses of the indefinite article

The indefinite article precedes a noun in the singular, or a pronoun (e.g. **a new one**) which:

1 expresses something previously unknown to the hearer or reader and possibly to the speaker or writer.
Is that really **a pink elephant** *I can see?*

2 refers to one of a number of possibilities.
She is **a cashier** *in* **a supermarket**. (There are many supermarkets, and several cashiers in this one.)

3 refers to a single member of a group who/which represents the whole group.
A Swede *speaks Swedish.* (and so do Swedes in general)

4 is a noun complement of the verbs **to be** and **to become**.
Stephen is **a student** *who hopes to become* **an engineer**.

5 is preceded by **in** or **on** and refers to a form of transport.
travel **in a bus/in a car/in an aeroplane/on a horse**
Compare: *travel by bus/by car/by air*
This also applies to various places of work:
work **in an office/in a factory/in a shop**

In certain cases, **a** may have the same meaning as **one**.

twice a week = twice in one week
eighty pence a metre
£5 a bottle

Practice

a You are sitting in a park in the sunshine, relaxing and watching what is going on around you. Describe some of the separate individuals, animals, birds and other things you can see and in some cases say what they are doing. In each case you are introducing the noun for the first time.

EXAMPLE
About fifty metres to my right, I can see a small oval-shaped lake where a boy is sailing a brightly-coloured boat and a swan is swimming slowly and gracefully.

Add about twelve more things you can see, each preceded by an indefinite article.

b Answer these questions and explain why you have used the indefinite article before the noun you have introduced into each answer.

1 Where do you buy petrol on a motorway?
2 What may you wear when you have to go out in the rain and what may you carry?
3 What must you have if you want to play tennis?
4 What do you do if you feel hot and dirty? (three possibilities)

c Rephrase each of the following statements.

EXAMPLE
Alex advises sick people. Alex is a doctor.

1 Barbara looks after sick people.
2 Christine is in charge of a university department.
3 Doug teaches in a college.
4 Emily works with children in a primary school.
5 Fanny makes ladies' clothes.
6 Gerald makes men's suits.

d Give short answers to these questions – just an article and noun, except on the last question. Suggest why an indefinite article precedes the noun in the various answers.

1 What bird carries messages?
2 What animal carries people? (four or more possibilities)
3 What type of ship carries goods? oil? people?
4 What person is a native of Greece?
5 Define a novelist – and also a novel.

e How often do you:

1 go on holiday?
2 have a meal?
3 get paid a salary, housekeeping or pocket money?
4 go to a hairdresser or a barber?
5 breathe?
6 blink?

(In each case use an expression related to **once a century**.)

f What is the price of these items in your country?

EXAMPLE
milk chocolate
Milk chocolate costs twenty pence a bar.

1 petrol
2 granulated sugar
3 full cream milk
4 matches
5 plain biscuits (packet)

Omission before uncountable nouns

a Many uncountable nouns are never preceded by the indefinite article, which may, however, precede a countable noun indicating a single example of the uncountable.

a piece of information/advice *a form of behaviour* *a case of typhoid*
an item of news *a type of knowledge*

Otherwise **some**, **any** or **no** or some other expression of quantity may precede an uncountable, or it may stand alone:

I hope you can give me advice/some/a little/a lot of advice.

b The indefinite article sometimes precedes certain uncountables – in particular those expressing abstract ideas or referring to commodities (= food and materials). It then expresses 'a kind of'.

a beauty that is unspoilt by time
a medicine recommended by doctors
an unusually fine silk
a wine that was drunk by the Romans
a steel of exceptional toughness

Practice

1 Suggest a useful piece of information you can get from a dictionary.
2 Now give a sensible piece of advice to a student looking up a word in a foreign-language dictionary.
3 Mention an interesting item of news you've read or heard recently.
4 What must happen if a doctor suspects he has a case of cholera?
5 What's the name of a cheese and/or a cigar you could recommend to a connoisseur?
6 What domestic animal is said to have a curiosity that may get it into trouble?
7 What can travel at a speed that is faster than sound?

3 The main uses of the definite article

The definite article precedes a noun or pronoun (e.g. **the new ones, the former**) which:

1 has already been referred to.
The pink elephant *may be visible to you, but I can't see it.*

2 refers to someone whose identity is known or is obvious from the context.
I went to see **the doctor** *yesterday.* (Compare: *You ought to see a doctor about that cough.* (The doctor is not specified.))
I put it on **the table.** (There is only one table, or we know which table.)

3 refers to a single definite idea, suggesting that it is the only possibility in the existing circumstances.
May I see **the manager** *of* **the sales department**? (The firm has only one sales department which has only one manager.)
You can buy this gift paper at **the stationer's** *near* **the Town Hall.** (There is only one stationer's near the Town Hall.)

4 is defined or in some way singled out.
The furniture *he sold us was worm-eaten.* (Compare: *He sells furniture.*)
the food *we eat* (Compare: *We eat food.*)

The defining of certain commodities may be understood and not indicated in words.
The bread/The milk (which we're going to eat/drink) *is on the kitchen table.*

This may apply also in the case of other nouns normally used without an article.
I left **the luggage** *in a locker.* (= the luggage I was carrying)

I put **the money** *in the safe*. (Compare: *Money can't buy everything*.)
the English *spoken by a Cockney*

Many abstract nouns are preceded by the definite article when defined.
the beauty *of the countryside*
the beauty *that endures*
the value *of good advice* (Compare: *This is good value*.)

The following nouns preceded by the definite article are in fact being defined:

the sun (= the sun in the Solar system)
the moon
the sky
the Arctic (not the Antarctic) *Circle*
the North (not the South) *Pole*

The British Museum
the National Gallery
(and other places defined or described – compare Trafalgar Square – a name)

the BBC
the Common Market
the World Bank

the United States (a description)
America (a name)
the Soviet Union (compare *Russia*)
the Netherlands (= the Low Countries, compare *Holland*)

the Bible
the Koran

Friday the thirteenth
Elizabeth the Second

5 is qualified by a superlative adjective, which in effect singles it out.
the most interesting story *in the book* (Compare: *I'm reading a most interesting story*. (**most** = very))

6 indicates a point or period of time that is being defined.
the last week of the year
the next Thursday after Easter
Compare: *last week, next Thursday*

7 in a singular form represents a group that is being considered scientifically or in a purely abstract way.
The dodo *is now extinct*.
The lamb *has long been regarded as a symbol of innocence*.

Other uses of the definite article

1 **the former, the latter**
Mac and Pat are friends. Oddly enough the former is an Irishman and the latter is a Scot.

2 Before a comparative adjective or adverb in expressions of the following type:
The cheaper the better.
The shorter the speeches, the happier I am.
The more fashionable the dress, the shorter the time (or: *the less time*) *you can wear it.*
The more she hears, the less she speaks.
The more carefully you listen, the more effectively you learn.
The less you spend on cigarettes, the less money you burn.

3 In contrasting making use of and visiting certain buildings.

USING	VISITING
in school (learning)	*in the school*
in church (worshipping)	*in the church*
in prison (as a prisoner)	*in the prison*
in hospital (as a patient)	*in the hospital*

4 Compare: *hear something on the radio*
with: *see it on television*

Practice

a Define each of the following nouns and add extra information to complete a sentence.

EXAMPLE
train
The train (arriving) (that is standing) at Platform 4 will call at Clapham Junction and Waterloo.

1 sportsman
2 actor
3 glove
4 experience
5 message
6 telephone kiosk

b Finish the following, using **former** and **latter**:

The Himalayas and the Alps are both impressive mountain ranges, but . . .

c Compare Everest with all other mountains.

d 'I had the most unpleasant experience the other day.' Briefly, what happened?

e What, in your opinion, is the most unpleasant colour for the walls of a room?

f Complete these sentence openings.

1 Last year . . .
2 The last day . . .
3 Next week . . .
4 The next day . . .

g Answer these questions.

1 What wild animal do you consider the most dangerous to man?
2 What large mammal spends most of its life in water?

h Complete these sentence openings.

1 The breakfast . . .
2 The language . . .
3 The poverty . . .
4 The water . . .
5 The medical students are spending today observing operations in . . .
6 The space . . .

i Complete each of the following suitably.

EXAMPLE
the more loudly he shouts
The more loudly he shouts, the more unwilling I am to obey him.

1 the higher the price
2 the older he gets
3 the less I eat
4 the higher you fly
5 the more quickly she types
6 the more work you do
7 the longer you wait to buy it
8 the fewer questions you ask
9 the more heavily he sleeps
10 the more grammar I learn

4 No article

No article is used before:

1 most abstract nouns that are not defined.
Nobody has a right to **happiness.**
Success *does not always depend on* **intelligence,** *but often on* **luck.**

2 many things considered as an amount or compound rather than a separate unit when they are undefined. These uncountable forms include:

SOME FOODS	**bread** (compare *a roll*), **meat, sugar**
LIQUIDS	**water, milk**
MATERIALS FOR CLOTHES	**linen, cotton, velvet**
OTHER MATERIALS	**glass, wood, paper, plastic**
MINERALS	**iron ore, steel, salt**
GASES AND SOURCES OF POWER	**oxygen, air, electricity**

A wide miscellaneous variety includes **rubbish, footwear, stationery, dust, polish, grass, arson, travel, wheat.**

3 most illnesses, e.g. **bronchitis, influenza.**

4 subjects of study and interest, e.g. **history, psychology, music, literature, poetry, art.**

5 languages, e.g. **Chinese, Arabic, Greek** (notice the capital letters).

6 games, e.g. **ice hockey, chess, Scrabble.**
Compare: *play a game*
play football/bridge/patience
play the piano/the violin/other musical instruments

7 gerunds when the ACTION and not the result is being referred to.
Compare: *He enjoys painting.*
with: *He is looking at the painting.*

Note
All the above may be preceded by a definite article when being defined.
the oxygen we breathe

Compare the following omissions and inclusions of articles:

Nature (the creative force)	*the nature of the problem*
in space (in the universe)	*the space between these two chairs*
Life is interesting.	*the life of a man* *have an interesting life*
Work is unavoidable.	*a work of Dickens*
youth/old age (a time of life)	*a youth* (a young man)
change for a ten-pound note	*need a change* *the change between winter and summer*
Doctor White, Major Black (titles)	*send for the doctor*
Time passes quickly.	*a time to remember* *have a good time* *What's the time?*
Man learns slowly.	*A man* (the man you expected today) *telephoned.*
Rain/Fog/Snow made driving difficult.	*The rain was falling heavily.* *lost in the fog* *play in the snow*
I don't like cold weather.	*I don't like living in a cold climate.* *The weather here is often cold.*

Practice

a Complete these sentences. A longer line refers to a single word, a dotted line to several words to be added.

1 He claims his success is due to ______ but we think . . .
2 Three essential qualities needed by an ambassador are . . .
3 To make a cake you need at least three ingredients: . . .
4 Energy can be produced from ______, ______, ______ and the ______.
5 My two favourite school subjects were ______ and ______.
6 ______ is the disease that many people are most afraid of.
7 A Swiss may speak ______, ______ or ______ and sometimes also ______.
8 Algy, the sportsman, plays ______ while Andy, the musician, . . .
9 A clock tells us the ______ and this shows us how quickly . . .

b Answer these questions in complete sentences:

1 Do you always find life interesting or are you sometimes very bored?

2 Suggest the main purpose of work and the main value of play in the average person's life.
3 What is one reason why you would or would not like to travel in space?
4 Suggest a discovery made by early man that changed the history of the human race.
5 What is a pleasure of youth and what is a problem of old age?
6 Do you enjoy painting yourself or do you prefer to admire a painting by an artist?
7 Is rain or sunshine of more importance for a dairy farmer?
8 Does time pass too quickly or too slowly for you?
9 Which of the following qualities does a really successful businessman need: charm, determination, patience, courage, shrewdness, ruthlessness, physical strength, imagination, drive, sympathy, generosity, luck?
10 Suggest a suitable name for each of the following: a bad-tempered general
a lazy medical specialist
a prince in an operetta
an absent-minded professor

Geographical names

a There is no article before:

1 the names of continents and countries, unless they are descriptive (see **b** below): **Australasia, Asia, Norway, Indonesia.**

2 the names of mountains (but **the** before mountain ranges): **Fujiyama, Mount Olympus, Snowdon.** (Exceptions include **the Matterhorn, the Jungfrau.**)

3 the names of islands which stand alone: **Sardinia** (but **the West Indies**).

4 names of lakes: **Lake Ontario.**

b The definite article precedes the names of:

1 countries, when these are descriptive: **The United Kingdom.**

2 mountain ranges: **the Rockies.**

3 compound names of islands, or island groups: **the Isle of Wight, the West Indies.**

4 compound names of lakes: **the Lake of Geneva.**

5 rivers, seas and oceans: **the (River) Nile, the North Sea, the Pacific (Ocean).**

6 railways and motorways: **the Trans-Siberian Railway, the M1.**

7 **the Equator, the Arctic Circle, the tropics, the North Pole.**

Dates

a There is no article before the days of the week, months, festivals (**Christmas, Easter, New Year, Lent, Ramadan** etc.)

b The definite article precedes dates: **the fourth of May.**

Notes

1 *It's summer now.*
in summer (any summer)
(The) summer has almost gone.
in the summer (any summer, but also the coming summer)
The same applies to other seasons.

2 *the day before yesterday, the other day*

A use of the possessive adjective

Parts of the body and personal possessions are usually preceded by the appropriate possessive adjective and not the definite article. As the following examples show, the accompanying verb is not used reflexively as it is in some other languages.

She has broken her wrist.
I have hurt my shoulder.

The adjective **own** is preceded by a possessive form.

It's your own fault.
He always wants his own way.
Do the Marchants live in their own house?

5 Further notes on articles and possessive adjectives

Contrasts

These are additional to those suggested in the foregoing explanations.

a *One of* **the** *kittens is black and* **the other** *is tabby.* (There are two kittens.)
One of **the** *kittens is black,* **another** *is tabby and* **the other** *is ginger.* (Three kittens, the definite article preceding the last.)
It was a disastrous day – some of the London clubs lost their matches, **others** *only drew, and* **the others** *had to cancel because their pitches were waterlogged.* (Three groups of clubs altogether.)
Some players were injured and **others** *were badly off form.* (The total number of groups is unknown.)

b *'There's* **a** *James Bond on the telephone.'* (I don't know who he is.)
'Not <u>the</u> *James Bond, surely? He doesn't exist.'* (the famous one)
'Well, he just said he was James Bond.' (his name)

c *The concert is taking place in* **a** *week.* (after seven days)
Can they have it ready in **a** *week?* (in the space of a week)
After all, they can't practise in **the** *week, but only on Sunday.* (on weekdays)
I can do it in **a** *day.*
He works only in **the** *day, not at night.*
He works day and night.

d *most* (of the) *people* (no article) **the** *most sensible people*

e **both** is never preceded by an article.
both twins *I saw both of them.*

f *I don't want milk. I want fruit juice.* (alternatives).
Would you bring me some fruit juice, please. (a certain quantity)

Practice

The following suggestions offer varied practice of much of the material dealt with in this section.

a Explain the difference in meaning between these sentences:

He's whistling a tune he heard this morning.
He's whistling the tune he heard this morning.

Now make up similar pairs of sentences using the ideas suggested and explaining the difference in meaning between each sentence in the pairs. Add any other ideas asked for by the questions.

1 show you/photograph/take (what of? when?)
2 go/supermarket/buy (what?)
3 dog/steal/lamb chop (where was it?)

b Explain the difference in meaning between these paired sentences:

I must have left my gloves on the bus.
I must have left my gloves on a bus.

Make similar pairs of sentences using these words and explaining the difference in meaning between each sentence in a pair.

1 a bookshop/the bookshop
2 a prize/the prize
3 an embassy/the embassy

c In which of these cases could you find the speaker without difficulty and why?

Perhaps we can meet in a café near the beach.
Perhaps we can meet in the café near the beach.

d Finish each of these sentences.

1 Money can . . .
2 The money is . . .
3 Can you buy furniture . . .?
4 Did you choose the furniture . . .?
5 You can get information . . .
6 Was the information . . .?

e Each of the following sentence openings includes a noun that may need no article before it or may be preceded by **the** and/or **a** according to the meaning of the sentence as a whole. Complete each sentence in a suitable way.

EXAMPLES
Illness forced him . . . to give up his job.
He was worried about the illness . . . of his youngest child.
The doctor feared that this was an illness . . . that might be incurable.

1 Three highly-respected virtues are truth, . . .
2 Do you believe the truth . . .?
3 A truth that we should always remember is that . . .
4 Without education, a young person . . .
5 We discussed the education . . .
6 I want my daughter to have an education . . .
7 She wears jewellery only when . . .
8 She wears only the jewellery . . .
9 Heat can be measured . . .
10 Everybody slept during the heat . . .
11 He had lived in Central Africa, but this was a heat . . .
12 Science enables man to . . .
13 Dr Curall is qualified in the science . . .
14 Psychology is a science . . .

f Miss Sparrow, the secretary, is expecting an unknown visitor to the firm, whose name she has been given. When an extremely good-looking, though slightly sinister stranger appears, she gets so confused that she says: 'Oh, good morning. Are you the Mr Hawk?'
She quickly changes this to: 'Oh, I'm sorry. Are you a Mr Hawk?'
At last she gets it right and says: 'No, I don't mean that, of course. Are you Mr Hawk?'
What idea is being suggested in each of these similar questions?

g Each of these statements answers a different question.
Question: Which would you like, tea or coffee?
I'd like some coffee, please.
Question: What would you like to drink?
I'd like coffee, please.

Make sentences in pairs according to the above models using the words below (with and without **some**), and suggest the question each is the answer to.

1 roast potatoes
2 vanilla ice-cream
3 tea with lemon

h Answer the question which follows each of these statements.

1 'We can draw some money from the bank in a week.'
'And if we need it urgently before, what can we do?'
2 'I can easily get through £500 in a week.'
'What sorts of things do you spend it on?'
3 'You can draw money only in the week.'
'Why can't I get it on Sundays?'

i Some of the following things you may have with your breakfast, your lunch, your dinner or your supper; others you may have/eat/drink between meals. Some of them you may never eat or drink. Say which of them you have with a certain meal or between meals and which you never eat, adding the indefinite article where this is necessary together with any suitable comment.

EXAMPLES
banana cheese spaghetti
I sometimes eat a banana between meals.
I occasionally have cheese after dinner instead of dessert.
I never eat spaghetti as I think it's fattening.

1	bread	13	honey
2	porridge	14	roll
3	egg	15	dry biscuit
4	cup of tea	16	fruit juice
5	milk	17	caviare
6	coffee	18	marmalade
7	toast	19	tomato sauce
8	salad	20	strawberry
9	hot water	21	yoghourt
10	grilled herring	22	mineral water
11	smoked salmon	23	soup
12	sugar	24	chicken

j Suggest one or more items of clothing or other useful things that can be made of each of the following materials.

EXAMPLE
velvet Curtains and evening dresses are sometimes made of velvet.
wool A winter dress can be made of wool and so can gloves, socks and carpets.

1	cotton	3	nylon	5	fur	7	canvas
2	silk	4	linen	6	leather	8	felt

k Answer these questions in complete sentences.

1 What's an electric iron made of?
2 What's a knife-blade made of?
3 What's a wedding-ring often made of?
4 What's an expensive tea-pot made of?
5 What are plates usually made of?
6 What kind of fuel do you use in your home for:
cooking heating water heating rooms?

l Answer the following questions in complete sentences, introducing into your answers the word above the group with or without an article before it.
In the last group (youth), complete the sentence openings.

1 **life**
What might you say to cheer up a person of forty who thinks he is getting old?
What biography have you most enjoyed reading?
What kind of life does the mother of six young children have?
2 **time**
What two things do you sometimes waste?
How long does an ice age last?
For what reason do you look at your watch?
3 **man**
What is one important difference between human beings and animals?
Jeanette has just asked a stranger the way to the station and she is reporting to her friend what he has said.
Why is the security guard at a bank or other building almost always a man?
4 **nature**
What subject do naturalists study?
Before attempting to solve a problem what must a scientist fully understand?
Why is everybody very fond of Jenny?
5 **youth**
Youth is . . .
The youth is . . .
I was surprised when a youth . . .

m People have various advantages in life, some of which are listed below. Say which of these you think you have (or have had) already, which you would like to have and which you consider less important. When speaking about any one of them you will in some cases have to add an article before it.
Add any other advantages you can think of for yourself.

EXAMPLES
flair for foreign languages *respect for authority*
happy childhood
I had the great advantage of a happy childhood.
It would be very useful to have a flair for languages.
I'm not too sure about respect for authority, which must depend on the nature of the authority.

1 money
2 good education
3 well-paid job
4 popularity
5 commonsense
6 efficiency
7 good home
8 beauty (or good looks)
9 good health
10 intelligence
11 foresight
12 charm
13 sense of humour
14 physical strength
15 luck
16 self-confidence
17 ability to get on with people
18 free time

n Answer these questions about geography.

1 What river does Vienna stand on?
2 What's the name of the range of mountains that covers Switzerland and parts of France, Germany, Austria and Italy?
3 What's the highest mountain in the world?
4 Which ocean separates the continents of Europe and America?
5 Where is an explorer standing when he can't go any farther south? (at)
6 What and where are the Philippines?
7 What's the name of a lake in Africa?
8 How would you be travelling if you were on the M6?

o Dates and days.

1 Read aloud in full what this date is: 21st February, 1948 (It's . . .)
2 What month is Christmas in?
3 Which week of the year is New Year's Day in?
4 Express **the other day** in different words.
5 Which day of the week do you have a holiday on?

p In which cases is an article needed at the beginning of these word groups?

1 both pictures are priceless
2 most pictures in this collection are by Dutch masters
3 most beautiful picture in the collection is now on loan
4 other pictures are all here
5 most interesting Greek statue was discovered near here recently

q What is the difference in meaning between these two sentences?

Most important people travel first class.
The most important people travel first class.

Make up some more sentences which show this difference in meaning. Here are some suggestions:
intelligent people read
successful businessmen have got
up-to-date watches are made

r Answer the questions that follow the statements.

1 One group of tourists went shopping and another visited the church.
Were there any tourists who did neither? If so, what various things might they have done?
2 Some of the flowers were blue and others were yellow.
Were any of the flowers neither blue nor yellow?
3 Three of the directors are at the meeting but the other is ill.
How many directors are there altogether?
4 Some of the staff work in Birmingham and the others work in Bristol.
Do any of the staff work in London?

s The answers to the following questions should include a part of the body.

1 What does Sheila do after she has been working in the garden and before she starts cooking?
2 What do you clean before you go to bed?
3 What could an ice-hockey player break?
4 What do you use a comb to do?
5 What do dogs wag when they are pleased?

t The following word groups refer to everyday occupations, activities and ways of passing the time. Talk about each of them, saying possibly when you do them, why, what they involve, whether you enjoy or dislike doing them, how often, with whom or under what circumstances they are carried out.
It will be necessary to use a suitable form of the verb and in some cases to add an article before the noun.

EXAMPLES
(cut) grass *(play) golf*
(consult) railway timetable
As we haven't got a garden, I don't have to cut the grass.

I'd like to play golf but I haven't got the time.
I don't often consult a railway timetable as I already know the times of the local trains.

1 (do) housework
2 (play) tennis
3 (play) piano
4 (listen to) radio
5 (watch) television
6 (have) conversation with a friend
7 (discuss) politics
8 (read) newspaper
9 (go on) journey
10 (listen to) music
11 (do) washing-up
12 (do) washing (clothes)
13 (smoke) cigarette
14 (go to) dance
15 (play) chess
16 (do) needlework
17 (cook) meal
18 (waste) time
19 (go to) doctor
20 (read) book
21 (go to) cinema
22 (catch) bus
23 (spend) money
24 (do) nothing

Section C Pronouns

1 Personal and reflexive pronouns

Definition

PRONOUNS can be defined as words that can take the place of other nouns or pronouns, thus avoiding the necessity of repetition when it is clear what is being referred to.

I've been talking to {*George.* **He's** *just back from Australia.* / *George,* **who's** *just back from Australia.*}

A noun which has not been expressed may be clear from the context.
I *live here.* (the person speaking)
You *look tired.* (the person spoken to)
I'll take **this,** *please.* (The speaker is indicating an object.)

Some pronouns and adjectives are identical in form and related in meaning. These are explained in Section D. The forms introduced in this Section are either used only as pronouns or are unrelated in meaning to similar adjectival forms.

Personal pronouns

SUBJECT	**I**	**you**	**he/she/it/one**	**we**	**you**	**they**
OBJECT	**me**	**you**	**him/her/it/one**	**us**	**you**	**them**

These are learned in the early stages of language learning, and therefore need little attention here. Two things, however, should be noticed.

1 Except in the case of a command (where it is understood) any pronoun that is subject of the verb is always stated in English. (This is not true of all languages.)
He/She/It is in the next room.
(you) *Hurry up!* (you) *Don't worry.*

2 A verb may have a noun and a pronoun or two different pronouns as its subjects. In this case a first person singular pronoun usually follows a second or third person pronoun or noun.
An associate and I have started a business.
You and I must discuss this.

This rarely applies in the case of plural forms where a different construction may be used.
We must discuss this. (not: *You and we*)
We have started a business with an associate.

Reflexive pronouns

a **myself** **yourself** **himself/herself/itself/oneself**
ourselves **yourselves** **themselves**

b The reflexive pronoun expresses the idea that the subject and object of the verb are the same person.
Did **Bob** *hurt* **himself** *when he fell down?*
We *should criticise* **ourselves** *more often than we criticise others.*

c Reflexive pronouns can be preceded by verbal particles or prepositions.
He's always looking **at himself** *in the mirror.*
Old people *often talk* **to themselves.**

d Verbs are used reflexively much less commonly in English than in some other languages. If you speak one of these languages it will be important to remember this.

The following verbs are seldom used with a reflexive pronoun: **apologise, ask, awake/wake, close, escape, feel, hide, hurry, lay, lean, move, open, remember, sit, stand, stop, wonder.**
He felt ill.
He hid in the cellar.
Don't lean out of the window.
Please sit down.
The museum opens/closes at five.

The following verbs are sometimes used reflexively (as in the brackets) but the non-bracketed form is more usual. Where no bracketed form follows, the verb referred to is almost never used reflexively except in the cases indicated by the asterisk and explained below.

*__have a wash (wash oneself)__
*__have a bath__
*__shave/have a shave__
*__get dressed/dress (dress oneself)__
get changed/change (clothes)
clean/brush one's teeth
do/comb/brush one's hair
get used to (accustom oneself to)
get ready (prepare oneself)
get lost (lose oneself)
be mistaken (deceive oneself)

*In these cases the use of the reflexive pronoun emphasises the fact that the subject does the action himself – nobody does it for him.
He never shaves himself – he always goes to the barber's.
A dog is washed. A cat washes herself.

Notes
1 Both **commit suicide** and **kill oneself** are used.
2 **get married, get divorced** and **separate** are never used reflexively.

Practice

Each of the following sentences either includes or indicates by its meaning one of the verbs referred to above. Complete the sentences suitably, in most cases supplying additional information about the bracketed suggestions or questions.

1 Don't come to work tomorrow if you still feel ... (suggest advice)
2 Be careful! If you lean ... (what may happen?)
3 The escaped prisoner hid ... (where and for how long?)
4 When I next met her, I apologised ... (**for** + gerund)
5 As the door opened ...
6 When he went out to pick up his newspaper, the door shut ... (with what result?)
7 Montmorency is still in his dressing-gown. He never dresses ... (before or until when?)
8 There are half-packed suitcases everywhere. The family is ... (to do what?)
9 Look at those dirty hands! You must ... (before doing what?)
10 When I see those thirty-storey blocks of flats, I wonder ...
11 Where can Jock have got to? He went out for a walk three hours ago. I hope he hasn't ... (lose – why might this happen?)
12 Sorry I can't stop to talk. I'm hurrying ...
13 This dress looks awful. I must change ... (before what happens?)
14 I forgot to send him a birthday present. I never remember ...

15 He always carries a battery-operated electric razor in his pocket so that he can ... (under what circumstances?)
16 He was kidnapped by terrorists but he managed to escape ... (how?)
17 It was clear that the victim had been murdered and had not ... (why?)
18 I didn't enjoy the heat at first but I ... (how long did this take?)
19 No, I'm not the girl you met in Alexandria. You must ... (mistake)
20 After being engaged for twenty years Nick and Nina are now going to ... (how old are they?)

Some special cases

a **please yourself** = do as you like, make your own decision.
You can please yourself about what time you come.

b **behave yourself** has the same meaning as **behave**, and is probably used slightly more often.
You must behave yourself at Granny's.

c **enjoy oneself, amuse oneself**
He enjoyed himself at the party, even though he didn't enjoy the food.
On the few wet days of the holiday we amused ourselves by playing at cards.

d *make oneself do something* (unwillingly) (Compare: *force oneself to do something)*
make oneself ill by eating too much
make oneself a cup of tea
Make yourself at home. (Feel at ease in my house.)
Help yourself. *Make yourselves comfortable.*
teach oneself something *pay for oneself*
cut/hurt/injure oneself *buy something for oneself*
consider oneself important *keep oneself warm*
take oneself seriously *pull oneself together*
adapt oneself to a new life *look at/after oneself*
deprive oneself of food *feel sorry for oneself*
talk to/talk about/worry about oneself
put oneself out (take trouble to help someone)

Practice

Complete these sentences with a suitable reflexive pronoun and additional words, providing answers to questions where these are suggested.

1 I've just poured out this cup of tea for you. Please help ...
2 'Did you enjoy your tour of Europe?' 'Well, we enjoyed ...'
3 'What time would you like me to be down for breakfast?' 'Oh please ...' (why doesn't the time matter?)
4 When you go to live in another country, you have to be ready to adapt ... (to what?)
5 With all the present-day driving regulations, it would be quite impossible to teach ... (what must you do?)
6 A polar bear has a very thick coat to protect ...
7 I've left coffee and cream in the kitchen so if you feel thirsty, make ...
8 In my small cold bed-sitting-room it's very difficult in winter to make ...
9 Just because he's been to university, he considers ...
10 A century ago people usually amused ... (by doing what?)
11 Her youngest child was run over on the way to school and she can never forgive ... (for allowing)
12 I don't think we've met before. May I introduce ...? (who are you?)

13 On hot summer afternoons students may have to force . . .

The verbs in these sentences need to be followed by a preposition before the reflexive pronoun.

14 She says she's getting so old she's afraid to look . . .
15 You're now earning more than I am so you can pay . . . (and also . . .?)
16 People who can talk only . . .
17 Old people sometimes talk . . . because . . .
18 George, you must buy a new overcoat . . . (why?)
19 Now that she's working, she wants to leave home and . . .
20 She never has time to worry . . . (why not?)
21 I've wasted too much time feeling sorry for myself. Now I must pull . . . (and do what?)
22 Why should we go to a lot of trouble and expense entertaining your relatives? They never put . . .

---

2 Each other, one another

These expressions emphasise that the action referred to is shared or divided between two or more people considered separately.

According to strict grammatical dogma **each other** refers to two people, while **one another** refers to three or more people. In the spoken language at least, **one another** is used in both cases, and **each other** is not uncommon in referring to two people or groups.

Compare: *The boys hurt themselves while climbing.*
with: *The boys hurt each other/one another while fighting.*

Verbs commonly followed by each other, one another

admire/like/love/respect one another
dislike/distrust/envy/fight/hate one another
know/recognise/forget/remember one another
annoy/irritate/help one another
speak/talk/write/telephone (*to*) *one another*
look at one another
depend on one another
live near one another
work/live/associate/discuss things/share things with one another

There are a considerable number of other verbs which can be used in this way.

Some verbs can be used with or without **one another**. These include **meet** (**one another**), **quarrel** (**with one another**), **write** (**to one another**).
But notice: **we greeted one another** (or: **we exchanged greetings**).

Practice

Finish these sentences using **each other** or **one another** only when these are essential to the meaning of the sentence. Add information in answer to the questions or to fill in spaces.

1 They've been on bad terms for a long time and in fact haven't spoken . . . (for how long?)
2 The children of the two families quarrel . . . (when?)
3 In my country when people greet . . . (what do they do?)
4 It wasn't surprising that the brothers didn't recognise . . . as . . .
5 On the first day of a cruise passengers hardly know . . . but . . .
6 The farmers helped . . . (when?)
7 We haven't met . . . (for how long?)

8 Although they've never met . . ., the pen-friends have been writing . . . (for how long?)
9 People living in remote areas depend . . . much more than . . .
10 The cat and the dog looked . . . and then . . .
11 If business associates don't trust . . .
12 As we live near . . .
13 If people could only respect . . .

3 Emphasising pronouns

These are the same in form as reflexive pronouns, but express a different meaning. They are used to give special emphasis to other nouns or pronouns.

Well I **myself** *like the turquoise one, though you may not.*
We decorated the whole house, inside and out, **ourselves**.

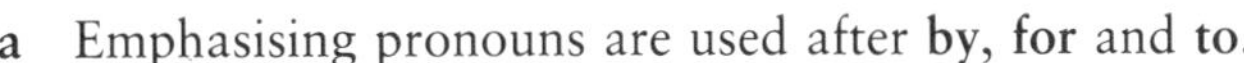

I SENT A LETTER TO MYSELF.

a Emphasising pronouns are used after **by**, **for** and **to**.
I did it **by myself**. (without help)
I live **by myself**. (without company)
I bought it **for myself**, *not for you.*
I sent a letter **to myself**.

b When the emphasising pronoun follows the related noun or personal pronoun immediately, a contrast with another person may be implied.
It was the manager himself who said that, not just one of his staff.

When the emphasising pronoun follows the verb, however, this may imply that only the person or people referred to by the related pronoun carried out (or did not carry out) the action.
He never takes his car to the garage. He always services it himself.
He didn't write his memoirs himself. A ghost writer wrote them for him.

Practice

Suggest the sentence (statement or question) which each of these statements follows.

EXAMPLES
No, I'm sorry. We need it ourselves.
May we borrow your caravan this weekend?
You can't carry it by yourself.
Let me help you with that trunk.

1 Well, I myself would choose the blue one.
2 Because you said you'd answer it yourself, Mr Brown.
3 Yes, indeed. The top Paris chef himself couldn't have cooked a better one.
4 Oh, did you? We ourselves didn't think much of it.
5 But there can't be a spelling mistake. I checked all the difficult words myself in a dictionary.
6 We earned every penny of it ourselves, by doing odd jobs for people. (collect)
7 No, indeed we didn't. The children made all the arrangements themselves.
8 No, I didn't. As usual I went on holiday by myself.
9 No, we don't. We mow the lawn, weed and tidy the beds, spray the roses and keep the plants in order by ourselves.
10 Well, I write reminder notes to myself and then I know I won't forget.
11 No, she didn't. She bought it for herself.

4 One, ones

The pronouns **one** and **ones** can be used in place of an already mentioned countable noun or pronoun in the following cases.

a Alone, i.e. without an article or adjective before.
I don't mind dogs on the whole, but my neighbours have got **one** *that never stops barking.*

b After an adjective of quality (e.g. **small, white, colder**).
'Can you recommend a good book?'
'Well, this is a very **informative one** *about Greek civilisation.'*
'I'm not keen on **informative ones**. *I prefer* **exciting ones**.*'*

one can, but need not, be used after a superlative form of an adjective.

c **one/ones** can, but need not, be used after **this, that, these, those, which, what, other.**
'Which (one) would you like?'
'I'll take this (one), please.'

But **one/ones** must be used when an adjective follows the above words.
I'll take **this new one**, *please.*
'Which rolls would you like?' 'I'll have **those long ones**, *please.'*

d **one/ones** is not used after **both** or possessive adjectives. It is rarely used after **either** and even more rarely after **neither.**
One flat was too small and the other (one) too expensive, so we didn't buy **either**/*so we turned down* **both**.
If you haven't got a programme you can look at **ours/mine**.

e **the one/the ones** is often followed by either an adverbial phrase or a relative clause.
I want the one in the window, please.
Is this the one (that) you lost?
I'll use the ones that have been opened already.

f After a number followed by an adjective, but not after a number without an adjective following.
'How many biscuits would you like?'
'I'll have three, please. May I have **three chocolate ones**?*'*

Note
one cannot be used to replace an uncountable noun. The noun has to be repeated.
'What kind of furniture did you inherit from your grandparents?'
'Only very old furniture in a bad state of repair.'

Practice

Answer these questions using **one/ones** where suitable in your answer. Suggest in which cases **one/ones** can be used but are not essential.

EXAMPLE
Which is the best qualified candidate?

Oh, undoubtedly Miss Paragon is not only the best qualified (one); she's also the prettiest (one), the most attractive (one) and in fact quite the most suitable (one). (Two of these **ones** would be the maximum!)

1 What colour roses do you like?
2 Have you got a large, medium-sized or small house or flat?
3 If Terry is hungry, which of the three cakes is he likely to choose?
4 Which letters should a businessman answer first?
5 Did Marcus give his fiancée a gold or a silver engagement ring?
6 Do you usually drink hot, lukewarm or cold tea (or coffee)?
7 Would you prefer boiled, baked or fried potatoes, sir?
8 How many cousins have you got?
9 You are packing to go on a long sea-voyage and very much enjoy reading. What kinds of books do you take with you?
10 Which do you prefer: rock, pop, light or classical music?
11 Would you prefer to sit on this metal and glass chair or in that armchair?
12 Would you choose black or brown shoes to wear with a green coat?
13 Which are you going to buy: these bananas which are hardly ripe or those that are already slightly soft and brown?
14 Which do you think are the more fattening: these milk chocolates or those filled plain ones?
15 Which look smarter: high-heeled or low-heeled shoes?
16 Where can you get the most reliable information about train timetables?
17 Where shall we have the meeting: in my small quiet room or in your large noisy one?
18 Please examine these photographs. Which of these men did you see leaving the bank?

5 Relative pronouns in defining clauses

A clause is a group of words which includes a finite verb – that is, a verb adapted to a subject (not an infinitive or gerund form). A sentence is an independent clause.

Dependent clauses have three functions.

1 NOUN CLAUSES do the work of a noun or pronoun as subject, object or complement of a verb, or serve as the object of a preposition.

2 ADVERBIAL CLAUSES provide information about the action of a verb: *how, when, where, why* (etc.) the action takes place.

3 ADJECTIVAL CLAUSES provide information about a noun or a pronoun.

RELATIVE PRONOUNS introduce ADJECTIVAL CLAUSES.

I know a child **who** *speaks four languages fluently.*
That's a colour **that** *suits you.*
Is he the boy **whose** *mother won the Nobel prize?*

Defining and non-defining clauses

a A noun or pronoun is identified by a following DEFINING CLAUSE, which is therefore essential to the meaning of the sentence.

The doctor who lives in our village is retiring soon. (**who lives in our village** identifies the doctor who is being referred to.)
The river which has its source here flows eventually into the Black Sea. (**which/that has its source here** identifies the river.)

b A NON-DEFINING CLAUSE, which is separated from the rest of the sentence by commas (as in this sentence), adds information to an already identified noun or pronoun and could in fact be expressed by a separate sentence.
Dr Leech, who is retiring soon, lives in our village. (The doctor is identified by name; the clause adds information.)
The River Danube, which has its source here, flows eventually into the Black Sea.
My father, who is now over eighty, is an enthusiastic skier. (The words **my father** refer to a known or identified person.)

Non-defining clauses appear mainly in writing or in formal speech and are therefore not dealt with in the following explanations.

Forms and usage of relative pronouns in defining clauses

a SUBJECT
who/that and **which/that** may be used as subjects of a following verb.
I know a man who/that keeps racing pigeons.
He has pigeons which/that fly from Budapest to Frankfurt.

b OBJECT
who/whom/that and **which/that** may be objects of a following verb or of a preposition. In this case, they are very often omitted.
He's the new teacher (whom/that) they've appointed.
Is this the most recent novel (which/that) you've written?
He's a fellow (whom/that) I used to work with.
I've found the letters (which/that) you were looking for.

Notes
1 In very formal speech it is just possible to express the third of the above examples as **with whom I used to work**, but you will never hear **for which you were looking.**
2 Whether **who** or **whom** is used as the object of a verb or of a preposition is a matter of personal choice, and in fact has little importance, as it is generally omitted anyway.

c **whose** showing possession may refer to both people and things and serve as a subject and object. **of which** (referring to things) is also possible, but is more formal.
I've just been speaking to a woman whose name I can never remember.
We had a wonderful view of the mountains, whose peaks (the peaks of which) were covered with snow.

d **what** is not used as a single relative pronoun, though it may have the meaning 'the thing(s) which/that which'.
I can't give you what (= the things which) *I haven't got.*

Summary

	PEOPLE	THINGS
SUBJECT OF A FOLLOWING VERB	**who** or **that**	**which** or **that**
OBJECT OF A FOLLOWING VERB OR PREPOSITION (very often omitted)	**who, whom** or **that**	**which** or **that**
POSSESSION (SUBJECT AND OBJECT)	**whose** or **of which**	

COMPOUND RELATIVE PRONOUN: **what** = the thing(s) which (never used after a separate related noun or pronoun)

Practice

a Finish each of these sentences with a relative clause in which **who/that** or **which/that** is the subject of the following verb (which may be active or passive in form).

EXAMPLES
You see that man over there? He's the one ...
who rode a bicycle from Ostend to Singapore.
Medchester is the company ...
that produces cars for speed and safety.

1 I spoke to one of the reporters ...
2 I'm looking for a shop ...
3 I've bought a watch ...
4 I'd like to speak to someone ...
5 A caretaker is a person ...
6 A thermometer is a device ...
7 I very much dislike people who ...
8 The firm produces robots ...
9 A kangaroo is an animal ...
10 He was one of the astronauts ...
11 The next time ...
12 The only town ...
13 The diamond ring ...
14 A few metres from the house ...

b Finish each of these sentences in two ways: (a) with a relative pronoun that is object of the following verb or a preposition, and (b) in a similar way but with the relative pronoun omitted.

EXAMPLE
He was rescued from drowning by the man ...
whom/who he had taught to swim.
he had taught to swim.
Medchester Motors produces the car ...
which/that your insurance company approves of.
your insurance company approves of.

1 This is the horror film ...
2 Would you like to see the photographs ...
3 Mrs Chatterley is the kind of woman ...
4 Were you listening to that story ...?
5 Did you find the telephone number ...?
6 A public lending library is one ...
7 I'm not someone ...
8 I hope this will be the last exam ...
9 Plantagenet Pickleberry is one of those names ...
10 It was a mistake ... (apologise)

c Complete each of the following sentences with a relative clause beginning with **whose**.

EXAMPLE
Julius Goldwell is the millionaire ...
whose fifth wife has just divorced him.

1 An anonymous work of literature is one ...
2 The singer ...
3 The vet was attending to a dog ...
4 Einstein was a scientist ...
5 During our walk we came across a lake ...
6 At the police station there was a tourist ...

d Relative adverbs
Forms:
where: to which/at which/in which
when: at the time which/during which
These can be used in a similar way to relative pronouns.

EXAMPLES
Perhaps we can find the house **where** he used to live. (he used to live in)
The Renaissance was an age **when** (during which) many great discoveries were made.

Complete each of these sentences with the relative adverb **where** or **when** as suitable, together with additional words.

1 I believe this is the office ...
2 The rush hour is the time of day ...
3 Can't anybody remember the exact date ...?
4 A museum is a building or open-air site ...
5 Can you recommend a restaurant ...?
6 The Stone Age was a period ... (tools/ weapons)
7 In many countries of the world, midnight of the 31st December is the moment ...
8 Present-day industrialised nations are very dependent on countries ...

Section D Pronouns and adjectives

1 Differing functions of pronouns and adjectives

The general characteristic of the forms dealt with in this Section is that they can function both as pronouns and adjectives (though possessives, the first group to be introduced, have different words when used as pronouns and adjectives).

A PRONOUN, by replacing a noun or another pronoun, avoids in most cases a repetition of the noun/pronoun when it is clear what is being referred to.

An ADJECTIVE provides information about a noun or pronoun which is usually present in the same sentence.

Consider these examples:

I don't think much of **these** *apples.*
How much are **those** *in the basket?*
The ADJECTIVE **these** informs the listener that the apples near the speaker are being referred to.
The PRONOUN **those** is used to avoid the repetition of the noun **apples.**
In the above example it also adds information – that the apples referred to are farther away from the speaker.

The PERSONAL PRONOUNS **I**, **we** and **you** are apparent exceptions, referring as they do to an idea in the speaker's mind: **I** = the person who is speaking, **we** = the group with which the speaker identifies him/herself, **you** = the person/people being spoken to. (See Part 1 Section C1.)

Pronouns may precede as well as follow the noun or pronoun they replace.
Which *of your children is more like you?*
This is the cheapest **one.** (The noun being referred to has been mentioned previously.)

2 Possessives

Forms ADJECTIVES

SINGULAR	PLURAL
my gloves	**our** dog(s)
your jacket	**your** country
his sister }	
her son }	**their** friend(s)
its cover }	
one's needs	

PRONOUNS	*These gloves aren't* **mine.**	*This dog isn't* **ours.**
	Is this jacket **yours?**	*Is this land all* **yours?**
	The house is **hers, not his.**	*Those awful children of* **theirs!**

Agreement There is no agreement between:
1 a possessive adjective and the noun or pronoun it qualifies
2 a possessive pronoun and the noun it replaces:

his *wife* **her** *husband*
Those two boys are **hers.**

his (ADJECTIVE/PRONOUN) refers to a male person or animal.
her (ADJECTIVE) and **hers** (PRONOUN) refer to a female person or animal.

Possessive adjectives with parts of the body In contrast to some languages, it is the possessive adjective and not the definite article that is used to qualify parts of the body when these form part of a specified person or animal (represented by a noun or pronoun). No reflexive pronoun is used.

He was holding his ticket ready in **his hand.**
She always wears her watch on **her right wrist,** *not on* **her left.**
Some animals change the colour of **their coats** *in spring and autumn.*
You've got dust in **your hair** *and a smut on* **your nose.**
I had only enough time to wash **my face and hands.**

Notes
1 When two parts of the body follow each other (as in the last example) there is no need to repeat the possessive adjective.
2 The DEFINITE ARTICLE is used when no person or animal is being referred to.

The eye *can often be deceived.*

Practice

a Answer these questions in complete sentences, using a possessive adjective.

EXAMPLES
Where do donkeys carry loads?
They carry loads on their backs.

1 Where does a married woman wear her wedding-ring?
2 What two parts of my head do my glasses rest on?
3 Where is Beatrice putting her necklace? (round)
4 Why doesn't Monty feel comfortable in his new shoes? (small for feet)
5 Where do criminals sometimes wear masks to avoid being recognised?
6 Do we wear slippers on our hands?
7 What parts of your body are you most likely to break when skiing?
8 What part of Sidney's face did the wasp sting?
9 What do you kneel on?
10 What does a dog wag when it's pleased?
11 What does a dentist do for you? (look after)
12 What must you do before you can go to sleep? (eyes)
13 How does an elephant pick up things? (trunk)

b Jenny has just got dressed in the morning. She hasn't had time for a bath or a shower but she has got ready in other ways, including a wash. What parts of her body has she:

1 cleaned (with a toothbrush)?
2 brushed and combed?
3 filed?
4 made up?

c Your motor-cycle has run into a wall with you on it and you are now in hospital for treatment. You are describing to an anxious relative what harm you have done to yourself. Describe your injuries. You have:

1 broken (or fractured)
2 cut
3 bruised
4 grazed
5 bumped
6 crushed
7 scratched
8 hurt

various parts of your body.

Here are some words that may be useful:
toe ankle heel knee thumb wrist elbow shoulder collar-bone knuckles chin forehead ribs
Use also any other parts of the body you can think of.

Begin like this:
Fortunately I was travelling slowly when the motor-bike and I hit the wall at more or less the same instant. Of course I fell off with the bike on top of me. The doctors say that fortunately I haven't **dislocated my hip** *or* **injured my spine**. *But I've certainly ...*

Possessive pronouns: examples of use

'Whose car shall we use, **mine** *or* **yours***?'*
'Oh, **mine** *will take at least five of us. Then if Roberta brings* **hers**, *there'll be room for everybody. Oh, here she is. Haven't you got your car with you, Roberta?'*
'No, I'm sorry. **Ours** *is at the garage just now.'*
'But the Bennets are sure to bring **theirs**. *And if Lucas turns up in his mini-bus, we shan't have to use either* **mine** *or* **yours**. *There'll be plenty of room in* **his**.*'*

Note
Possessive pronouns may be subject, object or complement of the main verb, and may also follow a preposition.
mine *will take at least five of us* (SUBJECT)
if Roberta brings **hers** (OBJECT)
the one at the garage is **ours** (COMPLEMENT)
there'll be plenty of room in **his** (after a PREPOSITION)

Practice

a Suggest what might be said in each of these situations, using a suitable possessive pronoun in your response.

EXAMPLE
After a party in your home you find a cigarette lighter and you're trying to work out whose it might be.
I wonder who left this lighter? Ivan smokes so it might be **his**. But it looks more like a woman's lighter. Sophie and Selina don't smoke so it can't be **theirs** and Stephanie's is a blue enamelled one so it isn't **hers**. It isn't one of **yours** by any chance?

You need introduce only one or two possessive pronouns in each case.

1 Someone is asking whether the car parked outside his house belongs to you. What might he say (using a possessive pronoun) and what might you answer if it doesn't?
2 Explain which of the cars in the street belongs to you. (Start with the pronoun).
3 Someone has asked you who Tom and Tessa's visitor is. You suggest that he may be a relation of Tom or of Tessa but you don't know which.
4 You're explaining that a factory belongs not to a friend's husband but to his wife.
5 You and your husband/wife are together explaining to someone who has to visit you the following day which house in the street to come to. The houses have no numbers.
6 You're explaining to someone that a bunch of keys doesn't belong to you but as your father often loses his keys, they might belong to him.

b Finish each of these sentences or suggest an additional one, introducing in each case at least one possessive pronoun.

EXAMPLE
Cedric and I both have property at the seaside, but . . .
his is a luxury villa while **mine** is a beach hut.

1 The dogs my neighbours and I own are different in breed, size and nature. . . .
2 George and Mary do the same kind of job but their salaries are very different. . . .
3 You and I ordered a meal at the same time but . . .
4 Maybe your children are better-looking than Eleanor's but . . .
5 Mr and Mrs Paternoster never invite their parents to dinner on the same day of the week. . . .
6 Both we and the Knights stayed in hotels in Geneva but . . .
7 Jack and Jill have lost their umbrellas in different places. He left . . .
8 You and McTavish speak quite different dialects. I can understand . . .

---

3 Interrogatives

Forms **who?** (PRONOUN)
what? which? whose? (ADJECTIVES AND PRONOUNS)

Usage a **who?** and **whose?** always refer to people.

b **what?** (ADJECTIVE) and **which?** (ADJECTIVE and PRONOUN) may refer to people, things and ideas.
What poet wrote these lines?
What other poems did he write?
Which sister/Which house in the village is the oldest?

what? (PRONOUN) refers to things and ideas, not to people.
What do you want?

c **which?** (PRONOUN) may be followed by **of**, but the other pronouns may not. (**who?** + **of** is very rare.)
Which of the puppies would you like?

d All forms can be used with (ADJECTIVE) or replace (PRONOUN) either a singular or plural noun or other pronoun.

what shop?	*what information?*	*what numbers?*
which shop?	*whose advice?*	*which numbers?*
whose coat?		*whose children?*

Who painted these pictures? (one or more artists)
What did you buy? (one or more things)
Which do you prefer? (one or more persons or things)

Notes
1 As **which?** suggests a choice between more than one item, it is rarely used before an uncountable noun.
2 **who?** is commonly followed by a singular form of the verb, though a plural form is possible.
Who's/Who is coming with me? (usual for one or more people)
Who are coming with me? (less usual, but possible)

what? which? a **which?** suggests that the number of possibilities is known or limited.
Which glove can't you find? (ADJECTIVE)
Which of your gloves can't you find? (PRONOUN)

b **what?** suggests an unlimited or unknown number of possibilities.
What make of car have you got?
What can I do for you?

Notes
1 It is, however, usual to ask: *What page is it?*
2 Adjectival **what?** is common in such phrases as:
what kind of . . .? what time . . .? what size . . .?
what colour . . .?

Practice

What might you say in each of these situations? Introduce adjective or pronoun **what** or **which** in your response: the part of speech to use is suggested in brackets.

EXAMPLES
As an employer, you're asking a job candidate the name of the school he attended. (ADJECTIVE)
What school did you go to?
As a host/hostess you're offering a guest tea or coffee. (PRONOUN)
Which would you prefer: tea or coffee?

1 You're asking someone about his choice of a present. (PRONOUN)
2 You're asking about the church a friend attends: there are four churches in the town. (ADJECTIVE)
3 Kim is asking Jim about his favourite opera. (PRONOUN)
4 A secretary's friend is asking about the make of typewriter the secretary uses. (ADJECTIVE)
5 You'd like to know the name of the town your friends spent their holiday in. (ADJECTIVE)
6 You're asking your guests whether they prefer apricot jam or orange marmalade with their breakfast toast. (PRONOUN)
7 You want to know the time of the train your colleague intends to travel by: you know there are eight trains during the day. (ADJECTIVE)
8 As a teacher you're asking a new Swiss student whether he speaks French, German or Italian as his first language. ((a) PRONOUN (b) ADJECTIVE)
9 You're asking the meaning of the word 'stock-taking'. (PRONOUN)
10 As a teacher you're asking about the words in a certain sentence that the students don't know the meaning of. (ADJECTIVE)
11 You want to know somebody's name. (PRONOUN)
12 When arranging an appointment by telephone, you ask whether the morning or the afternoon is the more suitable. (PRONOUN)
13 You're treating a friend to an ice-cream and want to know his/her preference. (PRONOUN)
14 You're asking whether a mile or a kilometre is longer. (PRONOUN)

Using other interrogative forms

PRONOUNS	ADJECTIVES
who?	—
what?	**what?**
which?	**which?**
whose?	**whose?**

Each of the statements below is the answer to a question which has been asked and which includes one of the above forms. Suggest what the question has been. Where both a pronoun or an adjective could be used, suggest two questions.

EXAMPLES
Oh, that's General Fabius Foote.
Who's that tall man with a loud voice?

He works as a surveyor.
What's his job? or: What does he do for a living?

I think it belongs to my neighbour.
Whose is that caravan outside? or: Whose caravan is that outside?

1 William Shakespeare.
2 I'm Mavis Merle Larksong.
3 We had vegetable soup, fish and chips and ice-cream.
4 We went to the Homefare Restaurant as the other one was closed.
5 The Alsatian? Oh, that's Dick's dog.
6 The Social Liberal party is more popular than either the Radical Democrats or the United Nationalists.

7 Well, it isn't ours.
8 I do.
9 Page 100.
10 At about three o'clock.
11 It's the twenty-ninth of February.
12 I'm next.
13 20 Meadowside Lane, Ambleford, Wiltshire.
14 562 8974103
15 The largest? I don't really know. Could it be Asia?

Whoever/whatever?
(**whichever** is seldom used)

When used as interrogatives, **whoever** and **whatever** express strong emphasis.

EXAMPLES
Whoever said such an extraordinary thing?
Whatever did you do when he pointed a gun at you?
Whatever are you talking about?
Whatever kind of music are they supposed to be playing?

In the second and third examples, **whatever** is being used as a PRONOUN, in the fourth as an ADJECTIVE.

Suggest questions beginning with either **whoever** or **whatever** that might be asked in each of the following situations.

1 You are served with some very strange-looking food.
2 Someone says he has heard another person describe you as an exceptionally intelligent person.
3 You see in a shop window some extremely expensive sandals and are wondering what kind of person would buy them.
4 On going into his room you find your colleague crawling about under the table.

5 Someone makes a very strange remark to you which you can't understand.
6 Someone knocks at your door at five o'clock in the morning.

Suggest a sentence containing an interrogative **whoever?** or **whatever?** each of which could follow the statements or questions below.

1 He says he's an old friend we haven't seen for years. ...?
2 Why are you crying? ...?
3 You've really bought a genuine Rembrandt? ...?
4 Someone told you this house is for sale. How odd! ...?
5 Why is the cat staring at that wall? ...?
6 I've lost every penny in the world. ...?

Notes
1 Adverbs **whenever, wherever** and **however** can suggest similar emphasis.
2 All the above forms ending in **-ever** can have the additional meaning of 'it doesn't matter who, what, when, where, how'.

---

4 Demonstratives

Forms	this	these
	that	those

Usage a These adjectives and pronouns suggest relative NEARNESS (**this, these**) or DISTANCE (**that, those**) in SPACE, TIME OF AWARENESS.

They agree in number with the nouns or pronouns they qualify (ADJECTIVES) or the ones they replace (PRONOUNS).

SINGULAR *this room* (I am in now)
this morning (now or the morning of today)
this money I've just found
this is where I live (here)
at that time (in the past)
I'd rather sit on that chair. (not the one you've suggested)
Could I look at that more closely?

PLURAL *these glasses* (I'm wearing now)
these days (the present time)
in those days (A fairly distant past is being referred to here.)
Do you remember those discussions we had at college?
I like these but I didn't think much of those we saw yesterday.

b **this** and **that** are often followed by **one**, except when referring to an uncountable noun, or, in nearly every case, by an idea (see the fifth example and (**c**) and (**d**) below).
This one seems to be broken.
I'll take that one, please.
This book is in French and that one is in German.
This money is French and that is German.
That sounds very funny. (possibly an incident or anecdote)

c **that** may sometimes refer to an idea which has already been expressed.
'I've been spending a month in China.'
'Oh, that must have been interesting.'

d **this** can refer to an idea (ideas) that will follow:
This is what you must do. Invite him to dinner, serve his favourite food, and then ask him.

Further examples *Do you think this scarf* (in my hand) *will go with that coat* (on the coat rail)*?*
These theories (which we're now discussing) *were suggested by astronomers centuries ago.*
In those days (years ago) *astronomers had not yet developed telescopes.*
I don't think much of that suggestion. How about this one?

Practice

Replace the dotted lines in the following statements and questions with a suitable word group containing **this, that, these, those** used as an adjective or pronoun. (Some suggestions as to which form would be suitable are shown in brackets.)

EXAMPLES
These roses in front of the window bloom earlier than . . . those over by the far wall.
'I've got a feeling that Toogood is leading a double life.' 'Yes, . . . (PRONOUN) that's what I think too.'
I can't find exactly what I want but I suppose . . . (ADJECTIVE) this blue one will do.

1 Which flowers shall we send her: those yellow tulips on the counter or . . . (ADJECTIVE)
2 I'm sorry. I'm tied up the whole time before lunch. Could you . . . (ADJECTIVE)
3 Can you reach . . . (ADJECTIVE)
4 'How about asking Bert what's wrong? He knows a lot about cars.'
'Yes, . . .' (PRONOUN)
5 I say, did you recognise . . .? (ADJECTIVE)
6 '. . . We'll hire a van and move the furniture ourselves. That'll be much cheaper.' (ADJECTIVE OR PRONOUN)

7 The peaches they're selling this morning look less ripe ... (PRONOUN)
8 Have you had any answers to ...? (ADJECTIVE)
9 I've bought two metres of material for my new coat. Do you think ... (PRONOUN)
10 'Is there anything else you'd like, madam?' 'No, thank you. ...' (PRONOUN)
11 We've been getting amazingly good pictures from our new space probe but ... are the best we had. (PRONOUN + SEVERAL WORDS)
12 Would you please hand me down ... (ADJECTIVE)

---

5 some, any
no, none
somebody/someone, something
anybody/anyone, anything
nobody/no one, nothing

Uses of some and any

a As an ADJECTIVE before an uncountable noun.
I've found **some money**.
He didn't give me **any useful advice**.

When the uncountable noun stands alone without **some** or **any**, the emphasis is on the NATURE of the thing itself, possibly in contrast to other things with which it is being compared.
Would you prefer cheese or fruit for dessert?
You'll need butter for that cake. I think margarine might spoil the taste slightly.
This isn't wood. It's plastic.

The additon of **some** or **any** implies that a PORTION OR AMOUNT is being referred to.
I've got **some very nice fish** *on the menu today.*
Could you lend me **some butter**. *I've run out completely.*
Haven't you got **any cheese**?

b Functioning as a plural of **a** before plural nouns.
Compare: *There are carrots, peas and onions in this soup, but no beans.*
with: *She bought* **some sandals** *to take on holiday.*

The difference in meaning resulting in the omission or inclusion of **some** and **any** is less evident in the above case.

However, a difference may exist:
He wrote books for children, not for adults.
He wrote **some books** *for children.*
In the second example there is a stronger suggestion that he wrote other books as well.

Note
In both cases (**a**) and (**b**) **some** is weakened in speech to /səm/.

c To indicate 'an amount of' or 'a number of' (ADJECTIVE and PRONOUN).
Pronunciation: /sʌm/.
I can let you have **some money**, *but not very much.* (ADJECTIVE)
I haven't got much money with me, but I can let you have **some**. (PRONOUN)
Some people *might agree with you, but certainly not everybody.* (ADJECTIVE).
I enjoyed **some** *of the records but not all of them.* (PRONOUN)

Notes

1 **any/no/none** suggest the absence of amount or number.
I didn't buy any (any fish, any strawberries).
He's got no money (no friends, none).

2 Compare:
Some *television programmes are educational.* **Others** *provide entertainment at various levels.* (There are other programmes which are not included here.)
Some *television programmes are transmitted live.* **The others** *have been pre-recorded.* (All television programmes are being referred to.)

I enjoy **some** *programmes, but not* **others**. (I don't hear them all.)
I enjoy **some** *programmes but not* **the others**. (I hear them all.)

d With the meaning 'it doesn't matter who/what/which'.

This use involves only **any** and its compounds **anybody/anyone, anything** and **anywhere** (ADVERB).
You can come any time you like. (It doesn't matter what time.)
Ask anybody and you'll get the same answer. (It doesn't matter what person you ask.)
Anything will do. I'm not fussy.
Sit anywhere. There's plenty of room.

Differences in meaning and usage between some/any somebody/someone anybody/anyone something/anything

There is no difference in meaning or usage between:
somebody and **someone**
anybody and **anyone**
nobody and **no one**
everybody and **everyone**

However, there is a difference between **anyone** and **any one**:
There doesn't seem to be **anyone** *waiting.*
He didn't stock **any** *(single)* **one** *of the items on my list.*

a **some** and its compounds most often appear in affirmative statements and commands.
I'll give you **something** *for that cough.*
Somebody *told me that you come from Australia.*
Bring me **some** *tonic water, please.*

any and its compounds most often form part of:
1 negative statements and commands.
I didn't need **any**.
Don't tell **anybody** *else that.*
2 affirmative and negative questions.
Was there **anything** *new about the strike on the one o'clock news?*
Didn't you have **any** *breakfast?*

b **some** and its compounds may appear in questions that:
1 expect an affirmative answer.
You are busy. Is **someone** *coming to lunch today?*
Are you looking for **something**?
2 are requests and offers in question form.
May I have **some information**, *please?*
Would you like **some help**? (OFFER) (Compare this with the question *Do you need any help?*)

c **any** and its compounds may form part of affirmative statements and commands when they have the meanings 'it doesn't matter who/what/which' (see (**d**) under 'Uses of **some** and **any**' above).

Any *bus will get you here.*
Take **any** *one.*

Practice

Suggest what you might say in each of these situations, using in your answer the word in bold type.

EXAMPLES
A friend asks you for a cigarette but you've left yours at home. **any** (PRONOUN)
I'm sorry. I haven't got any with me.
You're telling a rather new acquaintance that it couldn't have been you he claims to have met in Majorca. **someone**
But I've never been to Majorca. It must have been someone else.

1 You've got a bad cough. You don't know what to take for it so you're asking a chemist for some suitable medicine. **something**
2 You're giving advice about a suitable present for a mutual friend who has recently bought his/her own flat. **something** (PRONOUN)
3 You're asking a friend about new acquaintances he/she may have made while attending a recent conference. **anyone**
4 Your reply when your teacher asks you how much of a taped conversation you've understood. **some** (PRONOUN)
5 Having had no reply to a knock on a house door, you call out. **anyone**
6 You're offering refreshments to a visitor. **some** (ADJECTIVE)
7 You're telling a visitor that it doesn't matter where he parks his car. **anywhere**
8 You're explaining why you're lonely now you're living in the country. **anyone**
9 You're expressing surprise because on telephoning a large firm during office hours you can get no reply. **someone**
10 You're upset because you have no suitable clothes to wear at a very formal party you have to attend. **anything**
11 You're describing the kind of book you most enjoy reading. **something**
12 You're explaining why you couldn't buy a special kind of cheese when you were shopping. **any** (PRONOUN)
13 You're expressing surprise when, after trying on fifteen different dresses, a friend leaves the shop without buying one. **any one**
14 You can't find your gloves which you know are in the house. **somewhere**
15 You're asking the other students in your class if you can borrow a dictionary. **anyone**
16 You're describing the kind of man/woman you'd like to marry. **somebody**

no, none, nobody/no one, nothing

no (ADJECTIVE) and **none** (PRONOUN) express the absence of quantity and number.

I've got **no more time** *now.* (QUANTITY)
None *of the food was wasted.* (QUANTITY)
For once I've made **no mistakes.** (NUMBER)
She's got lots of presents, but I've got **none.** (NUMBER)

nobody/no one and **nothing** express the non-existence of people, things or ideas.

Nobody *would want to come as early as that.*
I've got **nothing** *in my pocket.*
I know **nothing** *about it.*

All the above forms may be substituted for related forms of **not any**. However, they tend to be less commonly used than the latter form, and may sometimes sound slightly dramatic and intense.

*I have***n't** *got* **any** *money or traveller's cheques.*
I've got **no** *money at all.*
*Are***n't** *there* **any** *of these pictures that appeal to you?*
No, I like **none** *of them.*
None *of the singers was worth listening to.*

I don't know **anybody** *who could help.*
Nobody *gave me any help when I needed it.*

*I'd rather not express an opinion. I have***n't** *got* **anything** *interesting to say.*
If you represent the Press, I've got **nothing** *to say.*

There's **no** *hope left.*
Nobody *will ever know the answer to that.*
Is there **nothing** *you can do about it?*

Notes

1 As subjects of a sentence, **no, no one, nobody** and **nothing** are the normal forms. A form with **not any** would rarely be used.
No changes have been made yet.
None of the furniture is valuable.
None/Not one of the pictures is valuable.
Nobody expressed an opinion.
Nothing can be done now.

2 In some languages the double negative (**not . . . no/none/nobody/nothing**) is common. The double negative is not used in English.

3 Similar usage to that described above applies to adverbs such as **never** and **nowhere.**
I've **never** *met him./I have***n't ever** met him.

4 These negative forms are less commonly used in questions. In many cases they would appear unnatural.
Couldn't your doctor suggest **any** *treatment?*
*Do***n't** *you want* **any**? (*Do you want none?* is extremely unlikely.)
*Did***n't** *you meet* **anybody**?
*Can***'t** *they find* **anywhere** *to live?*

Practice

Complete each of these sentences with several words, including the form in bold type.

EXAMPLE
It isn't my job to find a solution. Their problems ... **nothing**
have nothing to do with me.

1 I've tried twice to telephone the garage but ... **nobody**
2 I tried to find a skirt that was my size but there ... **nothing**
3 He wanted to make an omelette but ... **no**
4 Some lucky people get a large share of the cake while ... **none**
5 Most children get bored and restless when ... **nothing**
6 I asked at least twenty people where the church was but ... **no one**
7 I can't play golf while I'm staying here as ... **no**
8 Can I have some more coffee? Sorry, ... **none**
9 You may prefer tea but I consider there's ... **nothing**
10 He visited every hotel in the town but ... **nowhere**
11 That's a question ... **nobody**
12 He was afraid he might have to have an operation but the doctor said ... **no** (worry)

Expressions that may follow some/any/no compounds

a **else**
after **somebody/someone, something, somewhere**
anybody/anyone, anything, anywhere
nobody/no one, nothing, nowhere
Somebody else could do it for you.
Is there anything else to be done?
No one else can write so well.

b **at all**
after **anybody/anyone, anything, anywhere** (+ **not**)
nobody/no one, nothing, nowhere
There isn't anybody at all in the park today.
There's nobody at all in the park today.

c **more**
after **something, anything, nothing**
Would you like something/anything more?

d **left**
after **some, somebody, something**
any, anybody, anything
no (+ NOUN), **none, nobody, nothing**
Is there some/any cake left?
There was nobody left in the empty schoolroom.
I haven't got any money left./There's none left.

e Certain ADJECTIVES follow the forms listed in (**a**) above. The most common of these are:

important	**unknown**	**old**	**white** (and other colours)
suitable	**expensive**	**new**	**pleasant**
unusual	**cheap**	**good**	**unpleasant**
sensible		**bad**	**hot/cold** (for things)
well-known			

together with comparative forms: **something better** etc.

I want somebody sensible to give me some help.
I can't think of anything suitable to give him as a present.
He says there's nowhere interesting to go for a holiday.

f An INFINITIVE
after **some/any/no** and their compounds.
some work to do *anything to eat* *nobody to speak to*

none is less commonly followed by an infinitive.
There are none to use/to pick/to eat.

g A RELATIVE CLAUSE
After **some/any/no** compounds.
The conjunction **who/that** is very often omitted unless it is the subject of a following verb.
some people I know
somewhere we visited
something he said
anything you want
We saw none (that) we liked.
no one I knew
someone who/that speaks German
It's nothing that matters.

h **of**

after **some, any** and **none** (PRONOUNS).

These pronouns are normally followed by **of** + NOUN/PRONOUN, unless this noun or pronoun is obvious, in which case it can be omitted.

He attended some of the courses, but he wasn't really interested in any of the lectures.

There's still some Christmas pudding left. Does anybody want any?

Notes

1 **some, any** and **none** (PRONOUNS) replacing an UNCOUNTABLE NOUN may be followed by **of it**, though this is often omitted, as in the second example above.

2 **some, any** and **none** replacing a COUNTABLE NOUN may be followed by **of them** and this is usually included.

'What do you think of his cartoons?'

'Well, some of them are mildly funny, but none of them (not one of them) has ever been really original.'

Practice

a Complete each of these sentences with several words, using in each case either the word or an example of the form suggested in the brackets.

1 When caught doing a crossword puzzle, the clerk claimed that ... (**else**)
2 You've eaten far too much already: surely ... (**more**)
3 No, you can't have another helping of ice-cream: ... (**left**)
4 He went to the library, hoping ... (**interesting**)
5 I went to the railway bookstall ... (INFINITIVE)
6 I've asked dozens of people this question but I've found ... (**nobody** + CLAUSE)
7 Can you recommend ...? (**anything** + CLAUSE)
8 I'm almost starving: ... (**at all**)
9 I haven't been able to find ... (**of**)
10 From the red carpet and all the roses I'd say ... (**important**)
11 See if there's any money in the drawer: ... (**left**) where?
12 This is my business: it's ... (INFINITIVE)
13 On a hot day it's nice ... (**cool**)
14 The customs officer asked me if ... (INFINITIVE)

b Complete these sentence openings with at least six more words.

1 There's nothing at all ...
2 Opinions in the committee meeting were sharply divided: some of ...
3 If you want anything more ...
4 Nobody else ...
5 Some of the people she ...
6 I'm afraid (that) none of ...
7 If there's anything at all ...
8 Something unexpected ...
9 If you've got nowhere else ...
10 Don't you like any of ...
11 There's nothing worth watching ... (so ...)
12 If you've got some time to spare ...
13 I've just remembered something (that ...)
14 Couldn't somebody else ...?
15 If you've got any money to give away, ...
16 Is there anyone here who ...?
17 I'm looking for somewhere to ...
18 If there's anything left ...
19 I've nothing more ...
20 If there's anything nice ...
21 If you've got no work to do ...

6 All, every, each
all, everybody/everyone, everything, each
either, neither

all, every, each as adjectives

a **all** (+ **the/my/this**) may be used:

1 before an uncountable noun.
Did you really make all the/your/this furniture yourself?

2 before a singular countable noun.
I didn't read all the/my/that book.

the whole often replaces **all the** before a singular countable noun. **the whole of** may replace **all** before a possessive or demonstrative adjective or an article.
I didn't read the whole book.
I didn't read the whole of the/my/that book.

3 before a plural countable noun.
Did you write all the/your/those letters?

every/each may precede a singular countable noun.
Every/each child was given sweets.
There was a number on each/every door.

b 1 **all** + a singular noun suggests completeness.
We've finished up all the Cheddar cheese.
He spent all last year in Florence.

2 **all** + plural noun suggests a certain uniformity implying that an undifferentiated group is being referred to.
All the houses are new.
All four sides of a square are equal in length.

3 Differentiate between **all** and **all the**:
All trees have branches. (a general rule)
All the trees have been recently planted. (those in a particular group)
All cheese is made from milk. (cheese in general)
He has eaten all the cheese. (the cheese that was available, not all the cheese that exists)

Notes

1 **all people**, though semantically possible, is rarely used in present day English. **everybody** is the normal expression.
Everybody enjoys an occasional change.

2 Constructions which follow adjectival **all** and **each** are referred to in the section dealing with corresponding pronoun forms on pages 164–6 below.

Practice

a Each of the expressions in column B should be combined with a suitable expression in column A together with additional words to form a complete sentence. The expression in A may be used either as subject or object of the sentence.

EXAMPLES

A	B
all telephone boxes	*painted red*
all the telephone boxes	*occupied*

All telephone boxes are painted red to make them look conspicuous.
All the telephone boxes were occupied so I had to wait several minutes before I could make my urgent call.

all chocolate	*melted*
all the chocolate	*cocoa beans*

All chocolate is made from cocoa beans, sugar and milk.
All the chocolate melted in the intense heat and we had to throw it away.

	A	B
1	all drivers all the drivers	hold a driving licence (before ...?) travelling slowly (why?)
2	all fish all the fish	swim (why must they be able to?) ate (who?)
3	all correspondence all the correspondence	already dealt with (who?) filed for reference (where?)
4	all medicine all the medicine	didn't take (why not?) kept away from (whom?)
5	all birds all the birds	have wings (but ...) singing (where?)
6	all rivers all the rivers	flow (what direction?) frozen (which rivers? when?)

Note
all is seldom followed by a negated verb.
Not **all** *birds can sing.*
Birds can't **all** *sing.* } normal
not: **All** *birds can't sing.* (which could in fact have two meanings according to intonation when speaking)

b Complete each of the following sentences with the word(s) in brackets preceded by **each** or **every** (whichever in your opinion is more suitable: either might be possible) together with several other words.

EXAMPLES
Scientists are investigating the possible existence ... (planet)
of life on each planet in the solar system.
In the General Election ... (adult citizen)
every adult citizen has the right to vote.

1 You would have to spend a long time in the National Gallery if ... (picture)
2 He has hung a different wallpaper ... (wall – of which room?)
3 She was wearing an expensive ring ... (finger of her right hand)
4 I've spent ... (penny)
5 At the end of the oratorio a bouquet was presented ... (soloist)
6 He knows the name ... (flower)
7 The hotel manager makes a practice of ... (guest – when?)
8 Only a few delegates attended the three-day conference so ... (speech)
9 She invited only a few people to her birthday party but naturally ... (guest – did what?)

---

all, each
everybody/everyone
everything

a **all** (PRONOUN)

1 **all** very often appears next to or very near:

a) a noun or plural personal pronoun.
The spectators/The crowd/They all went home.
I told you all to be quiet.

b) **it.**
'Where's the coffee?' 'Oh, I've drunk it all.'

c) a singular or plural demonstrative adjective or pronoun.
All this has to be carried up three flights of stairs.

"DID YOU REALLY DO ALL OF THAT YOURSELF?"

2 When **all** is followed by **of**, the idea of completeness and universality may be stronger.
He's renting all of the house, not only the upstairs flat.
I want all of you to sing not only those with good voices.
(In *I want you all to sing* there is less emphasis on **all**.)
Did you really do all of that yourself? (**all that** is possible.)

3 **all** seldom stands alone, that is to say without a nearby related noun, pronoun or related clause.
'Is that all?' 'Yes that's all.'

Alone it may sound over-dramatic.
All is over between us. We can never meet again. (**everything** would have been rather more natural.)
All have deserted. Now we must stand alone against the world.

4 Pronoun **all** may refer to quantity and number.
He used it all up./He used them all up.

b **each** (PRONOUN)

1 **each** (**of**) is often used in similar circumstances to **all**, though only together with a plural noun or plural personal pronoun. It is rarely preceded by a demonstrative adjective or pronoun.

2 **each** emphasises the individual unit rather than the whole group:
Each of the flowers is a different colour.
We each got a different present.
We were each given a different present.
I only hope that each of the committee members has now made up his mind.

Note
the position of **each** unaccompanied by **of**:
a) before a single verb word (see the second example above).
b) after the first of two or more verb words (see the third example above).

3 **each** may form part of a sentence predicate, separated from its related noun or pronoun. It then conveys a strong idea of distribution.
You can have ten pounds each.

Notes
1 **each** rarely if ever appears as subject of a negative sentence.
2 **each** is not followed by a relative clause or (with rare exceptions) by an adverbial phrase.

c **everybody/everyone, everything** (PRONOUNS)

Compare these with **all** in usage. The pronoun **all** more often refers to a certain defined group of people, things or ideas and it appears in the same word group as the noun or pronoun it replaces.
All the rioters were shouting and throwing stones though not all of them knew what they were rioting about.
That's all. I won't be able to carry any more.

The idea that **all** refers to is sometimes understood and not expressed:
He saved all (the money) he earned for doing overtime.

This can also be expressed as:
He saved everything he earned for doing overtime.

everybody/everyone and **everything** are less specific, the first two often implying 'every possible person' and the third 'every possible thing', without necessarily defining who the people or what the things are.

Everyone is talking about what happened.
He has lost interest in everything.

In these cases **all** would sound completely unnatural in English, though its use is in fact not ungrammatical.

Compare:
a) *The picnic things are all in the hamper.*
b) *Everything (needed) is in the hamper.*
and:
a) *'What did he do with his money?'*
'He left that all to his son.'
'And how about his pictures?'
'He left them all to his sister.'
'What did he do with all the other things he had?
b) *'He left everything to charity, as a matter of fact.'*

Notes

1 **all** is regarded as singular or plural according to the noun or pronoun it refers to.
All of the information was false.
I don't think all of the committee are here yet.

2 **everybody/everyone** and **everything** are always singular.
Everybody/Everything is in the garden.

3 In some cases (apart from the possible singular/plural variation), **everybody/everyone** and **all of them/they all** are more or less interchangeable.
'Where are all our guests?'
'Oh, they've all gone home.'
or: *'Oh, everybody has gone home.'*

d Constructions that commonly follow **everybody/everyone** and **everything**:

1 **else** *They've already checked everything else.*

2 Certain adjectives including:

(everything/everyone)	**intelligent** **interested** **qualified**	**concerned** **involved** **alive**	**willing** **present**
(everything)	**necessary** **essential**	**possible** **ready**	**available**
(everybody/everything)	**suitable**	**important**	

3 Adjectival and adverbial phrases including:
everybody with a family/out of work/on duty
everything for children/made here/left on a bus
everybody in the classroom/at the meeting/from another country
everything under the sun/on the table

4 Relative clauses.
who/that are usually omitted unless they are the subject of the following verb.
Everyone who visits the Far East . . .
everybody you meet
everyone we know
everything he does

Notes

1 Both **all** and **everything** may be followed by a relative clause, but in some cases a slight difference in meaning is expressed in the choice of pronoun.

I'm taking everything with me. (not just a few things)

This is all I've got. (I haven't got any more, though I'd like to have.)

2 **everybody/everyone** and **everything** are followed by a singular verb form, and in formal writing any related pronoun or possessive adjective is also singular.

3 **everybody** and **everyone** are always interchangeable.
everyone and **every one** are different in meaning.

Every one of you will be questioned.

He counted the banknotes and then put every one (each) in a separate envelope.

Practice

Answer each of the following questions in as many different ways as are suitable, using pronoun forms of **all, each, everybody/everyone, everything** and **every one.**

EXAMPLES

Which of your friends gave you a present on your twenty-first birthday? (4 possibilities)
They **all** did. **All** of them. **Everybody** (did). **Each** of them (did).

How much of your money did you spend when you were on holiday? (2 possibilities)
I spent it **all**. **All** of it.

What would you miss most if you had to leave your country to live abroad?
Everything.

1 How many windows in Lucia's flat face south? (4 possibilities)
2 How much of the story do you believe? (3 possibilities)
3 What will the police want to know about what happened? (1 possibility)
4 How much of your furniture will you take with you to your new flat? (3 possibilities)
5 Which students should be able to pass tomorrow's exam? (3 possibilities)
6 How much of the poem have you learned by heart? (2 possibilities)
7 Which of us will they want to question? (4 possibilities)
8 Who's likely to listen to the President's televised speech? (1 possibility)
9 How much of his speech is likely to be controversial? (2 possibilities)
10 How many of you want to go on tomorrow's excursion? (4 possibilities)
11 If the twenty biscuits are divided evenly among the five children, how many will Alec, Bernice, Charlotte, Dolly and Ethel get? (1 possibility)

---

either, neither **either** and **neither** can each be used as (a) a PRONOUN/ADJECTIVE, (b) an ADVERB, or (c) a CONJUNCTION.

a ADJECTIVES and PRONOUNS

either may indicate a choice from or distinction between a set of two.

You may have either.

Conversely **either/neither** may indicate similarity.

I don't like either. Neither is new.

'But there are two television programmes I want to see.'
'Well you can watch either but I don't see how you can watch both.'
(PRONOUN – choice)

'In any case, neither of them starts before eleven which is well after your bedtime.' (PRONOUN – similarity)
'We offer courses in Secretariat Training and also in Interpreting: you can enrol for either course.' (ADJECTIVE – choice)

Notes

1 **either** when used affirmatively and suggesting similarity can sometimes be replaced by **both**:
Either colour suits you./Both colours suit you.
Either suits you./Both suit you.
But **either** cannot be replaced by **both** in a question.
Do you think that either suits me? (one or the other)
Do you think that both suit me? (both of them)
and also in any case where a meaning change results:
You can have either. (one of them)
You can have both. (two of them)

2 **neither** would sound quite unnatural in a question or command.
Don't you want either? Don't buy either.
Even in a statement **not + either** is more usual.
I don't want either.
This sounds more natural than **I want neither**, which is slightly dramatic.

3 **either** and **each**
When **either** suggests similarity and not distinction it can be replaced by **each**.
There are trees on either/each side of the road.
When **either** suggests a distinction or choice, it cannot be replaced by **each**, as this would result in a meaning change.
You can wear a watch on either wrist.
You can wear a watch on each wrist.

b ADVERB
too can be used (most often at the end of a sentence) to express affirmative similarity between ideas associated with two different people, things, ideas or groups.
A secretary has to be able to type well and she must be efficient too.

In a negative sentence of this kind **either** is used to express similarity.
My secretary can't type well and she isn't efficient either.

The second part of the sentence can be expressed alternatively with a different word order and using **neither/nor** instead of **either**.
My secretary cannot type well and neither/nor is she efficient.

The use of **either/neither/nor** is dealt with in more detail in short responses in Part 1, Section A8.

c CONJUNCTION
either . . . or and **neither . . . nor** are used as conjunctions to express choice or distinction. Compare the following examples.

You can have either roast or boiled potatoes.
You can have both roast and boiled potatoes.

Most people live either in the town or the country though some try to combine the two by living in a garden city.
He either walks two kilometres or runs one kilometre before breakfast every morning.
Either keep quiet or go out.
I neither want it nor need it.

Notes

1 The use of **either . . . or** emphasises that a choice must be made.

Would you like a sandwich or cake? (It's not impossible to have both.)

You are entitled to either fruit juice or tea with your meal on the plane.

Neither the affirmative nor the negative form is commonly used in everyday speech, **neither . . . nor** even less commonly than the affirmative form. Where they are used, they may serve a dramatic or similarly intense purpose.

The examples below would more likely appear in the written language or in formal speeches.

He's satisfied neither with his job nor his accommodation.

The Government has solved neither the problems of unemployment nor the difficulties of controlling inflation.

Neither the Government nor the Opposition can make any practical suggestions about how to deal with either problem.

In more colloquial speech the first two of the above examples would possibly be framed as:

He's dissatisfied with both his job and his accommodation.

The Government hasn't solved either the problems of unemployment or inflation.

Practice

a To each of these questions suggest a possible reply which will include **either** or **neither** as a pronoun or adjective (as suggested in the following brackets). Add an extra sentence.

EXAMPLE

'Who was elected chairman for the coming year: Smith or Brown?' (PRONOUN)

'**Neither** of them. They elected Robinson.'

1 Which of your two daughters takes after her mother? (PRONOUN)
2 How shall I pay you: in cash or by cheque? (PRONOUN)
3 Was it in Kandahar or in Peking that we met? (ADJECTIVE + place)
4 Shall I buy an ivory or a pale blue blouse to go with my new grey skirt? (ADJECTIVE + colour)
5 Which do you prefer: the red tie with yellow spots or the pink one with orange stripes? (PRONOUN)
6 Which of the two main parties is likely to get an overall majority in the coming election? (PRONOUN)

b Finish each of these sentences with a suitable group of words containing **either** as an adverb. A clue is given in 6.

EXAMPLE

I dislike uncomfortably hot weather . . .

and I don't enjoy freezing cold weather either.

1 Ostriches can't sing . . .
2 He's not particularly intelligent . . .
3 The department store escalator isn't working . . .
4 The weatherman says it isn't going to rain today . . .
5 No newspapers have appeared today . . .
6 You mustn't sound your car horn in a built-up area . . . (maximum speed there?)
7 No trains are running today . . .
8 I doubt whether I'll get a rise this year . . .

c Complete each of these sentences suitably.

EXAMPLE

He doesn't speak either ...
Dutch or Danish.
During our coming holiday we're considering either ...
exploring the remote tundra of Lapland or relaxing on the beach at Brighton.

1 Could you buy something for supper while you're out: either ...
2 With five young children to look after she can neither ...
3 As the train approached the frontier Hank was in despair as he could find neither ...
4 When I leave school I can either ...
5 There's no need for you to carry that, Granny: either ...
6 It's impossible to get into the building: neither ... (unlocked)
7 In this arid desert land neither ... (survive)
8 To achieve success in a political career one needs either ...

Section E Adjectives

1 Pre-noun and predicative adjectives

a Adjectives normally either:

1 precede the noun they qualify (PRE-NOUN ADJECTIVES), or:

2 are separated from the noun they qualify – in this case usually forming part of the sentence predicate (PREDICATIVES).

I'll be taking the **large brown leather** *suitcase.*
The food/It was **badly cooked, almost cold** *and* **quite uneatable.**

Note
available is one of the very few adjectives that can either precede or follow a noun, with little if any meaning change.
all the available accommodation/all the accommodation available

b Certain adjectives can be used only predicatively. These include:

afraid	**alight** (of a	**alone**	**asleep**	**ill**
ajar	fire or gas)	**ashamed**	**awake**	**well**
	alive			

Pre-noun adjectives related to some of these are:

frightened (**afraid**)	**living/live** (**alive**)	**sleeping** (**asleep**)
similar/identical (**alike**)	**solitary** (**alone**)	**burning** (**alight**)

Only **frightened** is a *near* substitute.

All the above can be used predicatively.
My grandfather, who is still **alive**, *is the last* **living** *member of his generation.*
The child was **alone** *in the house.*
Now at last our baby is **asleep**. *A* **sleeping** *child looks very helpless.*

Near substitutes for **ill** and **well** are **sick** and **healthy**, though **ill** and **well** may also refer to temporary conditions.
She feels **ill** *today, but she still has to look after her* **sick** *husband.*
A **healthy** *person does not always feel* **well.**
feel seasick/homesick
feel sick after eating too much rich food

Note
ajar, ashamed and **awake** have no single word substitutes.
She could hear everything from outside the door, **which was ajar.**
The prisoner, **who was still awake,** *heard approaching steps.*

Practice

Replace the dotted lines in these sentences with a suitable one of the above adjectives, together with any additional words needed. Use the predicative form wherever this is possible.

1 I'll call a doctor if . . .
2 When the last of his noisy guests left, he was thankful . . .
3 He spent his evenings in the hotel: . . . walk in the narrow unlit streets of the town.
4 I haven't seen my great-uncle for years and I don't even know . . .
5 Large parts of the earth are covered with desert where no . . .
6 I won't disturb him if . . .
7 The mother explained . . . child that the big dog was really quite friendly.
8 In the hot afternoon sun the street was quite empty apart from . . .
9 Sport and games are popular with . . .
10 After taking a sedative, . . .
11 Of course we've got problems: most people with a large family . . .
12 Identical twins are . . .
13 A vet (veterinary surgeon) is a doctor who . . .
14 She's worried that her house may be on fire as she's just remembered . . .

2 Adjectives after certain verbs

look sound taste feel seem appear get become turn

Compare the two sentences in each of the following pairs:

This report looks quite **thorough**.	*He always looks through reports* **thoroughly**.
This soup tastes/smells **good**.	*The chef always tastes/smells the soup* **critically**.
Those motor-scooters sound very **noisy**.	*The man sounded the gong* **noisily**.
The doctor, who was feeling **tired**,	*felt the broken bone* **gently**.

In the word groups on the left, the predicative word (**thorough, good, noisy, tired**) qualifies its preceding noun or pronoun (**report, soup, motor-scooters, doctor**). They are therefore ADJECTIVES.
In the sentences and word groups on the right, the words **thoroughly, critically, noisily** and **gently** show how the verbal action was carried out, and are therefore ADVERBS.

The use of the predicative adjective may seem more obvious in the case of the verbs **seem** and **appear**.

The local people seem **kind** *and* **honest**.
The teacher appears quite **young**, *though he's really over fifty.*

kind and **honest** qualify the noun **people**, and **young** the noun **teacher**.

Verbs which express change, such as **get, become** and **turn**, may be followed by adjectives qualifying an earlier noun.

Father/He always got/became very angry when contradicted.

Note
well can be an adjective as well as an adverb.
Mandy doesn't look well. (ADJECTIVE)
Mandy doesn't look after her dog well. (ADVERB)

Practice

Answer each of these questions with a sentence which contains the verb in bold type together with a following adjective or adverb as suitable. Adverbs such as **very, rather, really, extremely** etc. can be introduced additionally in several cases.

EXAMPLE
polite/politely
What did your pen-friend **sound** *like when he spoke to you on the telephone?*
He sounded extremely polite.

Group 1

Adjective/adverb possibilities:
nice/nicely careful/carefully
anxious/anxiously cold/coldly

1 How did your boss **look** at you when you arrived late this morning?
2 What does the new student in your class **look** like?
3 How did you **feel** when the doctor said you must have an operation?
4 How does a person **feel** his way downstairs in complete darkness?

Group 2

Adjective/adverb possibilities:
funny/funnily immediate/immediately
suspicious/suspiciously horrible/horribly

5 How does a customer in a restaurant **taste** strange-looking food?
6 What does castor oil **taste** like?
7 When did the sentry **sound** the alarm when he spotted the enemy?
8 What did Manuel's broken English **sound** like?

Group 3

Supply your own adjectives or adverbs here.

9 What does your new landlady **seem** like?
10 How did she **appear** when you told her you couldn't pay the rent?
11 How did the impatient motorist **sound** his horn?
12 What happens when you work too hard? (use: **get**)
13 What do you think the weather will be like tomorrow? (use: **turn**)

3 Adjective substitutes

Nouns Nouns are often used before other nouns when, as they provide additional information about the noun they qualify, they serve as adjectives. Their special function is to identify the following noun.

Compare: **a wine bottle, a beer bottle, a medicine bottle, a milk bottle**
(In each case the bottle is identified or named.)
with: **a large broken green stone bottle** (In this case the bottle is being described. (For the order of adjectives see Part 2, Section E8.))

Note
In the case of MATERIALS the noun and adjectival form are usually identical (with the exception of **woollen** and **wooden**).

Compare also: **a car door, a cheese flan**
(In this case the door and the flan are identified.
with: **a door of a car, a piece of cheese**
(In this case a part, section, amount or component is being referred to. See Part 1, Section B1/3.)

Note
a coffee cup – identifying the cup
a cup of coffee – referring to the contents

Further examples:
a stamp/coin/butterfly/matchbox/fossil collection
a railway/bus/fire/police station
a detective/love/fairy/adventure story
a car/glass/textile/plastics/furniture factory
a bus/train/theatre/season ticket

This use of the noun as an adjective is largely a matter of usage, and no defining statement can be made about the categories that can be used in this way.

The passage of time and/or shortness of the words involved has in many cases created single NOUN + NOUN compound words:
lamplight bookcase banknote bathroom raincoat
Longer words may be linked by a hyphen:
safety-pin motor-scooter lorry-driver window-cleaner

Practice

Each of the nouns in the A lists can be used adjectivally before one of the nouns in the accompanying B list. Combine suitably the noun–adjectives and nouns and say what you could do or (using your imagination) couldn't do *with*, *about*, *in* or *at* the object, place or idea expressed. In most cases an article or possessive adjective will probably precede the compound noun.

EXAMPLES

A	B
garden	*site*
caravan	*wall*

I could grow roses against my garden wall.
I couldn't go for a long walk on a caravan site.

	A		B	
1	street	crossword	puzzle	orchestra
	library	football	match	sandwich
	egg	symphony	book	plan

	A		B	
2	travel	income	buffet	towel
	shop	ocean	tax	window
	bath	station	liner	office

	A	B
3	telephone	car
	birthday	cruise
	evening	account
	bank	present
	Mediterranean	directory
	sports	class

Participles and gerunds

a PARTICIPLES
Besides forming part of verbal tense forms, participles may be adjectival. A present participle has an active meaning:
an **exciting** *story* (the story provides excitement)

A past participle has a passive meaning:
excited *children* (something has excited the children)

Examples given of the adjectival use of the participle sometimes sound unnatural. The following expressions are uncommon in everyday speech:
a barking dog a ringing bell a singing bird

The present participle, however, frequently forms part of certain commonly-used expressions, for example:

rising/falling prices, birthrate, costs
freezing fog
pouring rain
a moving staircase (escalator)
a revolving door
running water (from a tap)
a flying visit (a very short one)
coming events
the following sentence
the preceding word
a standing arrangement
a sleeping partner (who takes no part in running a firm)
the developing world

Present participles suggesting an appeal to the mind or the emotions are in common use. These include:

interesting **fascinating** **boring** **amusing** **tiring** **surprising**
annoying **irritating** **shocking** **alarming** **terrifying** **frightening**

Some past participles can be used with any suitable noun, as in these examples:

a **broken** *toy/cup/promise/engagement/heart*
a **typewritten** *manuscript/letter/statement*
a **well-cared-for** *animal/house/garden*

Various past participles often form part of commonly used expressions including:

mass-produced goods
stolen goods/property
lost property
a stamped addressed envelope
cut prices
an unemployed person
(under)developed areas
worn-out clothes
haunted houses
fried fish

b GERUNDS
These verbal nouns are commonly used as adjectives. As nouns, they have neither an active or passive meaning but they very often suggest the purpose of the noun they qualify.

a walking-stick (a stick for walking with)
a waiting-room
playing cards
a hearing-aid
a writing-desk
slimming tablets
a driving-school

The following examples show some slightly different uses:

a singing-lesson (in which singing is taught)
a dressing-gown (worn before dressing)
a skiing contest (one which involves skiing)

Note
While a hyphen often separates a gerund–adjective and noun qualified, this is far from universal and may depend on the individual writer or printer.

Practice

a For each of these expressions suggest two possible meanings, which will depend on whether the adjective is a participle or gerund.

1 a moving van
2 a recording tape
3 a freezing compartment
4 a dancing student
5 an acting teacher
6 a profit-making advisory service

b Explain the difference in use and therefore meaning between the adjectives in the following pairs.

1 changing fashions/a changing room
2 a visiting statesman/visiting hours
3 a running commentary/a running track
4 a closing door/closing time

c Replace the dotted lines before or after these word groups to form interesting sentences. Each word group includes a present participle.

EXAMPLE
... depressing weather
We decided to cancel our picnic because of the depressing weather.

1 A leading playwright has suggested ...
2 One of his annoying habits is to ...
3 I enjoy soothing music when ...
4 Growing anxiety is being expressed about ...
5 ... I needed a relaxing holiday.
6 ... the gathering clouds.
7 ... in good working order.
8 The town is now split into opposing groups: those who ...
9 The Managing Director believes that ...
10 ... the burning house.

d Answer the following questions with a complete sentence. Each of the questions includes a past participle used adjectivally.

1 Why do few housewives in industrialised societies produce home-made bread nowadays?
2 On average, who has the harder life: a married housewife or a single working woman?
3 Which do you prefer: bearded or clean-shaven men?
4 What is one advantage of being able to buy frozen food?
5 What is the main purpose of the United Nations Organisation?
6 What's the difference between full-cream and skimmed milk?
7 Which takes the least time to cook: a boiled egg, a poached egg, a fried egg or a scrambled egg? How long does it actually take?
8 Which is usually easier to let: a furnished or an unfurnished flat?

e Answer each of the following questions, introducing into your answer the noun in brackets at the end of the question together with a suitable gerund adjective.

EXAMPLE
What do most women take with them when they go shopping? (bag)
They take a shopping bag.

1 What does a driver move to change the direction of his car? (wheel)
2 Where does a doctor see his patients? (room)
3 What do you often have to put money into when you leave your car in a town? (meter)
4 What kind of light do many people prefer to read a book by? (lamp)
5 What kind of organisation may young people with bicycles join? (club)
6 What's used to repair a hole in a sock? (wool)
7 What do mountaineers wear? (boots)
8 What was used to produce the words on this page? (machine)

Phrases **a** These may precede the noun qualified and then are usually hyphenated. Plural nouns expressing age, weight, measurement, quantity and similar ideas lose the final plural -s.

a five-year-old child
a ten-ton lorry
a hundred-metre race
a twenty-pound note
a ten-floor building
a hundred-watt lamp
the sixty-four-thousand-dollar question
a long-distance runner

Phrases may consist of an adjective – participle preceded by an adverb. These forms are usually hyphenated.

strongly-expressed opinions
a brightly-lit street
a well-known actor
a hair-raising story

Note
Certain nouns may add **-d** or **-ed** and, when preceded by an adverb, be used adjectivally.
a green-eyed cat *a long-eared rabbit* *a short-sighted boy*

b Many adjectival phrases cannot be expressed in this hyphenated form and these follow the noun they qualify. They may also be used predicatively.

a family **with four children** | *a lecture* **on three different topics**
a song **without words** | *a picture* **by an unknown artist**

The adjectival phrase may be used predicatively:
The lecture will be **on three different topics.**
or it may begin with a participle–adjective:
an old farmer **leading his cow**
a cake **divided into four parts**

Note
A phrase does not contain a finite verb (with subject). See 'Clauses' below.

Practice

Add an adjectival phrase to each of these nouns. A possible first word of a phrase is suggested in brackets but you can use a phrase with a different opening word if you prefer.

EXAMPLES
an old house (*in*) a bad state of repair
a message (*written*) in large capital letters
a garden (*full*) of tropical flowers and plants

1 a paper-bag (with)
2 an opera (composed)
3 an ashtray (made)
4 an untidy boy (wearing)
5 highly-secret documents (left)
6 two coffees please (without)
7 a large china bowl (containing)
8 a new student (from)
9 a telephone box (painted) (do not use **in**)
10 a party of tourists (on)

Clauses Adjectival clauses usually follow immediately the nouns they qualify.
the actor **who won last year's Oscar**
the castle **which/that once stood here**
the newspaper **most people read**
a comedian **whose programmes have long been popular**
the cupboard **where I keep the cleaning things**
the time **when he won't be able to work any longer**

A clause is often used instead of a corresponding word or phrase.
I was kept awake by a dog **that kept barking.** (instead of **a barking dog**)

A clause may qualify a pronoun.
Bring me the one **that's on the top shelf.**

But its use after a personal pronoun may sound overdramatic, as in:
We, who have lived long, are wise.

Practice

Add an adjectival clause to each of these expressions and then if necessary complete the sentence.

EXAMPLE
The hymn (that) they were singing was one ...
I remembered from my childhood.

1 The many unexpected questions ...
2 One of my uncles, ...
3 Can you describe the exact place ...
4 May I introduce you to Mrs Mandeville Stoke, whose ...
5 I'm really looking forward to the day ...
6 Can you show me please the Ming vase ...
7 This isn't the one ...
8 People ...
9 Puddlepool and Watermarsh are two villages not far from the town of Coldbrook: the former, ...
10 I don't think much of the hotel ...

4 Adjectives expressing quantity and number

This section does not deal with numbers as such, which appear in 7 below (see page 186).

Adjectives that suggest a large or sufficient quantity or number

Forms:

SINGULAR ONLY	**much, a good deal of, a great deal of**
PLURAL ONLY	**many**
SINGULAR AND PLURAL	**a lot of, plenty of, enough**

a **much, a good deal of, a great deal of**
These can be used only with UNCOUNTABLE NOUNS.

a great deal of often suggests a larger quantity than **a good deal of.**
As a civil engineer working abroad, he earns a good deal of money.
He hasn't a great deal of money, but he's still quite well off.

much is normally used only in negative and interrogative sentences, though **very much** and **too much** can appear in affirmative statements.
Has much progress been made with your travel book?
Not much progress has been made with the book, but a great deal of time has been spent in gathering material for it.

b **many** is used before PLURAL NOUNS. It can be used in affirmative statements, though **a lot of** is more commonly used. **a great many** is a very large number.

'Has he got many friends?'
'Well, no. In fact he's got a lot of enemies and certainly not many friends.'

These stone axes must have existed for a great many years.

c **a lot of** and **plenty of** can be used with uncountable nouns and also with plurals.
a lot of/plenty of fruit **a lot of/plenty of apples**

plenty of may have a suggestion of more than enough.
I've had a lot of work/jobs to do today.
We needn't hurry. We've got plenty of time to spare.

a lot and **plenty** are often used without **of.**
'Have you got enough to eat?' 'Yes, thank you. I've got plenty.'

Adverbially **a lot** and not **plenty** is normal.
He travels a lot.

d **enough** normally *follows* an adjective or adverb, and *precedes* a noun.
There's enough soup for everyone, but it's not hot enough and I can't heat it quickly enough as the fire's almost out.

Practice

Suggest what you might say in each of these situations, using the word given in bold type together with one of the expressions that have been explained above. Use **a lot of** or **plenty of** only when one of the quantity number expressions is not suitable. (In some cases **plenty of** is more exact than **a lot of**.)

EXAMPLE
people
You're telling an English person he'll easily make himself understood when he visits Norway.
Don't worry. You'll find **plenty of/a lot of/a great many** Norwegian people speak good English.

1 **money** You're giving advice to a friend who wants to start his own business.
2 **hard work** You're congratulating someone on the beautiful garden he's made.
3 **information** You're saying how satisfied you are with your visit to the tourist office.
4 **luggage** You're referring to what you'll have to take with you on a world cruise.
5 **help** You're saying that Sonja, who has a job and a home to run, has a very co-operative husband.
6 **days** Christmas is getting rather near. (Begin: There aren't . . .)
7 **clever** You're explaining why Fred will never get very far in life.
8 **material** You're explaining why you can't make a long-sleeved dress.
9 **opportunities** (+**for** + GERUND) A tourist brochure describes the attractions of a holiday resort.
10 **progress** A teacher is writing a report on a rather unsatisfactory pupil.

SCHOOL REPORT
PUPIL:- Abel Little
Class 3

ENGLISH	Poor
MATHS	Bad
HISTORY	Weak
SCIENCE	Finds it difficult
GEOGRAPHY	Only fair
BIOLOGY	Hopeless

TEACHER'S COMMENT:- Abel could do a lot better.

11 **time** (+ **to** + VERB) An elderly person is dreaming of his retirement.
12 **suggestions** The Committee members weren't very helpful about ideas for the annual club outing.
13 **often** You're explaining why Student X hasn't learned much English during the course.
14 **difficulty** (+ **in** + GERUND) A handwritten letter has been almost impossible for you to read.
15 **room** You're explaining why you can't invite a lot of friends to a party in your small flat.
16 **glasses** You wouldn't even be able to give everybody a drink.

Adjectives that suggest a small quantity or number

a (a) **little** indicates quantity and is therefore used with uncountable nouns.

b (a) **few** indicates number and is therefore used with plural nouns.

a little / **a few** } =some **only a little** / **only a few** } =not enough **little** / **few** } =almost none

little
The police have **a little** *information about the murderer, including his approximate age and height.*
The police have **only a little** *information about the murderer: all they know is that he is a tallish man.*
The police have **little** *information about the murderer as he left no clue and was unseen.*

few
A few *people have been able to give the police some useful information.*
Only a *(very)* **few** *people were in the area at that time.*
Few *people in that area are willing to go out at night now.*

Practice

Answer the questions that follow the two groups of sentences and are in each case related to them.

1 I can give you a little information about the town.
I can give you only a little information about the town.
I can give you little information about the town.

What information might you then give in each of these cases?

2 She has a few qualifications for a secretarial post.
She has only a few qualifications for a secretarial post.
She has few qualifications for a secretarial post.

What qualifications might she have in each of these cases?

Comparatives and superlatives of some/little/few		
	WITH BOTH SINGULAR AND PLURAL NOUNS	**some, more, most**
	WITH UNCOUNTABLE NOUNS	**little, less, least**
	WITH PLURAL NOUNS	**few, fewer, fewest** (**the smallest number of**)

I have **some** *free time in the evenings,* **more** *free time at weekends and* **most** *free time during my holidays.*
She eats **little** *butter/***few** *cream cakes.*
She ought to eat **less** *butter/***fewer** *cream cakes.*
Last year the firm made the **least** *profit/got* **the smallest number of** *new orders for the last decade.*

Notes
1 **little** with countable nouns means small: *the little finger*
2 **the smallest number of** commonly takes the place of **the fewest**

Practice

more most less least fewer
the smallest number of

Complete these sentences in such a way as to include in each one of the above words followed by the noun in brackets and additional words.

EXAMPLE
One day he'll be able to give up smoking altogether . . . (cigarettes)
as he's trying to smoke fewer cigarettes every week.

1 A good-tempered person ... (enemies)
2 A job with a larger firm would offer ... (promotion possibilities)
3 This article is too long. You ... (words)
4 I'm still hungry. May ... (potatoes)
5 Our lazy son has ... (progress)
6 It is a highly-developed industrial country that ... (investment)
7 The country's high exchange rate is discouraging foreign tourists. This year we can expect ... (visitors – since 1950)
8 It isn't always the hardest workers ... (money)
9 It's often the people with least money ... (children)
10 I can't finish this today. I ... (time)

5 Comparison of adjectives

Forms a SINGLE SYLLABLES

POSITIVE	COMPARATIVE	SUPERLATIVE
cold	**colder** (**than**)	**coldest**
cold	**less cold** (**than**)	**least cold**

Exceptions:

bad	**worse** (**than**)	**worst**
good	**better** (**than**)	**best**

Note:

far	**farther**	**farthest** (distance)
far	**further**	**furthest** (to a greater extent – but also used for distance)

b THREE OR MORE SYLLABLES

comfortable	**more comfortable**	**most comfortable**
comfortable	**less comfortable**	**least comfortable**

c TWO SYLLABLES
No exact guidance can be given, as in many cases either of the above forms can be used.

windier/ more windy	**windiest/ most windy**
stupider/ more stupid	**stupidest/ most stupid**

The general tendency is for words ending in **-y** (**noisy**), **-er** (**clever**), **-ant** (**pleasant**), and **-ow** (**shallow**) to add **-er** and **-est**, and for words with other endings to be preceded by **more** or **most**.

Some of the adjectives preceded by **more** and **most** are:

careful	**distant**
correct	**foolish**
normal	**active**
afraid	**formal**
rapid	**silent**

and all participle adjectives.

Note
All participles, including those with one syllable, are usually preceded by **more** and **most**:
tired/more tired **bored/more bored**

Comparative construction	*A mountain is*	**higher**	**than** *a hill.*
	Today I'm	**less tired**	**than** *I was yesterday.*
	Life in London is	**more exciting**	**than** *in the country.*
	Watching television is	**less expensive**	**than** *going to a cinema.*

Practice

Compare the people and subjects shown, using the adjectives suggested together with any additional ones you can think of.

EXAMPLE

old active thoughtful carefree sensible healthy well-behaved childish

Granny is older than Lucy and she needs a walking stick.
She is less active than Lucy but she manages to get about quite a lot.
She is more thoughtful than Lucy and has more to think about.
She is less carefree than Lucy, but she is usually cheerful.
She is more sensible than Lucy, but not so imaginative.
She is less healthy than Lucy, but isn't often really ill.
She is better-behaved than Lucy as is to be expected.
She is less childish than Lucy and isn't yet in her second childhood.

Granny

Lucy

1 Begin each sentence: **The thriller/It is . . .**

small thick heavy educational popular intellectual silly exciting widely read expensive new cheap modern

the thriller

the dictionary

2 Begin each sentence: **Marilyn/She looks . . .**

beautiful pretty friendly cheerful attractive sensible sophisticated spoilt

Marilyn

Sophia

The more . . . the better This type of comparative construction may involve a wide range of adjectives, adverbs and clauses.

The older he becomes, the more energetic he seems to get.
The sooner you leave, the sooner you'll arrive.
The more you buy, the more you'll have to carry home.
The less we speak, the more we hear.
The longer people have to wait, the more impatient they become.

Practice

Complete each of these sentences with a comparative construction of the type described above.

1 The higher the price, . . .
2 The larger one's garden, . . .
3 The darker it got, . . .
4 The farther you have to travel, . . .
5 The more I see of him, . . .
6 The more I try to teach him, . . .
7 The less I have to work, . . .
8 The faster he spoke, . . .
9 The fewer people you tell about this, . . .
10 The more time you spend learning English, . . .

Constructions with superlatives

a A noun qualified by a superlative is followed by **in** before a PLACE, and **of** before a GROUP. Either **in** or **of** can be used before time expressions.
He always sits in the most comfortable armchair in the room.
He is the least experienced member of the team.
The most brilliant man in/of his era.

b A noun qualified by a superlative can be followed by a word, phrase or clause.
the most interesting person there
the most interesting person in the room
the most interesting person I've met
the least interesting speaker I've ever heard

c When the superlative **most** is preceded by **a** (**an**) it means 'very'.
I've been speaking to a most interesting person.

Practice

Finish each of these sentences with a superlative form together with other words as suitable.

EXAMPLES
Everest is . . .
the highest mountain in the world.
The lunch cost £20 and was awful. It must have been . . .
the most expensive and worst I've ever eaten.

1 Methusaleh Mujihara, who is said to be 150 years old, must . . .
2 The two million pounds paid for the Rembrandt must be one of . . .
3 My baby brother, who is two days old, is . . .
4 This homework is full of unnecessary silly mistakes. It's . . .
5 The Prime Minister is said to be . . .
6 William Shakespeare . . . (of all time)
7 The twenty-first and twenty-second of June . . .
8 The winter in Central Siberia must be one of . . .
9 The present Miss Universe is supposed . . .
10 You never do a stroke of work. You're . . .
11 Everybody went to sleep during his lecture. It was . . .

Comparisons of equality

The following constructions involve both adjectives and adverbs.
Is St Paul's Cathedral **as** *interesting* **as** *Westminster Abbey?*
Is he **as** *busy* **as** *he always is?*
The traffic wasn't **so/as** *bad today* **as** *it was yesterday.*
You can't run **as** *quickly* **as** *I can.*

AFFIRMATIVE **as . . . as**
NEGATIVE **so . . . as** or **as . . . as**
WITH ADVERB **as . . . as**

Normally these expressions are used in making a comparison of similarity in standard. This is especially the case when two nouns are being compared. This usage is not always so obvious, however, when other parts of speech or following clauses are involved.

as soon as possible *as recently as yesterday*
as much as usual *He stayed as long as he could.*

the same as

Look. Try to hold your racket in **the same** *way* **as** *I'm doing.*
He's got **the same** *semi-digested ideas* **as** *most of the other students.*
They stayed for a week in **the same** *picturesque town (unchanged, it seemed, for several hundred years)* **as** *they had spent their honeymoon in.*

Note
Be careful! In some languages **than** after comparative forms and **as** after expressions of equality and after **the same** are represented by an identical word. Beware of using **than** in the latter cases and especially when **same** is separated from **as** by several other words.

Practice

Compare these things and ideas in a question, including **same**. Then answer your question in two sentences. An adjective or adverb that could be used is suggested in bold type. Use the two ideas in the same order as they are given.

EXAMPLES
the size of Denmark and of Great Britain **small**
Is Denmark the same size as Great Britain?
No, it isn't. Denmark is smaller than Great Britain.
the speed of sound and of light **fast travel**
Does sound travel at the same speed as light?
No, it doesn't. Sound travels much less fast than light.

1 the length of the River Amazon and the River Danube **long**
2 the height of Mount Fujiyama and Mount Everest **high**
3 the price by air from London to Paris and the price by train **high**
4 the depth of the North Sea and the Pacific Ocean **deep**
5 the weight of hydrogen and oxygen **heavy**
6 the temperature of boiling water and melting steel **hot**
7 the meaning of 'terrified' and 'afraid' **strong**
8 the colour of crimson cloth and pink cloth **dark**

6 Emphasis and comparison: such a, such, so

Constructions suggesting emphasis

a **such a**
BEFORE A SINGULAR COUNTABLE NOUN: *It's* **such a problem***!*
I'm reading **such an** *interesting* **book**.

b **such**
BEFORE AN UNCOUNTABLE NOUN: *He's got* **such energy**.
We had **such** *cold* **weather**.
This region has **such** *beautiful* **scenery**.

BEFORE PLURAL NOUNS:	*They're* **such idiots**! *He tells* **such** *extraordinary* **stories**.

c **so**

BEFORE **much** AND **many**, STANDING ALONE, or FOLLOWED BY A NOUN:	**So much** *travel must be tiring.* *He has to make* **so many** *journeys.*
BEFORE ADJECTIVES WITH NO NOUN FOLLOWING:	*Your news is* **so extraordinary**. *They were* **so kind**.
BEFORE ADVERBS:	*You spoke* **so well**. *You walk* **so quickly**, *I can't keep up with you.*

Note the request: *Would you be* **so kind as** *to help me with this?*

Uses of such and so

a Emphasising the following idea.

You've got a beautiful house.	*You've got such a beautiful house.*
I've got a lot to do.	*I've got so much to do.*
I felt tired.	*I felt so tired.*

b In comparisons in negative sentences

This isn't such an attractive house as we lived in before.
They don't serve such good food here as they do in Chez Louis.
I don't feel so tired as I did yesterday.
The new television series hasn't been so much appreciated as we expected.

Note
It would be rare to find in this construction an uncountable noun without an adjective preceding it:
such heavy luggage as . . . but: *such a noise as*

Practice

a What would you say in each of these situations which would include a form preceded by **such a**, **such** or **so**.

EXAMPLES
You've just returned from a very long walk. **such**
We've had such a long walk. or: We've walked such a long way.
You're complaining about your cold room. **so**
My room's so cold.

1 You've enjoyed the evening. **such**
2 You like your neighbours. **such**
3 You've been shocked at the price of something. What? **so**
4 You find London very noisy. **such**
5 The streets are crowded with cars, buses and lorries. **so much**
6 You're criticising someone's furniture. **such**
7 You're praising the pretty colour of your friend's dress. **such**
8 You want to know if it's really necessary to get up at five o'clock the following morning. **so**
9 This is the tenth time you've explained something. **so many**
10 You've got a high opinion of someone's voice. **such**
11 Your teacher is grumbling about the many mistakes you've made. **so**
12 You had to take four suitcases and three large bags with you on holiday. **so**
13 You didn't like last summer at all. **so**
14 You're admiring someone's hair. **such**
15 You're apologising for having caused someone a lot of trouble. **so**

b Finish each of these sentences using **such** or **so** (**much**) as a form of comparison. Some suggestions are given in brackets.

EXAMPLES

A dog hasn't got . . . (claws)
A dog hasn't got such sharp claws as a cat.
This year I haven't spent . . .
This year I haven't spent so much money as I did last year.

1 A junior clerk doesn't . . . (salary)
2 Yesterday she didn't do . . . (housework)
3 Dick's son isn't . . . (energetic)
4 This year the firm won't make . . . (profit)
5 Radio One doesn't broadcast . . . (programmes)
6 Sweden doesn't have . . . (weather)
7 She hasn't got . . . (eyes)
8 A horse can't carry . . . (load)
9 Her latest novel isn't . . . (popular)

---

7 Numbers, times, dates

Numbers

Points to remember:

1 There is no **-s** at the end of **hundred, thousand,** or **million** when there is a preceding number.
five thousand (but: **thousands of years**)

2 **and** between the hundreds and digits.
5,464,392 (pronounced: five million four hundred and sixty-four thousand, three hundred and ninety-two)

3 **one hundred/thousand/million** and **a hundred/thousand/million** are equally correct.

4 In everyday English usage, a **billion** is a million million (not as in the USA). Similarly a **trillion** is a million million million.

5 Fractions: ½ = **a half,** ⅔ = **two thirds,** ¾ = **three quarters** (etc.)

6 Decimals: 25·436 = **twenty-five point four three six**

7 $4 + 5 = 9$ **four plus five equals nine**
$5 - 4$ **five minus four**
$9 \div 3$ **nine divided by three**
$4 \times 3 = 12$ **four times three equals twelve**

8 X^2 **X squared** $\sqrt{X}$ **the square root of X**

Telephone numbers

2 21 6 33 30
two two-one six double-three three O

Pair the numbers in each group from the right and pause very slightly between each pair, reading from the left. Similar numbers in each pair are referred to as **double.** Similar numbers not in a pair are said separately.

Times

a The word **minutes** is often omitted after 5, 10, 20, 25 but not after other numbers.

9.35 *twenty-five (minutes) to ten*
9.38 *twenty-two minutes to ten*
10.03 *three minutes past* (not *after*) *ten*

b The twenty-four hour time system is used in timetables, but everyday usage still prefers the twelve-hour system.
8 a.m. is eight o'clock in the morning.
3 p.m. is three o'clock in the afternoon.
7 p.m. is seven o'clock in the evening.

12 o'clock is common in everyday speech, with **noon** or **midnight** following if a difference has to be made, or **twelve o'clock in the day** or **at night** might be heard.
4.45 is more common in timetables: **a quarter to five** in everyday speech.

c Be careful with the half hours: **8.30** is half past *eight*.

d **at** is the preposition usually preceding the exact time.

Dates a ORDINAL NUMBERS (**first, second, third** etc.) are used in dates: **22nd March, twenty-second of March.**

b Years are usually pronounced **eighteen forty-eight** (**eighteen hundred and forty-eight** is possible).

Practice

a Say the following numbers aloud:

1 15 3 33 5 599 7 3,484,229
2 50 4 108 6 1760

b Say the following, together with the answers of the arithmetical calculations:

1 $33\frac{1}{3}$
2 $21\frac{3}{4}$
3 99^2
4 $\sqrt{49}$
5 12.345
6 $18 + 22 =$
7 $114 - 11 =$
8 $12 \times 13 =$
9 $62 \div 3 =$

c Say these telephone numbers:

1 560 2443 2 877 5999 3 700 3322

d Say the following times in everyday speech:

EXAMPLE
9.30 a.m.
half past nine in the morning

1 4.15 p.m.
2 8.40 p.m.
3 6.13 a.m.
4 noon
5 11.30 p.m.

e Say these dates:

1 12.4.1853
2 23.2.1922

f Answer these questions:

1 What's the date of your birthday?
2 What's the first day of the year?
3 What's the last day of the year?
4 What date is Christmas Day?
5 What year did you leave (will you leave) school?
6 What year did the Second World War start?
7 Today is the eighth anniversary of Sam's wedding. What date did he get married?
8 What's today's date?
9 What's the exact date of the extra day in the next leap year?
10 The fortune-teller has promised you that you will be left a hundred thousand pounds by a mysterious benefactor in a year and a day from now. When will this be?
11 What will the date be in four days' time? (note the apostrophe)

8 The order of adjectives

The following table shows the normal order when more than one adjective precedes a noun. The examples that come after the table show that various conditions can change this order but in most cases odd effects can be created by an unusual arrangement.

For example, a reference to **an Alsatian police powerful large dog** would puzzle an English-speaker for a moment until he realised that **a large powerful Alsatian police dog** was being referred to.

Note
Two adjectives together are the usual maximum in everyday speech but more than two may sometimes be used, especially when one of them is a noun– or gerund–adjective.

	1	2 Number	3 Size and extent	4 Descriptive quality	5 Participle	6 Weight	7 Age	8 Colour	9 Shape	10 Nationality	11 Material	12 Gerund-adjective or noun-adjective	13 Noun
1	those	three		lively			young						children
2	the		long		interesting		new					detective	story
3	a	second	large-scale	important	developing					Australian		tin-mining	industry
4	their		large	beautiful									carpet
5		several		valuable	embroidered			blue (or 9)	rectangular (or 8)	Chinese	silk	head-	scarves

Variations The many possible variations in the order may depend on meaning, emphasis, sound, rhythm etc.

Examples

1 *cold* (TEMPERATURE) *heavy* (WEIGHT) *continuous* (DESCRIPTIVE QUALITY) *depressing* (PARTICIPLE) *rain* (NOUN)

2 *a refreshing* (PARTICIPLE) *cool* (TEMPERATURE) *lemon* (NOUN–ADJECTIVE) *drink* (NOUN)

3 *a useful* (DESCRIPTIVE QUALITY) *light* (WEIGHT) *leather* (MATERIAL) *expanding* (PARTICIPLE) *weekend* (NOUN–ADJECTIVE) *suitcase* (NOUN)

Predicatives The above order usually applies also to adjectives used predicatively. The last two adjectives in a predicative series are linked by **and, or** or **but** as suitable.

The football crowd was large, noisy and high-spirited.
The football crowd was large and noisy, but reasonably well-behaved.

Practice

Use at least three adjectives together, each belonging to a different category, to describe suitably the following nouns.

EXAMPLES
guide
an attractive well-informed young Swiss guide
tablecloth
a large white square damask tablecloth
safe
an enormous heavy grey metal safe

1 handbag
2 actress
3 candle
4 cat
5 vase
6 restaurant
7 school
8 island
9 apple
10 mountain
11 handkerchief
12 church
13 cigarette-lighter
14 hat
15 label

Section F Adverbs

1 Adverbs of manner and their corresponding adjectives

Forms

ADJECTIVE	ADVERB
careful	**carefully**
gentle	**gently**
heavy	**heavily**

Notice the omission of the final **-e** and the changing of **y** to **i**.

good	**well**

ADJECTIVE AND ADVERB
better **worse**
best **worst**
hard (*hard work*, *work hard*) (**hardly** = scarcely)
difficult **with difficulty**

For adjectives ending in **-ly**, the corresponding adverb is usually phrasal:
friendly/in a friendly way

Most participles have no **-ly** adverbial form.
A few exceptions: **hurriedly, excitedly, worriedly**.

Use of adverbs

ADJECTIVES qualify nouns and pronouns only.
ADVERBS modify all other parts of speech.

He **speaks well.** (VERB)
He is an **extremely good** *speaker.* (ADJECTIVE)
He speaks **extremely well.** (ADVERB)
Actually, he isn't a Greek; he's a Cypriot. (SENTENCE)

Adverbs of MANNER usually modify VERBS.

Notes
1 In some languages most adjectival and adverbial forms are the same. Speakers of these languages should therefore give special attention to the use of adverbial forms in English.
2 **taste** and **smell**
This **fish** *tastes* **good.** (the **fish** (NOUN) is **good**)
An expert **tastes** *food* **critically.** (this is *how* he **tastes** (VERB))
This **fish** *smells* **bad.**
The cook is **smelling** *the fish* **suspiciously.**
(See Part 1, Section A1.)

Practice

Answer each of the following questions with a sentence which includes one of these alternative adjectives or adverbs, which are listed in the same order as the questions.

good/well **slow/slowly**
leisurely/in a leisurely way
difficult/with difficulty
hard (ADJECTIVE)/**hard** (ADVERB)/**hardly**
extreme/extremely **loud/loudly/aloud**

Note
The adverb **hardly** appears most often in such expressions as **hardly ever** and **hardly any/ anything/anybody/anywhere.**

1 Why is Dr Curall so popular with his patients?
2 Why does Tessa have to wear glasses?
3 Muggins isn't very bright. What kind of progress is he making at school?
4 How should a car be driven (if at all) in thick fog?
5 What kind of walk do you go for on a hot afternoon?
6 Were the tourists hurrying past the souvenir shops?
7 When might a class ask their teacher to speak more loudly? (... to hear him)
8 Does Stan get about at all now that he suffers so much from arthritis in his legs?
9 Why's your dog having such difficulties in eating his biscuit?
10 Would it be easy for a European to learn Arabic and Chinese at the same time?
11 What kind of worker does a firm like to employ?
12 Why are you always so tired at the end of your day's work? (have to)
13 Do you often see your son and daughter-in-law in Australia?
14 How would you describe a winter temperature of −35°C and a summer temperature of +40°C?
15 How old would your great grandfather be if he were alive now? (You need not give his exact age.)
16 What kind of bark has a large dog usually got?
17 Why could everyone in the large hall hear what Clarence was saying?
18 How does Deborah keep her blind father interested in books and newspapers?

---

2 False form and meaning connections between adjectives and adverbs

In most cases an adjective and adverb related to it in form are related in meaning. In some cases, however, a meaning change can cause confusion.

ADJECTIVE	ADVERB	
hard	hard/hardly	*Not being a hard worker, he hardly ever works hard.*
late	late/lately	**lately** = recently
practical	practically	**practically** can also mean 'almost'
direct	direct/directly	**direct** = straight to (a place) **directly** = almost at once
present	presently	**presently** = soon
short	short/shortly	**stop short** = stop suddenly **shortly** = soon
high	high/highly	**highly** = very much (*highly dangerous*)
fair	fair/fairly	**play fair/fairly** **fairly** may mean 'moderately'
simple	simply	**simply** = 'in a simple way' or 'really' (*You simply must do it.*)

Further examples appear in the Practice on the next page.

Practice

Answer these questions using one of the words given in bold type.

EXAMPLE
simple/simply
Is it very difficult to play chess?
It's simple to learn, but very difficult to learn to play well.

1 **hard hard/hardly** Why does Theresa often feel very lonely?
2 **late late/lately** Why is Roy's boss often annoyed with him?
3 **practical practically** Why won't the new transport scheme work properly?
4 **direct direct/directly** How do racing pigeons fly from Oslo to Edinburgh?
5 **present presently** When may the busy waiter say he will come and take your order?
6 **short short/shortly** How did the hurrying policeman stop when he heard the shot behind him?
7 **high high/highly** Why does that aeroplane look so small?
8 **fair fairly** What must a referee be when making a decision?
9 **simple simply** What did I say when I was trying to persuade Sheila to come to my party?
10 **hard hard/hardly** How must you try if you find something difficult to do?
11 **late late/lately** What might you say when you meet someone you haven't seen for some time?
12 **practical practically** Why are the committee members beginning to look at their watches and gather up their papers?
13 **direct direct/directly** How soon should an ambulance arrive?
14 **short short/shortly** The manager is on the telephone. What could his secretary say to the visitor who is waiting to see him?
15 **high high/highly** How inflammable is petrol?
16 **fair fair/fairly** How might you describe your car when you've had it for three months?
17 **hard hard/hardly** Why do the audience ask the lecturer to speak up?

3 Whenever, wherever, however

Meanings Each of these adverbs has two distinct meanings.

a As an expression of emphasis. A feeling of surprise/shock may be suggested.
Whenever did you get home last night?
Wherever could I have put that letter?
However did you manage to open that safe?

b At any time/place or in any way.

whenever = at any time, it doesn't matter when.
He screams whenever I touch him.

wherever = at/in any place, it doesn't matter where.
Wherever we went, we saw smiling people.

however = in any way, it doesn't matter how.
However hard he pushed and pulled the drawer, it refused to open
However much I try . . .
However clever he is, he won't be able to solve this problem.
In each of these cases, the second half of the sentence suggests failure – he can't do it.

Note
however can also mean 'but/though'.
The quality of the goods was excellent. The prices, however,/However, the prices were far too high.

Practice

Finish these sentences with at least four more words in each case. The two suggestions in brackets are for use only if you have no ideas of your own.

1 What a marvellous sun-tan you've got! Wherever ... (spend)
2 Wherever did you buy ...?
3 As she is a widow with a job and four small children, nobody can understand however she ... (find time)
4 Sarah goes to the opera whenever ...
5 They pitch their tent for the night wherever ...
6 However much he ate, ...
7 Whenever I met him, ...
8 Wherever you are in the world, you ...
9 I'm not going to offer him the job, however (ADJECTIVE) ...
10 He's got no musical talent whatever. His sister, however, ...

---

4 Rather, fairly, quite

Meanings

a **rather** suggests a DEFINITE quality.

Last night's programme was rather interesting: we discussed it for a long time afterwards.
It's rather cold today: you'd better put your heavy coat on.

b **fairly** is less definite: it suggests a MODERATE quality.

Last night's current affairs programme was fairly interesting, though actually no new facts or opinions were given.
Last night was fairly cold, though there wasn't actually a frost.

c **quite** has two different meanings:

1 completely.
I'm quite ready now.
2 suggesting a definite quality, though this may be slightly less definite than that suggested by **rather**.
He's getting on quite well at school.

Examples

His piano technique is fairly good, though he still has a lot to learn.
His piano technique is quite good – better than I'd expected.
His piano technique is rather good: I should recommend him to study at the Royal College of Music in preparation for a musical career.

Practice

Finish each of these sentences in such a way as to show clearly the meaning of the word in bold type.

EXAMPLES

I'm **rather** *tired so ...*
I'm rather tired so I think I'll put off writing that letter till the morning.
Yes, I'm **fairly** *tired but ...*
Yes, I'm fairly tired but I don't think I'll stop yet.

1 Yes, I know him **rather** well so I can tell you ...
2 A holiday in Spain could be **fairly** expensive but ...
3 He's **quite** busy at the moment so ...
4 Our new house should be **quite** finished by July and then ...
5 The local shopkeepers are **fairly** honest though ...
6 He speaks English **quite** well though ...

7 The current at this point of the river is **rather** strong so ...
8 I'm **quite** sure ...
9 My grandfather is **fairly** old but he ...
10 My grandfather is **rather** old so he ...

Note
I'd rather (= **I should/would rather**) = I'd prefer to: *I'd rather play chess than football.*

Sentence modifiers

Certain adverbs modify a whole sentence or phrase. The following practice exercise introduces some of these. Suggest a second sentence (beginning with the adverb shown) which could follow the sentence given in each case.

EXAMPLES
Where have you been? Polly was asking about you the other day. Incidentally ...
Incidentally, talking about Polly, have you heard she's won a beauty contest in London?
Well, the job has some disadvantages like irregular hours and a certain amount of risk. On the other hand ...
On the other hand the pay's good and the work's extremely interesting.

1 I know Mr Marshall would very much like to meet you. Unfortunately ...
2 Well, most holidaymakers are completely happy with a good beach, a luxury hotel and lots of sunshine. Personally ...
3 You can't expect top quality at the lowest price. Obviously ...
4 Jake was due at six and it's now eight. Obviously ...
5 I wonder why Pat's so quiet today. Normally ...
6 But he never goes out after ten o'clock in the evening. Surely ...
7 The elder brother was lively, talkative and very self-confident. In contrast ...
8 He was carrying a suitcase, a ciné-camera and a cage with a canary in. In addition ...
9 Although they had very little money they longed to have a house of their own. Eventually ...
10 He was found unconscious and badly injured beside the railway track. Apparently ...
11 With good typing and shorthand speeds she'll be just the right person for the job. Moreover ...
12 I told you my husband was a University professor. Well, actually ...

Section G Word order

1 Basic order

Statements

SUBJECT	VERB	OBJECT	ADVERBIALS
I	*bought*	*these coffee cups*	*in Sweden, two years ago.*
I	*don't use*	*them*	*very often nowadays.*
I	*haven't broken*	*any of them*	*yet.*

a The subject almost always comes before the verb and the basic order is not affected by a preceding adverbial form except in the case of:

1 **here/there + to be.**
Here is (**Here's**) *the key.*
There were *several people absent.*

2 a negative adverbial which is usually followed by a subject–verb inversion, often with the purpose of creating a dramatic effect (see Part 2, Section G5).

Note
In a literary style an opening adverbial may occasionally be followed by a subject–verb inversion, usually to create a dramatic effect.
In the middle of the square stood the bronze statue of a powerful horseman.

b No individual word that forms part of a compound verb tense stands isolated from the rest of the verb at the end of the sentence either in a statement or a question.
This may happen, however, in a short sentence containing an inter-verb adverb: *He has not/now spoken.* (See Section G4 on pages 197–8.)
The same applies to the second of two associated verbs in a sentence.

He hasn't made that mistake before.
I can't read this untidy writing.
My neighbour lets me use his telephone.
He decided to do it again.
The antique dealer took the vase to the window to examine it more closely.
Will the weather be warmer tomorrow, do you think?

Questions

FIRST AUXILIARY OR MAIN VERB	SUBJECT	(VERB)	OBJECT	ADVERBIAL
Was	*he*			*here yesterday?*
Did/didn't	*the murderer*	*leave*	*any fingerprints*	*on the gun?*

Note
A reported question appears in statement form:

INTRODUCTION	SUBJECT	VERB	OBJECT
I don't know where	*I*	*put*	*it.*
He didn't say whether	*he*	*had enjoyed*	*the book.*

Practice

Finish the sentences starting with the following words or groups.

EXAMPLES
Immediately . . .
Immediately he saw me, he started shouting at me.
There in a corner . . .
There in a corner he sat, slowly drinking cold tea.
When the firm went bankrupt . . .
When the firm went bankrupt, some two thousand employees were made redundant.

1 In our local shopping precinct . . .
2 An hour ago . . .
3 Even then . . .
4 Occasionally . . .
5 During his visit to Japan . . .
6 Though he was reasonably well off, . . .
7 As soon as I saw him . . .
8 Wherever you go, . . .
9 Far from being tired . . .
10 Yesterday . . .
11 Fortunately . . .
12 Oddly enough . . .
13 In order to . . .
14 As I had no small change, . . .
15 What on earth . . .?
16 He asked me . . . (add a CLAUSE)

2 Position of the direct object

The direct object is rarely separated from its associated verb by an adverbial form.

He (very much) enjoys Chinese food (very much).
He (slowly) raised his right hand (slowly).

Exception A short adverbial may separate a verb and its object if the object consists of several words.

He read with some impatience the long and often untidy essays his many students had handed in.

Practice

Suggest in sentences
(a) what you very much **enjoy**, **admire**, **like**, **appreciate** and **dislike**, and
(b) what you did to something **carefully**, **quickly**, **quietly** and **curiously**.

EXAMPLES
what you very much hope
I very much hope that you can come.
what you did to something thoroughly
I (thoroughly) cleaned the kitchen (thoroughly).

3 The order of direct and indirect objects

The order in which these two types of objects are used depends on the associated verb.

a **ask**
Only one order is normally possible.

	INDIRECT OBJECT	DIRECT OBJECT
I asked	*the newspaper seller*	*the way to the station.*

In this case, the indirect object (without **to**) comes before the direct object.

b In the case of **say, explain, relate, describe, report, repeat,** and all methods of speaking, including **shout, whisper** and **murmur,** only one order is possible.

	DIRECT OBJECT	INDIRECT OBJECT
He said	*good afternoon*	*to me.*
He reported	*what he had discovered*	*to the police.*
He described	*the splendid procession*	*to the blind man.*

In this case, the direct object comes before the indirect object, which is preceded by **to** and **for**.

Notes

1 **for** used before an indirect object suggests 'for the benefit of'.
2 Where direct speech follows the verb, the direct object in effect comes after the indirect object.
He whispered to me, 'Keep out of sight.'
But more often than not, the sentence starts with the words spoken, followed by what, in the above example, is the introductory statement.
'Keep out of sight,' he whispered to me.

c With various verbs, including **give, bring, take, send, tell, write, buy, sell,** and **show,** both word orders – direct/indirect and indirect/direct – are normally possible. Whichever object is the more important normally follows the less important idea.

	INDIRECT OBJECT	DIRECT OBJECT
The postman gave	*the gardener*	*a telegram.* (What he gave him is important.)
	DIRECT OBJECT	INDIRECT OBJECT
The postman gave	*a telegram*	*to the gardener.* (not to the house-owner)
The postman brought	*a telegram*	*for the gardener.* (not the house-owner)

Note
to and **for** precede the indirect object when it follows the direct object. There is no preposition before the indirect object when it precedes the direct object. The emphasis resulting from the positioning of objects is illustrated by the form of the following questions:
'How much did you give (to) the cashier?' 'I gave him ten pounds.'
'Which assistant did you give ten pounds to?' 'I gave ten pounds/it to the cashier.'

Practice

In answering these questions use both a direct and an indirect object, introducing them in a suitable order.

EXAMPLES
What does one have to show an immigration officer?
One has to show him one's passport.

1 What did you give your favourite relative for his/her birthday?
2 What kind of questions does your teacher usually ask you?
3 Which people have you written letters to during the past week?
4 Mrs Rover has a son and a daughter. Which child has she bought a football for?
5 What has she bought for the other child?
6 What aspect of the use of the English language am I explaining to you in this section?
7 What did the small boy with no watch ask the policeman?
8 What did Mick take to his wife in hospital?
9 What did you pay the railway porter for?
10 What did you pay the ticket-collector? (excess fare)

11 What did the painter on the ladder shout to the passer-by as he dropped the pot of paint?

4 The position of adverbs in a sentence

Pre- or inter-verb positions

PRE- – before a single verb word.
INTER- – between two or more words forming a compound verb tense.

a Adverbs which may be used in these positions:

1 ADVERBS OF FREQUENCY (single words alone or preceded by **very, quite, almost, hardly** and **scarcely**). The most commonly used of these are:

always	**occasionally**	**generally**	**never**
sometimes	**normally**	**rarely**	**often**
usually	**seldom**	**frequently**	**ever**

2 certain ADVERBS OF MANNER when they are not emphasised, including:
slowly **carefully** **quietly**

3 various other adverbs including:

possibly	**really**	**now**	**last**	**scarcely**
probably	**still**	**then**	**suddenly**	**fully**
certainly	**soon**	**once**	**hardly**	**completely**
				also

Position with single word verb forms (pre-verb position):
Few trains **ever** *stop at this station.*
He **probably** *mistook you for someone else.*

Exception: single word forms of the verb **to be**:
Our neighbour's dog is **always** *in our garden.*

Position with multi-word tense forms (inter-verb position):
STATEMENTS:
The league champions have **hardly ever** *lost a match.*
Adam will **soon** *have been working for sixty years.*
He didn't **usually** *show so much interest.*

MODAL VERB CONSTRUCTIONS:
He must **now** *have a rest as he is very tired.*
I couldn't **possibly** *remember everything he said.*

QUESTIONS:
Don't you **ever** *get tired of doing housework?*
Have they **really** *been living here all their lives.*

SUMMARY
The adverbs referred to above can be used:
1 before a one-word verb: *he* **probably** *mistook*
2 after the first auxiliary (+ negative adverb) in the case of a compound tense: *he has* **hardly ever** *got lost*, or a negative statement: *he didn't* **usually** *show*
3 after a modal verb form (+ a negative adjective): *he* **must** *now have*
4 after the (first) auxiliary and subject in a question: *have they* **really** *been living? don't you* **ever** *get?*

Exceptions to 2 and 3:
possibly probably really certainly still
He **probably** *didn't want it.*
I **still** *can't hear you.*

b USAGE
1 When emphasised, adverbs normally appear at the end of a sentence or, in certain circumstances, at the beginning.
I'm afraid I forget people's names quite often.
He'll be coming home quite soon.

2 Certain adverbs, including **ever**, **never**, **hardly** and **scarcely** are rarely used at the end of a sentence (**still** is used in this way occasionally).

3 Adverbs are used in a pre- or inter-verb position when they add to the meaning of the sentence without special emphasis.

Notes
1 *He* **rarely** *has been out as late as this.*
They **always** *are out in the evening.*
In this unusual position the verb may express special emphasis but the usage is uncommon enough for students of English to avoid it.
2 Contrast the normal positions of **yet** and **still**:
He's **still** *working. He hasn't retired* **yet**.

Practice

Answer each of these questions in a complete sentence which includes one of the listed adverbs in a pre- or inter-verb position.

1 What do you always do before you go out on a very cold day?
2 When did you last go for a walk of at least eight kilometres?

3 What have you sometimes done when you've felt fed up with your daily routine?
4 What will you never have the chance of doing?
5 Where are you now and where will you be in two hours' time?
6 What are you doing now?
7 What will you probably be doing at this time tomorrow?
8 What additional money must you usually pay if you borrow money?
9 Why is Sadie having problems with her suitcase filled with heavy books? (manage + even)
10 What don't you normally do on a Sunday?
11 What are some places you probably won't ever visit? (never)
12 What haven't we finished doing yet?
13 Why did Father suddenly start shouting at Fred? (temper ... with)
14 Why didn't you invite your new neighbours to your house-warming party? (hardly)
15 How did the old man get from the ground floor to the attic? (climb)
16 How was the hunting cat moving in the garden? (creep)
17 What did the canary in a cage say to the cat watching it from outside? (never)

Final position This is a common position for adverbial phrases and clauses and also for several single-word adverbials which are not used in a pre- or inter-verb position. These include:
yesterday today tomorrow here there early late
together with various place adverbs such as:
upstairs downhill forwards sideways

More often than not, ADVERBS OF MANNER, especially when emphasised, are used at the end of a sentence.
He examined the X-ray photographs **slowly/carefully/thoughtfully.**

Very many adverbs of manner are never used in a pre- or inter-verb position. These include:
intelligently sweetly beautifully fast

Here are some examples of phrases which would rarely be used in any other position but the end of a sentence:
He'll be with you **in a moment/as soon as possible.**
A pendulum swings **backwards and forwards.**

Front position

a Certain adverbs can be used at the beginning of a sentence. These include:
1 various TIME adverbs (though not **always** or **ever**)
2 SENTENCE ADVERBS such as **fortunately** and **certainly**
3 SENTENCE MEANING LINKS such as **by the way** and **in that case**

Note
In a few cases the position of an adverb can affect its meaning in the sentence.
Now, are you all **ready?** (claiming attention)
Are you all **ready** *now?* (at this moment)
Really *I can't understand you.* (expressing slight impatience)
I can't **really** *understand you.* (completely)
Once *I might have helped you.* (at some time past)
I might have helped you **once.** (but not more than once, or at some past time)

b A dramatic effect (more often used in the written language) can sometimes be achieved by a front position.
Slowly *the tiger moved towards its prey.*
The tiger (**slowly**) *moved towards its prey* (**slowly**).

c ADVERBIAL PHRASES and CLAUSES are often used at the beginning of a sentence but this is probably less common in the spoken than in the written language.

Now and again I spend a few quiet days in the country.
When I have time, I do some gardening.

Greater emphasis is achieved by a final position.

Before the word(s) being modified

An exact meaning in written expression may depend on the position of **only**. This applies, though less commonly, to certain other adverbs such as **apparently** and **almost**.

Compare the various possible meanings of this sentence resulting from the position of the bracketed adverbs.

(**Only**) *the guide* (**only**) *occasionally*(**only**) *whispers* (**only**) *short instructions* (**only**) *in French* (**only**) *to the driver.*
An (**almost**) *fifty-year-old competitor* (**almost**) *defeated* (**almost**) *the only person who had* (**almost**) *equalled him previously.*

In speech **only** tends to precede the verb (unless **only** is modifying the subject), its true application being indicated by voice emphasis.

I only came a little late. (**little** is emphasised here by voice)

Practice

a Give information relating to the following queries, using an adverbial expression (single word, phrase or clause) at the beginning or end of the sentence, whichever you consider the more suitable position.

EXAMPLES
when you posted your letters
I posted my letters on my way to work.
what you did last Saturday
Last Saturday I gave my flat a thorough spring-clean.

1 how long you've been learning English
2 what you've been doing during the past five minutes
3 what the weather's usually like in Greenland and in Central Africa
4 how you behave when you're really angry
5 something that happened in the world a week ago
6 what time most of the local shops close
7 how long you usually have to wait between dialling an overseas telephone call and getting an answer
8 what you would most likely do if you had the chance of a highly-paid job abroad
9 what you can see on your left, on your right and in front of you
10 how you might spend your time while awaiting an interview that may affect the whole of your future career
11 which hand you usually put a glove on first
12 what you do if you can't stand a TV programme that all the rest of your family insists on watching

b Suggest sentences, using in each of them one of the following words or phrases, either at the beginning or end (in one case in the middle) as you consider most appropriate.

1 yet (= until now)
2 yet (= however)
3 also
4 four or five times
5 politely
6 inevitably
7 far from making a profit
8 at a dangerous speed
9 without interruption
10 slightly
11 for good (= for ever)

Grouped adverbs of manner, place and time

Normal order: MANNER PLACE TIME
(Note M.P.T. – alphabetical order.)

	MANNER	PLACE	TIME
He dozed	*peacefully*	*in the garden*	*for several hours.*

However, this normal order seldom applies completely, for the following reasons:

1 It is rarely necessary to use all three types of adverbials in the same sentence.
2 Such an accumulation of adverbs may appear clumsy.
3 TIME ADVERBIALS often appear at the beginning rather than the end of the sentence.
After reading the note, he quickly slipped it into his pocket.

Practice

Explain *how*, *where* and *when* (or for how long) the following things happened, avoiding where possible three separate adverbials together at the end of a sentence.

EXAMPLE
Miss Bella Cantata sang
Last Thursday Miss Bella Cantata sang magnificently at the Covent Garden Theatre.

1 the Cheltenham Chargers football team played
2 the exhausted explorers slept
3 snow fell
4 the newspaper reporter ran
5 we thought we could hear someone moving

Grouped adverbs of a) time b) place

The normal order with both types of adverb is of exactness, the most exact coming first.

TIME
At three minutes past ten on Monday the eighth of January 1985.

PLACE
He entered through the window of the dining room in Flat 5, 36 Shrub Street, Shrewsbury, Shropshire.

This order may vary as a means of suggesting special emphasis.
The First World War ended on the eleventh day of the eleventh month of 1918 at exactly eleven o'clock.

Practice

In answering these questions give exact details of *when* or *where* the events referred to happened.

EXAMPLE
When did the disastrous fire start?
It started at about half past two in the morning of the 29th December last year.

1 Where did the fire start?
2 When (approximately) were you born? (change the year if you prefer)
3 Where did the police find the stolen money?
4 When did the most recent serious earthquake (or an earlier one) happen?
5 Where exactly are you sitting now?

5 Subject–verb inversion after negative adverbials

Though most commonly used as a literary device in the written language, this construction may be heard sometimes in speech. On account of its more literary connections, however, only a short summary is given here.

Negative adverbials include:
1 single word adverbials such as **never, seldom, rarely** and **scarcely**
2 phrases such as **not even then, at no time, only then** (= not before)
3 clauses such as **not until I get home in the evening, only after I had studied the contract**

Adverbials of this kind may be used at the beginning of the sentence or clause group to suggest emphasis. In this case the normal statement order of the following subject and verb may be reversed.

Never before/Seldom/Rarely had we seen so many battered old cars.
Only then did we realise how badly the locals must drive.
Not only have my wife and eight children left me, but even my dog has disappeared.
Only when} I get home in the evening can I find time to read my
Not until } morning's correspondence.

Note
An example of a negative adverbial without emphasis (no subject–verb inversion): *Not far from the lake there is a half-ruined church.*

Practice

Suggest statements that might follow these sentence openings.

EXAMPLES
Scarcely had he sat down . . .
Scarcely had he sat down before the telephone started ringing again.

1 Never in my life . . .
2 Seldom in the history of this country . . .
3 Only after long years of research . . .
4 Not even with the most powerful telescopes . . .
5 Only in an emergency . . .
6 Nowhere else in the world . . .
7 On no account . . . (= for no reason)
8 Only if you diet methodically . . .
9 Under no circumstances . . .

6 Summary

In comparison with the order of words in some highly inflected languages (in which the form of a word shows clearly its function in a sentence) English word order may appear inflexible.

However, the relatively normal order of direct and indirect objects and of adverbs and even the basic pattern (SUBJECT – VERB – OBJECT) may be modified to express more appropriately and sensitively:
1 differing meanings and shades of meaning
2 the emphasis put on a particular idea
3 pleasing effects of sound and rhythm

Note
Two or more pre-noun adjectives are normally used according to a fixed pattern, but as this pattern involves only the adjectives concerned, and not the sentence as a whole, it is explained in Part 2, Section E8.

Part 3

Contents Prepositions and adverbial particles

Section A Prepositions at, in, on: contrasts

1 Place and time

Basic meanings

The following meanings apply in many but by no means all cases:
at a point
in within boundaries, surrounded
on supported from below, (partially) covering
(compare **over**: wholly covering)

at an address	*in a town*	*on the table*
at an exact time	*in the middle*	*It happened on Thursday.* (partially 'covering' Thursday)
	in this century	*on the wall* (covering a certain area)

Some exceptions

at sea	*in a minute* (with the meaning 'at the end of a minute')	*on the left/right*
at night (but *in the day*)		*on holiday*
		on the radio
		on the way

The following tables contrast some of the more commonly used forms.

Place	at	in	on
1	arrive/wait at a bus stop/ station/airport	arrive in a town/country wait in (= *inside*) a station	wait on a platform be/go on a journey/an excursion
2	live at 2 Park Avenue	live in a room/building/ street	live on the third floor be on the premises
3	at/on a street corner	in the corner of a room walk in the road	on/at a street corner walk on the pavement
4		be/travel | in/on a bus in a car/an aeroplane	be/travel | on/in a bus on a horse/a bicycle/a ship on board a ship come on foot (*more usual:* walk)
5	at sea (*travelling*) at the seaside	in the sea (*swimming*) in water in the country/(the) town in the sky/the (open) air everyone in the world in the rain/the sun(shine) in bloom/flower/blossom	on the sea (*floating*) on land work on the land (*farming*) on the ground/the earth everyone on earth on the beach

6	(be) at home *but*: arrive/come/leave home (arrive) at work (*the place*) (be) at work (*be working*)	live in an old people's home	
7	at/in school/church at/in the cinema/the theatre at a concert/meeting (*present*) *Note* at/in school (*learning*) at/in church (*for a service*) in hospital (*as a patient*) in prison (*as a prisoner*)	in/at school/church in/at the cinema/the theatre in a play (*performing*) at/in the school (*visiting*) at/in the church (*visiting*) at/in the hospital (*working or visiting*) at/in the prison (*working or visiting*)	on the stage
8	sit at a table/a desk	in bed (*probably asleep*) sit in an armchair	lie on the bed sit on a chair on the wall/the blackboard/the ceiling
9	have at hand (*available*)	in one's hand (*holding*) tears in one's eyes carry in a pocket/a bag	on one's hands/fingers/wrist/feet/head (*wearing*) on one's back (*carrying*) a scar on one's face
10		in a (the) newspaper/a book/a film/a play	on paper on page ten on television/the radio/the telephone (a doctor may be) on call
11	at the front/the back/the side (of) (= *beside*) at both sides (*not touching*) at my side at/on the right side at the foot/top/bottom (of) (a page, a letter) at the edge of (*by*)	in front (of) (*opposite*: behind) in the north (*but*: north of a named place) (stand) in a circle	on the front (of) on both sides (of the box) on/at the right side on my side (= *supporting me*) on (*possible:* at) the left/right (of) on top (of) (*standing*) on the edge (of) at the point of (*about to*)
12	(remain) at a distance of (ten metres)	(see) in the distance	

Practice

Answer each of the following questions in a complete sentence, introducing into your answer an expression that is the same as or is related to one of those shown in the table on pages 204–5 (the noun you may wish to use may be different from the one suggested). Suggest additional ideas to give interest to your sentence. Make a special note of and memorise any prepositional usage that you find you are not sure about.

EXAMPLES
Where do you expect to see gloves in cold weather?
You expect to see them on people's hands, if they haven't got their hands in their pockets.
Where do you usually find the enquiries room in a multi-storey office block?
You can usually find it on the ground floor, often just inside the main door.
Where are most children on Monday mornings?
If they're not on holiday or ill or playing truant, they're probably in/at school.

1 You can wear or carry a watch. Suggest two different places.
2 Why do ramblers (people walking in the countryside) prefer rucksacks to suitcases?

3 You can have a flat near the top, near the bottom or halfway up a twenty-storey block of flats. Where would you prefer to live? Suggest which floor.
4 Mr Fox the lawyer is having a discussion with a client who has been arrested. Where is Mr Fox and where is his client?
5 Where does the sun rise and where does it set in temperate latitudes in mid-September?
6 Where can you read and how can you hear the latest world news? Which of these sources do you consider the more reliable?
7 Presley, who lives in England, is about to propose marriage to a pen-friend in Australia whom he has never met. How can he do this at once and what answer will he probably get?
8 What is the characteristic feature of all amphibians?
9 Ben spends his holidays on the South Coast where he enjoys rowing a boat and swimming. Use three expressions ending in **sea/seaside** in describing where and how he spends his time.
10 Explain your exact position at this moment, beginning with 'I'm sitting on a chair' and continuing with the table or desk, their position, room, floor, building, number and street, town, county or province, country, planet, planetary system and ending with the universe.
11 Where is it possible to see birds and what are they possibly doing in some of these places?
12 Jack looks very wet and Jill looks very brown. Where is Jack walking and where is Jill lying?
13 Where do people on farms live or what work do they do?
14 What side of a British car is the steering-wheel and where is it in one of your local cars?
15 Is the rear mirror behind the driver? Why is it placed where it actually is?
16 Where are the headlights? Why?
17 Where exactly is the number of this page?
18 When could a glass easily slip off a table and what can be done to prevent this?
19 Which side of the bride does the bridegroom stand when they are being photographed?
20 Where do members of the Government and those of the Opposition sit in the British House of Commons? Why?
21 How far from his office does Archie live if he can walk to work in half an hour?
22 When does a ship or a car look very small? How can you see them more clearly?
23 Where do most working people (a) eat breakfast, (b) spend about forty hours a week, (c) spend a good deal of their childhood, (d) see films, (e) spend about one third of their existence?

Time	at	in	on
1	at the beginning/the end (of) (*indicating a point*) (TIME AND PLACE)	in the beginning/the end (ADVERBIALS FOR MORE GENERAL TIME) in the middle (of) (TIME AND PLACE) in the meanwhile/meantime in the interval in the course of	
2	at this/that time/ moment/instant	in an hour = **a** *in the space of an hour* **b** *at the end of an hour* in an hour's time	
3	at the right/exact time	in time (for) (= *early enough*) in time (= *gradually*)	on time (= *punctually*)
4	at the same time	in the same week/month/ year	on the same day
5	two at a time	two in a row (SPACE)	
6	at present at once (= **a** *immediately* **b** *at the same time)*	in the past/the future in future in due course	on the point of (= *about to*)
7	at weekends at eight o'clock at Christmas/Easter at the age of twenty	in the week (*not Sundays*) in June/summer/the eleventh century/1066 in the holidays in one's childhood/old age	on weekdays on Sunday/Christmas Day on her birthday on holiday on the first of May
8	at night/dawn at lunch	in the morning/afternoon/ evening in the day in daylight/darkness	on that/the following day

Practice

Each of the sentence openings in the following numbered groups should be completed with: a suitable time phrase from the correspondingly numbered group in the chart above, and additional words providing extra information. The longer line indicates the position of the time phrase: the dotted line the additional words.

EXAMPLE

A preface . . . _____ while there may be . . . _____

A preface often appears **at** the beginning of a book while there may be an appendix **at** the end.

1 He tried for months to learn Chinese but _____ . . .

Explorers must have many interesting experiences _____ . . . especially . . .

In hot countries people usually have a siesta _____ . . . as . . .

Everybody applauded enthusiastically _____ . . . which . . .

The doctor will be here as soon as possible; _____ . . .

2 If you can't finish my suit _____ (week), . . .
I can't make a decision _____: . . .
If you can telephone again _____, . . .

3 The new party has only a few members now but _____ . . .
If the performance doesn't start _____, . . .
Unless we hurry, . . . _____ (2 possibilities) . . .

4 Twins . . . _____ but not inevitably _____.
(2 phrases)
As our unfortunate country has experienced floods, a prolonged drought and an earthquake all _____; . . . (help)
Can you read a book _____ . . .?

5/6 If you all try to speak _____, . . .
He ran up the first four flights of stairs _____ but . . . _____
If his temperature gets any higher . . . _____
The parachutist was _____ . . .
Although we have no jobs available now, . . . _____
It was easy to find servants _____ but _____ . . . (2 possibilities)

7 (Individual words in the phrases may be changed.)
Although she rarely sends me a greetings card _____ . . . _____
Shops in my home town open _____ . . . _____
Mothers have far more free time during the school term as _____ . . .
_____ octogenarians try to remember . . . _____
Few people have time to visit museums _____ (2 possibilities) but . . . _____
Most children start school _____ and . . . _____
Tobias Tompkins was born _____ _____ _____ (time, date, year)
Alexandre Dumas, Queen Victoria, Garibaldi and Karl Marx lived _____
He spends Sunday afternoon working in the garden _____ and . . . _____

8 The town streets are deserted _____ but _____ . . .
You can take photographs both _____ and _____ . . .
Most workers leave home _____ and . . . _____
We went to bed early as . . . _____

2 After certain verbs

	at	in/into	on
1	look/gaze/stare/glance at	look into (*investigate*) look into (a mirror)	look on (*watch without taking part*)
2	get at (*be able to reach*)	get in/get into (a car, trouble) (a train) gets in (= *arrives*)	get on (a bus) get on (*make progress*) get on (*get older*) get on with (one's work, other people)
3	call at (a house)	call in (the police to help)	call on (a customer or acquaintance)
4		go in (= *enter*) go in for (a career, a sport, a hobby)	go on (= *continue*) go on with (one's work)
5		come in (= *enter*) (a fashion) comes in	come on (= *move forward* or ADVICE *to do something*)
6		take in (= *deceive*) take in lodgers	take on(= *undertake responsibility for*)

Practice

Suggest what might be said in each of these situations, using one of the verbal forms in the chart on page 208.

1 Somebody knocks at the door.
2 You are asking when a train arrives.
3 Instructions to the security officer in a factory when a lot of valuable equipment is found damaged.
4 Instructions to the security officer about what he must do if he can't find the cause himself.
5 A teacher's advice to a student who is depressed by his lack of success.
6 Silas explains why he is late for school.
7 Instructions to a newly-appointed door-to-door salesman.
8 Instructions by a teacher who is leaving the class alone for a short time.
9 An explanation by Uncle Sam about why he has to wear reading glasses now.
10 An explanation by a charity organiser of why she never has any free time.
11 Advice given to an elderly widow with a large house and too little money.
12 Advice to an inactive man who is putting on too much weight.
13 What Joe must be content to do now he's too old to play football.
14 An explanation of why medicines should be kept locked up when there are young children around.

15 A salesman's promise to an important customer who has telephoned about unsatisfactory goods.
16 Tony's explanation of why he is resigning from the club he joined recently.
17 An offer of help from a car driver to a neighbour who is carrying home a heavy basket.
18 In a hurry to catch a train, Paula speaks sharply to Peter, who stops to buy cigarettes.

3 Other forms

	at	in	on
1		in the way (as an obstacle) in this way (*like this*) in a way in an (interesting) way (*way* = *manner*)	on the way (to)
2	at a high speed at 180 kilometres an hour	in a hurry in a rush	
3	at risk at the risk of	in danger/an emergency in difficulty/trouble in need	on fire
4	at ease	in comfort in a good (bad) temper/mood	on one's best behaviour
5	at war live at peace with	in peace	

6	(sell) at a price/profit/ loss	(sell) in dozens/hundreds	a profit on sales
7	good/bad at	interested/absorbed in involved in	keen on
8		Is he in? (= *at home*) the train's in (= *has arrived*)	What's on? a play/film is on the cooker/radio/light is on The drinks are on me. (= *I'll pay*)
9	at all events (*whatever happens*)	in any case/circumstances (*whatever happens*)	on all accounts/on no account/on my account

Practice

Suggest a suitable instruction or piece of advice to follow each of these statements. The person making the statement or someone else may be speaking.

EXAMPLE
Well, I like him in a way but I don't really trust him.
Then you shouldn't get too friendly with him.
We want to be sure of living in comfort when we retire.
Invest your savings in some kind of reliable pension fund.

1 This table is in my way.
2 Don't speak to your mother in that rude way.
3 You won't have time to stop for a meal on the way to the airport.
4 You're driving at a dangerously high speed.
5 Don't write that letter in a hurry.
6 Your life is at risk if you continue driving in this broken-down old car.
7 You're in danger of catching typhoid if you drink this water.
8 You'll be in difficulty if you run out of money.
9 You'll be in trouble with the police if you don't do something about that rear light.
10 Some waste paper in the litter bin is on fire.
11 The boss is in a bad temper this morning.
12 The children must be on their best behaviour when we visit Great-uncle Croesus.
13 The country we are planning to spend our holiday in may soon be at war.
14 If only I could work in peace!
15 We're selling this soap powder at a loss, you know.
16 People are protesting in hundreds of thousands about the tax increases.
17 People never seem interested in what I have to say.
18 I'm always getting involved in quarrels and arguments.
19 I'm not keen on the colour of my kitchen walls.
20 I've lost my door-key so I've no idea what to do if there's nobody in when I get home.
21 Our train won't be in for half an hour.
22 I'd like to know what's on at the Rex Cinema tonight.
23 There's nothing interesting on television this evening.
24 I'm not very good at using these prepositions correctly.

Section B Prepositions and adverbials: further uses of at, in, on

1 At

After verbs

smile/laugh at a joke
laugh at a person = make fun of
aim/shoot at a target
smile at a person (as a greeting)
frown/shout at him
point at (or **to**) a person or thing

Compare: **throw a snowball at** (to hit with)
with: **throw a ball to** (to catch)

Other phrases

a After certain adjectives and participles:
angry/annoyed/surprised at (something that happened)

Note
about (sometimes: **by**) is also used:
He was angry about what you said.
He was annoyed (surprised) by/about it.

b **at first, at last**
Compare the two sentences in each group.

1 *A new student feels lonely* **at first** *but he soon makes friends.*
First *she cleared the table, then she washed up and finally she mopped the floor.*

at first warns of a contrast to follow.
first introduces a following sequence.

2 *He took his driving test four times and* **at last** *he passed it.*
Write your full name, your date of birth, your home address, your passport number and last your signature.

at last introduces the end to a period of waiting.

last suggests the end of a preceding sequence.

c **at least, at most**
This manuscript is at most/at least eight hundred years old.

d **at best, at worst**
At best/at worst we'll have to pay a fine.

e **at all** (emphasis with a negative implication)
none/nothing/nobody/nowhere at all
Is there anything at all left?

Practice

a Answer the following questions using one of the above forms in each of your answers.

EXAMPLE
How many new jobs does the government hope to provide by subsidising the synthetics industry?
It's aiming at twenty thousand in the near future and possibly another twenty thousand within three years.

1 How can you greet a friend who isn't near enough to speak to?
2 What shouldn't you do when you're annoyed with a small child?
3 How was that window broken? (somebody)
4 How did you know the speaker was referring to you?
5 How can you see that a joke you tell isn't considered funny?
6 The would-be assassin is now under arrest. What crime did he commit?
7 How is Fred distributing the oranges and sweets among the children?
8 What should be the maximum and the minimum number of students in a language class to ensure effective teaching, learning and discussion? (2 phrases)
9 How much water is there on the moon?
10 What are the best and worst things that can happen to you if your car is stranded on a lonely road in a blizzard?

b Complete these sentences suitably.

1 At first he enjoyed living in this quiet village . . .
2 First he went to the post office to send off his parcel . . .
3 . . . and at last I found someone who could tell me.
4 . . . and last he checked his case to make sure he hadn't forgotten anything.

---

2 In

in forms part of a very large number of expressions of which only the most commonly used can be explained here.

in, into

a Theoretically **in** indicates EXISTING POSITION and **into** indicates MOVEMENT INTO POSITION. But **in** is commonly used in both cases.

put/pour/empty milk into a jug	*the milk is then in the jug*
go/come/break into a house	*be in a house*
put/fall into water	*be in water*
in common use:	*put your hands in your pockets*
	he fell in the river

Compare: *Thieves went/broke* **into** *the house.* (PREPOSITION)
with: *Thieves went/broke* **in.** (ADVERB)

Note
run into a room (not *enter a room (in) running*)
Similarly:
hurry past an angry crowd
stroll/stride along a street
swim across a river

b Compare these forms:
run in *a car* (drive it slowly when it is new)
The car **ran into** *a tree.*
I **ran into** *an old friend.* (met by chance)

c Other verbs which can be followed by **into**:

change/transform/ convert a storeroom **into** a workshop	**come into** effect/(**be**) **put into** effect
get into trouble	**burst into** tears
run into difficulties	**divide into** parts
go into detail	**get into** touch with

Note also: *four into twenty equals five*

Other forms are introduced in the tables at the beginning of Part 3 Section A.

Practice

Use a phrase introducing **in** or **into** in your answers to the following questions. The phrase should be included or related to those included in the above lists.

EXAMPLE
What did Mrs Jones do with her shopping at the check-out?
She put it into her basket.

1 Where do you pour the following: medicine, tea, milk for the cat?
2 What sometimes happens when a person is water-skiing?
3 Where did you meet your old school friend?
4 What do you have to do with some of your money when you visit France?
5 How did you get that black eye?
6 What may happen to someone who cycles without lights after dark?
7 Why is there a delay in the scheme to introduce complete automation in the power station?
8 When did the wearing of car safety belts become compulsory in your country? (law) (2 possibilities)
9 The Prime Minister has been given five minutes' television time to explain the government's programme. What won't he/she be able to do?
10 Ann and Brian with their three children are having a picnic. What is Ann doing with the large fruit cake?

---

in after certain verbs	**believe in** *ghosts* (but *believe a story*)	**fill in** (or **out**) a form
	join in the singing (but *join a club*)	**invest in** a company
	succeed in finding	**share in** the profits
	result in danger	**persevere/persist in** an attempt
	take part in a discussion	**confide in** a friend (but *trust someone*)

Practice

Respond to these questions and instructions with at least one complete sentence, introducing into your answer the words in brackets where given.

1 Suggest which of the following forms of investment you might choose for your savings and which you wouldn't choose. Suggest why or why not.

a a savings bank
b shares in an oil company
c the development of solar energy
d a new fringe theatre an acquaintance is opening
e the purchase of a house

2 Explain why you do or do not believe in any one of the following:
  a telepathy
  b the effectiveness of acupuncture treatment
  c the possibility of colonising other planets
3 Do you think that the workers in a company should decide company policy? (take part)
4 What is the attitude of some workers towards the use of company profits?
5 Suggest two occasions when you have to complete a form.
6 What is something you have never managed to do?
7 Which of the following can you **join** and which can you **join in**:
  a a discussion **d** disco-dancing
  b a political party **e** English classes
  c an orchestra **f** choral singing
8 What was the result of the football match between the Cup winners and your local team? (victory)
9 What kind of person would you tell your secrets to?
10 Why were you annoyed with the door-to-door salesman (what was he selling?) who kept you standing at your door?

Prepositions

in comparison with
in contrast to
(be) **in need of**/(go) **in search of** food
in charge of children
in command of a regiment
in spite of difficulties
in accordance with the law
in addition to his salary
in reply to your letter
in pursuit of the fugitive
in order to

Practice

Complete each of these sentences.

1 In comparison with Jupiter and Neptune, the earth . . .

2 In reply to your letter of the 12th January, . . .
3 In spite of the freezing weather . . .
4 We wandered along the main street in search of . . .
5 In accordance with traffic regulations . . .
6 As he was in urgent need of more money, . . .
7 People who spend their lives in pursuit of money . . .
8 In the course of his career as a lawyer . . .
9 Miss Langley, who is in charge of our Reference Department, can . . .
10 In contrast to the dryness and bareness of the desert area in the south, . . .
11 He recorded the lesson on tape in order to . . .

Other phrases

express **in words/in speech/in writing**
speak **in a whisper/in a loud voice** (compare: *aloud*)
illustrate **in colour/in ink/in sound/in music**
a book is **in** (opposite: **out of**) **print/in preparation**
goods are **in stock/in store/in reserve**
write **in English/in a formal style/in a notebook** (compare: *on paper, on tape*)
pay **in cash** (compare: *by cheque*)
in evening dress
dressed in black
in fun
in earnest
in love (with)
in my opinion
in my experience
in my life
in a conversation with

hear **in a radio news bulletin** (compare: *on the radio*)
(describe) **in general/in detail**
(refer to) **in particular**
(have characteristics) **in common (with)**
in theory
in practice **in effect**
in fact **in brief**
a metre **in length/in width/in height/ in depth**
study **in depth**
in a good condition/state
in good health/form/spirits
(gasp) **in surprise**
(hesitate) **in doubt**
(live) **in hope**
(a law is) **in force**
(demonstrators arrive) **in force**
(a government is) **in power**
(keep children) **in order**
(a room is) **in disorder/in a mess**
(arrange) **in alphabetical/numerical order**
in (good) **working order**
(be) **in a class**
(serve) **in the army** (try) **in vain**
(answer) **in turn** (sing) **in tune**

Practice

Complete each of the following sentences with at least six more words.

1 I cannot express either in words or in writing . . .
2 Please don't speak in such a loud voice . . .
3 In this solemn music the composer is trying to express . . .
4 I'm sorry to say this book is no longer in print but . . .
5 We haven't any of that material in stock just now but . . .
6 Although the instructions for use are in German . . .
7 She was in ski-trousers and an anorak when I saw her, so I suppose . . .
8 I never know whether he's speaking in fun or in earnest . . .
9 In my opinion smoking . . .
10 I have never in my life seen . . .
11 If you describe everything that happened in such detail . . .
12 The speaker lectured on the developing world; in particular . . .
13 France, in common with Italy, . . .
14 I understand how to hang wallpaper in theory but . . .
15 During the interview I tried to appear calm and collected but in fact . . .
16 I've given you a detailed account of the discomforts and drawbacks of working in this area: my opinion in brief is . . .
17 As the mountain is around four thousand metres in height, . . .
18 As the second-hand furniture wasn't in a particularly good condition, . . .
19 As the President hasn't been in good health for some time . . .
20 He stared in horror . . .
21 The government in power at present . . .
22 This kitchen is in a mess but . . .
23 Names in a telephone directory are arranged in alphabetical order so that . . .
24 To make sure your car engine is in good working order, you . . .
25 Instead of waiting in turn to . . .
26 He tried in vain to get a better job but . . .

3 On

After verbs and certain nouns

put on a light/the radio/a coat
you're **putting it on** (= you are pretending or exaggerating (illness or strong emotion))
keep (on) asking questions
tread on someone's toe
give an opinion/a judgment/a lecture on (also **about**)
write a book **on** (also **about**)
concentrate on one's work/writing
insist on perfection/seeing the director
depend on/rely on friends/getting help
live on/feed on fish
wait on guests

Practice

Answer these questions in complete sentences. For additional practice use the words in bold type in your reply.

EXAMPLES

When might you hesitate to **rely on** *someone's promise to help?*
I might not rely on his promise if he has already let me down.

1 What does a retired person usually **live on**?
2 When might you **put on** an electric fire?
3 When might you carry a mackintosh, and when would you **put** it **on**?
4 What different things do you **insist on** getting if you pay a lot for a restaurant meal?
5 What do country people without cars usually have to **depend on** to get to the nearest town?
6 What is the rest of the football team **congratulating** the centre-forward **on**? (score)
7 Why do drivers on a long journey often **put on** the car radio?
8 What should you do if you **keep on** getting headaches?
9 What different things can you **feed** a dog **on**?
10 What's likely to happen if you **tread on** a cat's tail?

---

on + gerundial constructions

On entering *the house, he took off his hat.* (= when he entered)

Note
The construction **on the point of** (**doing**) = immediately before doing.
He was on the point of entering the house when he stumbled on the doorstep.

Practice

Suggest constructions using **on** + a gerund, which could precede or follow the sentence openings and endings below.

EXAMPLES

... he gave a sudden exclamation.
On reading the message he gave a sudden exclamation.
You should always get a receipt ...
You should always get a receipt on paying your bill.

1 ... he took it immediately to the police station.
2 I expressed my deepest sympathy to him ...
3 ... he discovered a mouse inside.
4 I was completely horrified ...
5 ... he realised to his horror he had left his key inside the house.

Adverbial and other phrases

(be) **on one's knees**
(stand) **on one's own feet** (= be independent)
live/do things **on one's own** (= alone)
hit/wear/carry **on the head**
take (something) **on oneself** (= take responsibility for)
on paper
on a list
on trial
on a committee
(goods are) **on order**
(goods are sent) **on approval**
(act) **on instructions/on orders/on advice**
on request/on demand (= if it is asked for)
on account (= as part payment)
on my account (= for my sake)
on my account (= for my own purposes)
on no account (= in no circumstances)
on one/this condition
on these terms
on good/speaking terms
on purpose

on the contrary
on the whole (= for the most part)
on average

on and on (= without stopping)
on and off (= at intervals)

Note
on one condition = if this condition is accepted
in a good condition = in a good state

Preposition **on account of** (= because of)

Conjunction **on condition that** (= if)

Practice

Suggest what either you or the person or people referred to might say in each of the following situations introducing one of the above phrases into each of your responses. Not all the phrases given under this heading are included, but those that are will be in the same order. Some additional words and changes in wording are necessary.

EXAMPLE
A teacher is explaining to students what they must do if they want to take part in a school excursion. (*on a list*)
If you'd like to take part please write your name on the list on the notice board by the office.

1 You're giving advice to someone who depends too much on other people.
2 A couple are explaining that they have created their garden without help from anyone else.
3 You're giving advice to someone who's thinking of undertaking a full-time job besides her normal one of looking after a family of six.
4 The radio announcer is explaining what is happening now to the Kent Killer, arrested some weeks ago.
5 A shopkeeper is assuring a customer that the knitting wool she wants will soon be available in the shop.
6 A journalist is explaining to his critics why he wrote a very unpopular article. (editor)
7 A mail order firm is explaining in an advertisement how customers can examine goods before paying for them.
8 A notice in a hotel about the provision of TV sets in people's rooms.
9 A suggestion from a shopkeeper to a customer who wants to buy a dishwasher but can't pay the whole price immediately.
10 A mother is giving a strong warning to two children she must leave alone in the house for an hour or so. (Begin: You must . . .)
11 Father is telling fifteen-year-old Marlene the time she must be home if he allows her to go to a disco.
12 You're explaining why you can't invite both Sadie and Sarah to your dinner party.
13 You're disagreeing with a friend who finds London a boring place to live in.
14 You're describing the health of an elderly relative who is only occasionally ill.
15 You're giving information about the hours of sunshine to be expected daily in your locality in June.
16 You're criticising a boring lecture which continued for far too long.
17 On a day of intermittent rain you're describing the weather to a friend on the telephone.
18 You're explaining why someone has gone to live in a warmer climate. (where?)

Section C Prepositions to and for

1 Contrasts between to and for

General explanation

to refers to the delivery or handing of something to another person.
for can refer to providing something for the help, use, or advantage of another person.

I took some flowers to the hospital **for** *my wife, but as she was still undergoing an operation, the nurse promised to give them* **to** *her when she came round.*
What can I do **for** *you?*
What did that mob do **to** *you? You look awful.*

Verbs followed by to and for with contrasting meanings

take/send/bring a present **for** someone or **to** someone
write instructions **for** someone (to read later) or **to** someone (in a letter to him/her)
sell/carry goods **for** someone (he/she has asked you to do this)
sell/carry goods **to** someone (also: *sell someone goods*)

Note
1 **buy** *something* **for** *somebody* is the only possibility.
2 Compare: **leave** *something* **for** *someone* (to be given to him/her)
with: **leave** *money* **to** *someone* in a will for a certain purpose (e.g. a child's education)

Practice

Answer each question in a sentence which includes the words in bold type.

EXAMPLE
What kind of car did the salesman **sell to the millionaire**?
He **sold** a Rolls-Royce **to the millionaire.**

1 What contribution did Gwyn **bring to the party**?
2 What **magazine** might you **send** an article on sport **to**?
3 What present did he **bring for his hostess**?
4 What kind of medicine did Mrs Vickers **buy for her husband** when he had a bad cough?
5 What do you **write to your friends** when you are on holiday?
6 Why did Angus **write** an extra large cheque **for his wife** last week?
7 What does Mike the dog **carry for his master** when they come home from the newsagents?
8 What does he **carry to his master** when they're playing in the park?

Some other verbs followed by to suggesting delivery or handing over

speak to someone
explain the meaning **to** someone
relate (a story) **to** someone
describe (a place) **to** someone
telephone (the news) **to** someone (but *telephone someone*)
give (money) **to** someone (but *give someone money*)

Note
pay someone **for** something:
I paid the cashier for the things I had bought.

Practice

What person do you pay for each of these things?

EXAMPLE
an air letter
I pay the post office clerk for an air letter.

1 a meal in a restaurant
2 a bus ticket
3 the flat you rent (landlord)
4 carrying your luggage
5 a journey in a taxi
6 cutting or setting your hair

Suggest something you might pay:

7 a baker for?
8 a booking-office clerk for?
9 a solicitor for?
10 a garage mechanic for?

Some other verbs followed by for suggesting help, use, advantage

provide for a family
contribute/donate money **for** flood victims
supply steel **for** industry
produce goods **for** overseas buyers/overseas markets

Other verbs include **make, manufacture, design.**

2 To

In verbal phrases

get to a place (*Where has my bag got to?* (It's lost, or mislaid.))
get up to mischief (as when children do things they shouldn't) (*What have you been getting up to recently?* (sometimes used jokingly as a friendly greeting))
come to after an anaesthetic or faint (also **come round**)
look forward to what should be a pleasant future experience
attend to a customer in a shop/a matter that needs attention/what is being said (**pay attention to**)
see to things that must be done (e.g. arrangements for a party)
refer to information, a dictionary, notes etc.
agree to a suggestion, arrangements, terms (= accept)
point to (= indicate with the finger)
prefer a well-paid job **to** a poorly-paid one
take to someone (= decide one likes him/her soon after a first meeting)
give in to (= accept unwillingly what someone stronger wants)
belong to the owner (a book which belongs to me is mine)
turn to someone for help (**turn into** = become something different)
go up to/come up to a thing or person (= go/come very near)
turn to the right at the next turning
compare someone's voice **to** music (**compare** a copy **with** an original)
tend/be inclined to talk too much/tell lies (=do it rather often)

Practice

Answer these questions in complete sentences, making use of the form in bold type.

1 Kahdeksan Company suggested an agent's commission of 8% but the agents wanted 12%. What compromise did the two firms **agree to**?
2 What happened to the badly-managed and unprofitable Nogo Company after Mr Super Sparks took over the management? **turn into**
3 Why do you write your name on certain books, files and papers? **belong to**
4 Which suits you better: an outdoor or an indoor life? **prefer to**
5 Which people do most youngsters **turn to** when they're in trouble?
6 What kind of person do you usually **take to** at first sight?
7 Which question have we **got up to** now?
8 What time do most office staff have to **get to** work each morning?
9 What might the employees do if the management refuses to **give in to** their demands for higher wages?
10 What are some of the things a secretary has to **see to** for his/her boss?
11 'Please **attend to** these letters, Miss Able.' What does Miss Able do about the letters?
12 Two policemen are waiting at the hospital for an unconscious man to **come to.** He has been attacked by wage thieves. What do the policemen want to hear?
13 What can we **compare** a juggernaut lorry or van **to**?
14 Describe the early months of spring in your country. **tend to**
15 'He is **inclined to** lose his temper if anyone argues with him.' Does he always do this?
16 Do you still **look forward to** your birthday or do you dread it slightly?
17 How can a teacher show which word on the blackboard he/she is talking about? **point to**
18 There's a traffic diversion ahead. What must the motorist do when he gets to it? **turn to**
19 Slipslop the spaniel has been getting up to something. Suggest what this might have been. (You need not repeat **getting up to.**)

In noun phrases	the **key to** the garage door/the mystery/this book an **answer to** a question the **entrance to** the hall
Various other phrases	**To some extent/To a certain extent/To a large extent** I agree with you. Brighton is **to the south of** London. **three minutes to four** **on the way** to the airport count **from one to ten** **To my surprise** he let me have what I wanted.

Practice

Form phrases by combining words in the two columns (though not in the same order as at present), adding **to** where necessary. In your answers to the questions below, include one of the phrases you have formed.

A	B
twenty-four minutes	eight
an answer	of the Alps
a certain	the safe
the entrance	work
the key	the church
the north	ninety-nine
on the way	extent
ten	his letter

1 What's the cashier looking for?
2 Where are most of Bavaria, Munich and Lake Constance?
3 What's another way of saying 7.36 in the morning?
4 How far can you count using only two-figure numbers?
5 When do most people buy their newspapers?
6 How far are you interested in politics?
7 Where were the bride and bridegroom photographed?
8 Henry has written to apply for a job. What's he waiting for now?

In adjectival phrases

used to/accustomed to cold weather/working long hours (so he/she probably doesn't mind this)
Isn't this (**un**)**related to** the subject?
Are you **related to** the other Mr Peppercorn in our company?
A hare is **similar to** but not the same as a rabbit.
A polar bear is **adapted to** Arctic conditions
He is **married to** an heiress.
opposed to change
(**un**)**kind to/cruel to** animals
indifferent to love and hate
The weather's **likely to** be cold at Christmas time.

Practice

a Express each of these sentences in a different way, using one of the adjectival phrases given above.

1 This has nothing to do with the matter.
2 Eating with chopsticks is nothing new to him.
3 Jeremiah Jones belongs to the same family group as Ezekiah Evans.
4 Mr Polipop will probably win the election.
5 An Alsatian dog is rather like a wolf.
6 Her husband is an archaeologist.
7 Some parents treat their children (very) badly. (2 possibilities)
8 Most animals are at home in their natural surroundings.
9 He is against vivisection.
10 He doesn't care about what other people think of him.

b Join these word groups suitably, adding one of the expressions, **owing to**, **thanks to**, or **due to**.

EXAMPLES
He had to cancel his visit **owing to** his wife's illness. (PREPOSITION)
Thanks to his excellent health, at eighty he can still work hard. (PREPOSITION)
His ability to work is **due to** his good health. (**due** is an ADJECTIVE referring back to the noun **ability**.)

1	His success	A	the heavy snowfall
2	The train was late	B	excellent teamwork
3	The breakdown	C	disagreements with his parents
4	He left home	D	a favourable wind
5	They won the match easily	E	an electrical fault
6	The yacht reached the harbour safely	F	hard work

---

3 For

In verbal phrases

look for something lost
ask for something needed
apply for a job
apologise for causing trouble
feel sorry for someone unhappy
hope for a better future
fight for what one wants/one's country (but *fight* **against** *an enemy/fight* **about** (*a cause of disagreement*)
care for a sick or elderly person

not care for something one dislikes slightly
provide for the needs of one's family
punish someone for wrongdoing
send for a doctor
set out for (= begin a journey to a destination)
go for a walk
an angry dog might **go for** a person
the letters C.O.D. **stand for** Cash on Delivery
take someone **for** someone else (= think he is someone else)
What do you **take** me **for**? (= Do you think I'm so stupid as to believe you?)
go in for a sport or hobby

Practice

Answer each of these questions with a complete sentence, introducing into it the words in bold type which appear in the question. Some suggestions are shown in brackets but your own ideas may be more interesting.

EXAMPLES
Linda is turning out her handbag. What's she **looking for**?
She's probably looking for her key.

1 When might you **send for** the police?
2 What are those three dogs **fighting for**?

3 How did the manager **punish** the clerk **for stealing** office equipment? (by dismissing)
4 What time do you usually **set out for** your English class?
5 What colours don't you **care for**?
6 Who **cares for** patients in a hospital?
7 What did you do when the Alsatian dog **went for** you?
8 What winter sport do a lot of Austrians **go in for**?
9 What do the letters UNO **stand for**?
10 When do you **feel sorry for** yourself?
11 What should you do when you **apply for** a job? (letter of application)
12 Which of these people would you most like to be **taken for**:

a film star	a successful politician
a model	a well-known sportsman
a pop star	a glamorous spy?

13 What do you say (introducing the words **take for**) to someone who asks you to lend him your car for a bank robbery?
14 What is one thing you **hope for** in the future?
15 What do you usually **ask for** when a waiter first comes to your table?
16 What day of the week do you usually **go for** a walk?

Used for

Answer these questions in complete sentences.

EXAMPLE
What's a kettle used for?
It's used for boiling water in.

Notes
1 Note the use of the gerund (**-ing**) form after **for**.
2 Note the use of the preposition (where necessary) at the end.

What are these things used for?

1 a door key
2 an ignition key
3 a corkscrew
4 a camera
5 a suitcase
6 an envelope
7 a compass
8 a paper clip
9 insect repellent (keep away)
10 a wallet
11 a tuning-fork
12 glue (stick together)
13 a garden spade
14 a carving knife

In noun phrases

a **cure** for rheumatism
a house **for sale** (but: *a house to let*)
a game **for three people**
show **respect for** a person
feel **affection for** a person
have a **liking for** a person or thing
make an **apology for** something
feel a **need for** something (e.g. a change, a holiday)
the train for York is standing at Platform 5

Practice

Complete each of these sentences or suggest an additional one introducing all or part of one of the noun phrases already suggested.

1 Three people aren't enough to play bridge....
2 You should hurry if you want to catch ...
3 When she's hungry, my cat shows a lot ...
4 I'm very fond of cats but I haven't the same ...
5 We've been renting a flat for too long. Now we're looking for ...
6 Children of today show less ...
7 Medical research scientists are trying ...
8 After working hard all the week, most people feel ...

In adjectival phrases

It's **good/bad/difficult/important/unusual for** me to have a lot of exercise.
He's **grateful for** your help.
I was **thankful** for my warm coat.
He's **responsible for** the accident.
He's **responsible for** keeping the building in good condition.
He's **sorry for** neglected children. (compare: *Sorry about being late.*)

Practice

Answer these questions in complete sentences, introducing the words in bold type.

1 What kinds of food do you think are **good for** you?
2 Why is it **necessary for** you to have a job?
3 Why isn't it **safe for** people to walk on frozen lakes in the springtime?
4 What kind of person might you feel **sorry for**?
5 What are parents **responsible for**? (looking after)
6 Why aren't children always **grateful for** their parents' advice?
7 Why is it **difficult for** you to speak English perfectly?

In other phrases

Time:
for good (= for ever, for life)
That's all **for now/for the present.**
Are you staying **for long/for a long time/for dinner**?

Price:
I sold/bought it **for five pounds.** (often not the usual price)
I got it **for nothing.**

Others:
He's coming tomorrow **for sure/for certain.**
I'm afraid we're **in for** a difficult year/bad weather etc.
He put pepper in my ice-cream **for a joke/for fun.**
I must see it **for myself** before I buy it.

Practice

Answer these questions in complete sentences, introducing the words in bold type.

1 Is there anything in the world that can last **for ever**?
2 What might cause someone to leave his country **for good**?
3 Solly the Slayer has been sent to prison **for life**. How long might this be for in your country?
4 A friend asks to borrow your tennis racket. Suggest a possible answer, which should include the words **for now**.
5 Have you been learning English **for long**?
6 Harriet bought a fur coat in a sale. How much did she **get it for**?
7 Your landlord is asking you for some unpaid rent. How might you answer him, introducing in your reply **for sure** or **for certain**?
8 How can you tell that you're **in for** a bad cold?
9 What is something a small boy might do **for fun** or **for a joke**?
10 What is it advisable to do **for yourself** before you buy a villa abroad that you've never seen.

Various expressions These include:

But for (if there hadn't been) your help, I should never have finished.
I agree **for the most part**, but not entirely.
Are you **for or against** the plan?
That's **for him to decide**, not me.
I know most people think he's a great artist, but **for my part**, I think he's a fraud.
I've no idea what nationality he is: **for all I know**, he's a Martian. (I don't know and I'm not really interested.)
'Change those shoes at once, Tom.' '**What for**?' (an impolite way of saying **Why**?)

Practice

Finish each of these sentences with words which include one of the above expressions.

1 I can't thank you enough for lending me this money: ...
2 Part of his speech was highly controversial but ...
3 I don't know anything about the proposed scheme so I can't be ...
4 You may believe there will be mass unemployment next spring but ...
5 It's no use asking me where my husband is: ...
6 Whether your wife has a job is not ...

Section D Prepositions about and of

1 About with the meaning 'concerning, dealing with, connected with'

After verbs

ask (someone)/**learn**/**teach** (someone)/**tell** (someone)/**find out**/**know about** computer programming
think/**read**/**write**/**hear**/**speak**/**argue about** social problems
But: discuss social problems (no preposition) = have a discussion about social problems

Notes

1 *What do you think of this book?* = What is your opinion of it?
2 *He doesn't* **care about** *my feelings.*
Her job is to **care for** *children.*
I don't **care for** *those two colours together.*

worry about the possibility of being unemployed
How do you **feel about** spending a year in Central America? (Would you like this or not?)
remind someone **about** a forgotten arrangement (compare: *You remind me of your father.*)
see about something (= make arrangements for it to be done) (*I'll see about dinner now.*)
I'll **see about**/**think about** it. (= I'll consider it, think it over.)
But: *I'll see to it.* = I'll do what is necessary. (*I'll see to all the arrangements.*)

Note

learn a language/how to do something
learn about (some aspect of) a subject (*We're learning about the French Revolution*).

Practice

Answer these questions, repeating in your answer the words in bold type, which may in the answer be separated by other words where this is necessary.

EXAMPLES

Why didn't village people in the distant past **hear** *much* **about** *what was happening elsewhere?*
They didn't hear much about what was happening because there was no radio and few people travelled about the country.
What can you **tell** *me* **about** *China?*
I can tell you very little about China as I've never been there.

1 Where can you **find out** about postal charges?
2 What are you **learning about** now?
3 Who can **tell** us **about** today's news? (a newsreader)
4 What instruments do scientists use to **find out about** the universe around us?
5 How much do you **know about** astronomy?
5 Where can we **read about** world events?
7 What do people **talk about** when they don't know one another very well?
8 What do journalists **write** a lot **about** in newspapers?

9 What do you think that ordinary people **worry about** most?
10 What's the difference between **discussing** a subject and **arguing about** it?
11 How would you feel about having ten children? (You need not repeat **feel about.**)
12 Who **reminds** a businessman **about** his day's appointments?
13 What room does a housewife **see about** lunch in?
14 Father answers Ben's request for a new bicycle with the words: 'I'll see about it.' What's he promising to do? (You need not repeat **see about.**)

After adjectives

angry (with) someone **about** what he/she has done
sorry about what has been done (compare: **sorry for** = feeling pity for)
enthusiastic about a hobby or interest
worried/anxious/concerned about his father's health

Practice

Complete each of these sentences suitably.

1 You'd better apologise to Mr Wright. He's angry about (your being/coming/forgetting etc.) . . .
2 What are you worried about? Well, I'm rather concerned about . . .
3 Many people in the world are anxious about . . .
4 The audience wasn't particularly enthusiastic about . . .
5 I'm afraid I probably disturbed you last night I'm sorry about (making) . . .

---

2 About (preposition/adverb) with the meaning 'here and there'

move/walk about the room
travel about the world
too ill to **get about** much
Stop **running about**!
leave things about (= not put them away tidily)
The scissors must be **somewhere about.**
There wasn't **anybody about** at that time of night.

Practice

Answer these questions.

1 You can hear somebody moving about in the house. What might he be doing?
2 When do schoolchildren have a chance of running about? (the break)
3 What kind of person is always leaving things about?
4 'My briefcase must be somewhere about.' What problem has Mr Hare got?
5 'Poor Cedric can't get about much any longer.' What can't Cedric do and possibly for what reason?
6 What time of day is there usually nobody about in a small town?

---

3 About (adverb) with the meaning 'close to'

He's **about fifty**.
He'll be here **about nine o'clock**.

Practice

Answer these questions in sentences.

1 If grandmother is about fifty-five, between what ages is she likely to be?
2 'I'll come about two o'clock.' What's the earliest time you expect Kim to arrive?
3 'It's about time you were up.' What's another way of saying this, using the words 'by now'?
4 'The race is about to start.' How soon will it start?

4 Of

With the meaning 'belonging to, part of, referring to'

These are a few of the many possibilities:

a branch **of** a tree/of a bank
the name **of** a country
the price **of** food
the uses **of** a tool
a photograph **of** my family
the force **of** the wind
the problem **of** saving energy
the difficulty **of** meeting rising costs

With the meaning of position (which may also suggest 'part of')

the north **of** England
at the back **of** the hall
at the side **of** the house
at the beginning **of** the lesson
in the middle **of** Manchester
at the end **of** the journey

Practice

a Add one or more words to the following:

1 the first page of . . .
2 the spelling of . . .
3 the size of . . .
4 a view of . . .
5 the captain of . . .
6 the edge of . . .
7 the depth of . . .
8 the height of . . .
9 the length of . . .
10 a description of . . .
11 the foot of . . .
12 the summit of . . .
13 in front of . . .
14 the colour of . . .
15 the importance of . . .
16 the necessity of . . .
17 the strength of . . .
18 a feeling of . . .
19 a question of . . .
20 the loss of . . .
21 the last of . . .

b Complete each of the following sentences using one of these expressions, not necessarily in the same order. Add any other words necessary.

piece of **top of** **temperature of** **sheet of**
crowd of **title of** **rest of**

1 You'll need a thermometer to find out . . .
2 The letter was written on . . .
3 I can't remember . . .
4 He was eating . . .
5 He made his way with difficulty through the large . . .
6 Can you help me to get off . . .?
7 We shall move on to Portugal for . . .

After certain verbs

get rid of/dispose of an unwanted object (= throw it away)
cure a patient **of** an illness
die of pneumonia (**from** is sometimes used)
Hamish **reminds** me **of** his father. (Hamish is like his father in some way.) (compare: *Please remind me about that appointment tomorrow.*)
I don't **think** much **of** it (= I've a low opinion of it.)
take care of one's belongings (= look after them) (also **take care of** children)
care of (c/o) Mrs Smith (used when addressing a letter to someone living in another family's house)
What do you **make of** this? (= Can you explain something which seems strange to me?)
What do you **make of** him? (= What's your opinion of this rather unusual person?)

Practice

Answer these questions, introducing into each reply (though not necessarily in the same order) one of these phrases:

take care of **get rid of/dispose of**
cure (somebody) **of** **die of**
remind (somebody) **of** **think much of**

1 What do you do with shoes with holes in the soles?
2 Why is James very grateful to Dr Leech?
3 What's your opinion of a lot of TV programmes?
4 What might be the cause of the death of someone with a weak heart? (a heart attack)
5 Why is Tom's car in such a bad condition?

---

made of/made from/ made out of/ made with/made by

A table is **made of** wood. (The wood itself has not changed.)
Paper is **made from** wood. (The wood itself no longer exists.)
She made the child's pinafore **out of** one of her old dresses. (She used an already made thing to make something else.)
He **made** the holes **with** a drill.
This cupboard was **made by** my son.

Practice

Answer these questions, repeating in your reply the words in the question in bold type.

1 What's a window **made of**?
2 What's cocoa **made from**?
3 What could a kettle-holder be **made out of**?
4 What kind of person is bread **made by**?

After certain adjectives

ashamed of bad behaviour
proud of his clever children
unsure of/uncertain of success, winning a race
confident of one's own ability (compare: **show confidence** in a junior employee by trusting him with a difficult job)
tired of a dull job/waiting (compare: **bored with** a dull job)
fond of cats/flowers
(un)afraid of the dark

(**un**)**suspicious of** strangers
(**un**)**worthy of** praise (compare: *worth a lot of money*)
That's very **kind/nice/thoughtful of** you.
unaware of/(**un**)**conscious of** somebody else's presence/one's faults/problems

Note
aware of and **conscious of** usually have the same meaning.
awareness often applies to physical things or danger.
consciousness refers to mental or emotional states.

Practice

Answer these questions, using in each reply one of these adjectives + **of**.

afraid ashamed confident fond very kind proud unsure suspicious tired unaware worthy

EXAMPLE
Why's your dog barking at that black-bearded stranger?
My dog's always **suspicious of** black-bearded strangers.

1 Why does Kevin keep looking at his map?
2 Why has Karin decided to become a kindergarten teacher?
3 Why don't the villagers go into the forest even on moonlit nights?
4 Why have Mr and Mrs Field decided to move from London to a quiet country town?
5 What does Mrs Lime say in answer to Mrs White's offer to do some shopping for her?
6 What does Ernest Goodman say when he turns down the offer of a knighthood? (honour)
7 What did the team manager say about his football team just before the Cup Final match?
8 Why is the mouse that's happily eating the cheese in great danger?

9 Why is Mrs Dove always talking about her wonderful husband, the bank manager?
10 Why wouldn't Esme allow the rough-looking stranger into her house to read the electricity meter?
11 Why hasn't Sid told his parents about not passing his exam? (failure)

Section E Prepositions from, by; with, within, without

1 From

After certain verbs

a Getting something from a person, place or idea:

get/borrow books **from** the library
get a letter **from** James/**from** home
It's **reported from** Brussels that . . .
learn the truth **from** somebody/**from** experience
hear the news **from** a friend
keep/take something (**away**) **from** somebody (**keep** medicines **away from** children)
keep a secret/bad news **from** somebody
borrow something **from** somebody
gather an idea **from** what one hears

b Suggesting absence, separation:

be/stay away from work/home
separate the sheep **from** the goats (distinguish between good and bad people)
save/protect/rescue from danger
(**take**) **shelter from** the rain
dismiss/resign/retire from a post
withdraw from a competition
He **comes from** Denmark.
take ten (**away**) **from** twelve
change from winter to summer time

c Other meanings:

suffer from rheumatism
recover from influenza, a shock
judge someone **from** his/her appearance/behaviour (**by** is also possible)

Practice

Complete each of these sentences, using the word **from** and at least three additional words.

1 'How did you know about the Chairman's resignation?'
'I heard about it . . .'
2 'For a near-beginner, you play chess very well.'
'Well, I learned how to play . . .'
3 'This is our special correspondent in Spain reporting . . .'
4 'If you don't take that knife away . . .'
5 'When I run out of eggs or butter, I can always borrow . . .'
6 When my secretary is away . . .
7 To separate one garden . . .
8 A passer-by picked up the child on the edge of the sea-wall to save him . . . (**from** + GERUND)
9 I keep a large dog to protect . . . (an OBJECT should precede **from**)
10 The picnickers took shelter . . . (where?)
11 When he was dismissed . . .
12 There is a considerable difference between the English of people who come . . . (and those) . . .
13 The answer isn't nought if you take . . . (what is it?)
14 As he suffers . . .
15 He may well never fully recover . . .

Time and place a Time:

from January
from 1800 to 1880
from two o'clock onwards
from birth
from morning to/till night
from childhood

b Place:

wander (about)/move **from place to place**
move **from side to side**
come home **from work/school**
arrive **from Australia/abroad**
a letter **from India**
a radio programme **from Scotland**
fall **from a tree**
jump down **from a wall**
a wind/gale **from the south-west**
(see/come) **from a distance**
(disappear) **from sight**

Note
AFFIRMATIVE STATEMENT: *It's a long way from here.*
NEGATIVE STATEMENT: *It isn't far from here.*

Practice

Make a statement about each of these pictures, using one of the above expressions suggesting time or place. In some cases, the expression may have to be changed slightly.

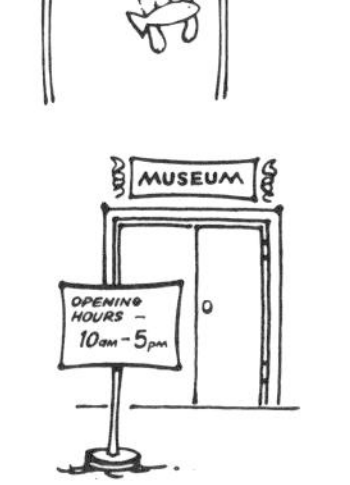

Adjectival and other uses

different from
divorced from (but: *she divorced him/they got a divorce/got divorced*)
From my/our/the firm's point of view, the strike will be a disaster.
From what I've heard (but I've no personal experience) the firm is losing money.

made from

Bread is **made from** *flour.* (The flour no longer exists in its original form.)
Shoes are **made of** *leather.* (The leather remains unchanged.)

Practice

Which of these things are made from something/made of something? Add a second sentence explaining what each is used for.

EXAMPLES
scissors paper
Scissors are made of steel. They are used for cutting things.
Paper is made from paper pulp, which is made from wood. It has many uses, including writing and printing on, wrapping things and covering the walls of rooms.

1 a pullover
2 an envelope
3 sugar (sugar cane, sugar beet)
4 a bottle
5 gunpowder (saltpetre, sulphur, charcoal)
6 a table
7 tyres

2 By

After certain verbs

get by = to pass somebody or something with difficulty (*Can you move a little? I can't get by.*)
= to just manage to live on one's income
enough light to **see by**
learn by doing
an honest face is nothing to **go by** (can't always be trusted)
judge by/from appearances (similar in meaning to **go by**)

Expressing the way something is done

travel by road/sea/air/underground
travel by car/bus/train/boat
send by post/airmail
deliver by hand

Note
in a car/a bus/a train
on a horse/bicycle/motor cycle
go on foot (more usual: *walk*)

Expressing who or what does something (passive)

examined by an expert
powered by electricity
heated by gas
generated by steam
blown by the wind

In a certain way/to a certain extent

I found it **by chance/by accident**
learn/know **by heart**
do it **by oneself** (= without help)
little by little
the table **by the window**
sit **by me**
walk **two by two**
live **by oneself** (alone)
by far the best/the most interesting
buy **by the dozen**

Note
Not **nearby**, which is an adverb: *He lived nearby.*

Time

by day/night (compare: **in darkness**)
finish it **by tomorrow**
He should be home **by now/by and by.** (= later: *I'm busy now. I'll help you by and by.*)
by then

Other expressions — **by the way** (used to suggest a change of subject that is in some way related to what has just been said)
by all means (used when giving permission)

Practice

In each of the following groups of words, one of the above expressions appears in bold type. Either add an extra sentence or complete the unfinished one in such a way as to show you understand the meaning of the expression.

EXAMPLE
First the members of the group were photographed **one by one,** . . .
First the members of the group were photographed one by one and then a photograph of the whole group was taken.

1 Excuse me, I can't **get by.** . . .
2 Even with my wife working we only just manage to **get by.** . . .
3 Can you **see by the light** of that lamp or . . .?
4 Londoners travel **by bus** or **by underground** but Venetians . . .
5 I want to send this parcel **by air mail.** . . .
6 'Do you really believe he met you **by chance** or . . .?'
7 In deciding how well educated a person is, you can often **go by/judge by** . . .
8 Although the operation was carried out **by** . . . (distinguished surgeon)
9 As all the hotel rooms are cooled in summer **by** . . .
10 When I have to learn something **by heart,** . . .
11 He's recovering from the operation **little by little** but . . .
12 Did you go to the theatre **by yourself** or . . .?
13 Did you redecorate this room **by yourself** or . . .?
14 Your dog's standing patiently **by your car** waiting . . .
15 He prefers to work **by night** because . . .
16 **By the end of this year** . . .
17 They've already been building the sports stadium for three years. **By now** . . .
18 I had dinner with Harvey yesterday. He was talking about his new job. **By the way** . . . (be remembered to)
19 'May I open a window?' '**By all means.** . . .'
20 I may try for a better job **by and by** but just now . . .

3 With

Showing what is used to do something with — We can sew **with a needle.**
Meals are eaten **with knives and forks** in Europe, and **with chopsticks** in the Far East.

Practice

Answer the following questions in complete sentences.

What do you:
1 write with?
2 see with?
3 cut with? (two possibilities)
4 pay for things with?
5 take the temperature with?
6 bite with?
7 kick with?
8 clean your teeth with?
9 do your hair with?

What can you do with:
10 a camera?
11 a telescope?
12 a gun?
13 knitting needles?
14 a corkscrew?
15 glue?
16 a map? (find your way)

Be together with live/stay/work/play/travel/go/come/go to a concert/go on holiday/associate/ be friendly **with** somebody
have/take/bring/carry something **with** you
have a camera/no money **with** you
take an umbrella/bring your book to class **with** you
carry a shopping bag **with** you

Compare: *married* **to** *somebody*

Practice

Suggest answers in complete sentences to each of the associated questions in the two following groups:

1 Which of the people below does Mr Barnaby, the solicitor:
- **a** live with?
- **b** stay with on holiday?
- **c** travel to work with?
- **d** work with?
- **e** occasionally have dinner with?
- **f** go to concerts with?
- **g** associate with?
- **h** Which is he friendly with?

his musical daughter
important clients
his wife
his partner
other solicitors
people he gets on with
friends who have a villa in Spain
the man who lives next door

2 What do you have/take/carry/with you when you:
- **a** go on holiday?
- **b** go shopping?
- **c** go abroad?
- **d** go to an ice-rink?
- **e** attend an English class?
- **f** visit a friend in hospital?
- **g** climb a steep mountain?
- **h** go swimming?
- **i** go to an opera?

Used descriptively a man **with** a beard/**with** brown eyes/**with** grey hair/**with** a long nose/**with** a pleasant smile/**with** his hands in his pockets/**with** a deep voice (Compare: speak in a deep voice)
a woman **with** a large family/**with** many responsibilities/**with** a lot to put up with
a town **with** a long history etc. etc.

Practice

Describe yourself, using at least nine descriptive phrases including **with**:

EXAMPLE
I am a man with short hair, with green eyes, with large ears, with a long black moustache, with a bass voice, with a wife and ten children, with a small house, with little money, and with no car.

In adjectival phrases	**(dis)pleased with**	**(dis)satisfied with**	**friendly with**	**angry with**
	annoyed with	**acquainted with**	**(un)familiar with**	**connected with**
	associated with	**combined with**	**mixed with**	**safe with**
	filled with (compare: **full of**)			

Practice

Answer these questions, introducing the words in bold type into your replies.

1 Why was Charlotte **pleased with** her present?
2 Why was Ben Pratt **dissatisfied with** his hotel?
3 What kind of people are you most **friendly with**?
4 How do you behave when you are very **angry with** someone?
5 When might a teacher get **annoyed with** a student?
6 Are you **acquainted with** many people or only a few?
7 What building are you most **familiar with**?
8 What war is Abraham Lincoln **associated with**?
9 What building is an actor's job **connected with**?
10 What's a balloon **filled with**?
11 What's an empty room **full of**?

After verbs

interfere with someone's belongings (compare: **interfere in** someone's business/affairs)
get on (**well**) **with** someone
be on good terms with someone
put up with rather unpleasant things
compare/contrast one thing **with** another
mix flour **with** eggs
mix/associate with other people
associate/connect one idea **with** another
part with a valued possession
dispense with something unwanted
provide/supply (someone) **with**
deal/cope with a difficulty
manage with little money
green **goes with** brown (= it looks pleasant)
What have you **done with** my bag? (= Where have you put it?)
I could **do with** a coffee. (= I'd like to have one.)
What do you **want with** me? (= Why do you want to speak to me?) (note: **speak to me**)
It rests with you to decide.

Practice

Make complete sentences using the disconnected words and adding any information asked for.

EXAMPLE
not sympathise you (why?)
I'm not going to sympathise with you: it's your own fault you're hard up.

1 not often agree him (why not?)
2 why people compete one another? (what could they do instead?)
3 never quarrel my relatives (why not?)
4 who interfere stamp-collection? (how do you know?)
5 Rob not get on anybody (why not?)
6 People living in large blocks of flats put up (what?)
7 can't compare life today (what with?)
8 if mix blue yellow (what colour do you get?)
9 politicians have to associate (what kinds of people?)
10 hotels provide guests going on full-day excursions (what with?)
11 must buy a scarf to go (what with?)
12 I know what done your gloves (where are they?)
13 when Avery has to deal problem (what does he do?)
14 so tired that do (what with?)
15 now that have car can dispense (what with?)

Various other expressions Would you come to lunch on Sunday? Yes, **with pleasure.**
with best wishes from
with love from
fall in love with
with care (printed on something breakable)
with his help
with difficulty
with ease

Practice

What do you do:

1 with difficulty? 2 with ease? 3 with someone's help? 4 with pleasure?

4 Within

General meaning Up to but not beyond a certain point.

Place **within reach**
within walking distance

Time **within two days** (= in not more than two days)

Also I'll do anything for you **within reason**. (= help as much as can reasonably be expected.)

5 Without

I went out **without** any money/a coat/any idea of where I was going.
I'll do it **without fail** (= for certain)/**without delay**/**without difficulty.**
Everybody **without exception** agrees.
I haven't got any coffee so we'll have to **go without** it/**without** having any.
However little money he's got, he never **goes without** his cigarette.
How can you **manage without** a fridge?

Practice

Finish each of these sentences suitably.

1 You can't travel by train without ...
2 The committee elected Parsons as Chairman without ...
3 I'll write to you on Monday without ...
4 Flowers can't do without ...
5 A short-sighted person can't manage without ...
6 If you're too fat, it's best to go without ...
7 He looks really ill. He should consult a doctor without ...
8 He solved the problem without ...

Section F Prepositions up, down, over, after, back, round

1 Up

In verbal expressions

bring up a subject in a meeting (= introduce it)/children in the home
put up your hands to answer a question/an unexpected visitor for the night
put up with small discomforts (less strong than **bear**)
get up in the morning
stay up/sit up late at night
get up to mischief (= do something childishly naughty) (*What have you been getting up to?*)
stand up (opposite: **sit down**) (but: *People stand in a queue.*)
stand up to hardship/very cold weather/an aggressive attacker
turn up at a meeting or party (= attend)
take up a new interest or hobby/an offer (= accept it)
look up a word in the dictionary/the time of a train in a timetable
catch up with someone or something (= get level)
come/go up to somebody (= approach very closely)/London (from the surroundings)
run up bills by overspending
ring someone **up** (= telephone)
pick up something lying (compare: **pick flowers, fruit**)
pick up a language (= learn it by practice rather than study)
make up a story (= invent it)/a quarrel (= end it)
do up a house (= redecorate it)/a coat (= button it up)
hold up (= delay)

With the meaning 'completely'

use up everything one has
eat up all the food
burn up/tear up old letters
up in the sky/in the air
upstairs
up there
wind up a watch (fully)
streets **dry up** after rain
Time's up. (= You must stop now.)
move up and down (vertically)
walk up and down (horizontally)
an up train (into the city) (**a down train** – from the centre to the surroundings)

Other expressions

What's up? (=What's the matter?)
It's up to you. (= It's your responsibility; you have to decide.)
not up to the mark (= not good enough)
not up to much (= of poor quality)
up against difficulties
hard up (= short of money)
up-to-date (= modern)
make-up (= cosmetics)
a hold-up (= a robbery, often in the street, by threat of force)

Practice

Finish these sentences or add a further sentence. Most of the given examples already contain an expression with **up**. Where this is not the case, include a suitable expression in the words you add.

1 Although he was now a millionaire, he had been **brought up** . . .
2 People living in hot countries have to **put up** . . .
3 The television programme was so interesting that he **stayed up** . . .
4 Because the children had been **getting up to** mischief, . . .
5 In order to remind people to **turn up** . . .
6 After his holiday Bert had to **catch up** . . .
7 He **came up to** me and . . .
8 I watched a tiny aeroplane moving . . .
9 **'What's up?'** . . .
10 It's **up to** you to . . .
11 I'm not feeling . . ., so . . .
12 She keeps her diary **up-to-date** by . . .
13 Some people find it easier to **pick up** a language than . . . (to do what?)
14 He **picked up** one of the apples which were . . .
15 If you can **ring** me **up** tomorrow, . . .
16 Children who **make up** stories, . . .
17 If only he would **take up** . . . (why?)
18 While he was waiting he walked **up and down** (why?)
19 I've **used up** all the eggs, so . . .
20 He gave the rest of the meat to the dog, who . . .
21 He says he's **hard up**, but . . .
22 You can **look up** . . .

---

2 Down

After verbs

a machine breaks down (a **breakdown**)
a house may **burn down**
put down what one is carrying
write down a word in a notebook
take down a letter in shorthand
sit down on a chair
lie down on a bed
get down from standing on a table
bend down to pick up something (= stoop)
fall down from a standing position (compare: **fall from above**)
knock down something standing (e.g. a vase)
turn down an offer (= refuse it)
let someone **down** (= fail to do what one has promised)
run down a person (= say bad things about him/her)
a machine may **run down** (= lose power)
look down on someone whom one considers inferior
sounds **die down** (= become less) (compare: **die away** = gradually disappear)

Other uses

ADJECTIVES
down and out (= without any money and possibly begging)
down to earth (= plain and matter-of-fact)
a down train (away from a large city centre)

VERB
down tools (= refuse to work any longer)

Practice

Answer each of these questions with a sentence containing one of the above expressions.

1 What did the waiter do with his loaded tray?
2 Why has Maurice been going to work by bus all this week?
3 When may fire insurance cover be useful?
4 What did Maureen do when Max proposed to her?
5 What do you use your notebook for?
6 For what three reasons is Mabel unpopular? (use three expressions)
7 What must a tall man do when he goes through a low doorway?
8 The taxi-driver had promised to come at seven o'clock but still wasn't there at a quarter past. What was I afraid he had done?
9 What happened when the teacher went into the classroom?
10 Does rain fall or does it fall down?
11 Why couldn't the old man afford a bed even in the cheapest hostel?
12 What kind of person must a nurse be?

WHAT MUST A TALL MAN DO WHEN HE GOES THROUGH A LOW DOORWAY?

3 Over

After verbs

get over an illness, shock, sorrow = recover from the effects
turn over a page
a lorry could **overturn** in an accident
hand over an object or responsibilities to someone else
take over another person's job/another firm
overtake (= catch up with and pass a person or vehicle in front)
run over someone with a car
overrun (= be everywhere (weeds may **overrun** a garden)/ take longer than the time allowed)
fall over/knock over an object
lean over a bridge
jump over a river
think over something before deciding (**think it over**)
see over/look over a house one might buy
look over another person's book/shoulder
oversee (= direct work in progress) (**an overseer**)
overlook (= forget to do something or agree to forget a wrongdoing)
show someone **over/show** someone **round** a house or factory

As a verbal prefix

a With the meaning 'too much':

overeat	**overwork**	**overdo** things (= try to do too much)
overestimate	**overheat**	**overstrain**
overwork etc.		

(**do overtime** = do extra work but not necessarily too much)

b With the meaning 'be stronger than':
overcome **overpower**

Here are a few of the many adjectives whose prefix **over-** has the meaning 'too', 'too much':
overweight **over-confident** **over-tired** **overfed**
Notice the adjective **overdue** (= later than planned or expected).

Amount have food (**left**) **over** (= too much to use)
over ninety years old
over and above what I asked for

Time and place stay **over the weekend**
have paint **all over** one's hands and face/**all over** the place
he lives **over the road** (= on the other side of)
(But: *from London to Paris* **via** *Dover*)

Completion the programme's **over** (= finished)
We'll get the speeches **over** quickly and then have refreshments.

Practice

Finish each of these sentences using a suitable form of one of the above expressions. Include information relating to the questions in brackets.

1 He's had scarlet fever but now ... (what's happening?)
2 She admired the picture on one side of the postcard and then ... (what did she do and why?)
3 While the manager was on holiday, ... (who did his/her job?)
4 As she jumped on to the table, the cat ... (what did she do and what happened as a result?)
5 Clive's had an accident: ... (what happened?)
6 He narrowly escaped a collision with an oncoming lorry while he ...
7 I delayed giving a final answer as I said I wanted ... (for how long?)
8 Having moved last week, my friends want ... (what will they do when I go to see them?)
9 If you have any bread ... (what can you do with it?)
10 He's now been in hospital ... (how long?)
11 I wish you wouldn't leave ... (where?)
12 When the meeting is ... (what will happen?)
13 I'm driving from London to Venice next week, but I haven't decided which route to take. I can go ... or ... (France/Germany)

4 After

After verbs **look after** children/belongings so as not to lose them, or to keep them in good condition
take after (= resemble – usually a relative)
run after somebody who is running away
ask after (= ask for information (health etc.) about an absent person)

Other uses **after all** means:
1 something must be considered:
We must help him now. After all, he helped us in the past.
2 even though this was not expected:
He passed the exam after all.

one after another/one after the other
This may be used with some annoyance:
People keep disturbing me one after another/the other.

the day after tomorrow
the week after next

Practice

Combine each of the verbal forms shown below with a suitable one of the phrases in the following list. Then use the word group you have formed (adapted if necessary) in a sentence.

EXAMPLES
look after **run after**
the bus *the suitcases*
She asked him to look after the suitcases while she bought the tickets.
He had a heart attack while he was running after the bus.

look after **take after** **run after** **ask after**

1 a friend's son who is living abroad
2 a bag-snatcher
3 patients in a hospital
4 a mouse
5 a colleague's family
6 his father but not his mother
7 his garden

5 Back

After verbs

go back/come back (home, to school etc.)
be back (*He's just back from Canada.*)
give back/bring back/take back what has been borrowed
bring back old memories
take back what one has said
pay back money borrowed
I'll **pay** you **back**. (= take revenge)
send back/put back/get back something lent or lost
keep back (= not move forward/not allow to move forward)
look back (= look behind/think about the past)
turn back (= turn round to come back to the starting point)

Other uses

PREPOSITIONAL
at the back of the hall
on the back of a donkey

ADVERBIAL
back to back
back to front (wearing clothes the wrong way round)
there and back (a return ticket takes you there and back)

Practice

Using one of the above expressions, suggest what you would say or do in each of these situations.

1 You are asking for a book a friend has borrowed. (3 possibilities)
2 On returning home you discover a record you've just bought is scratched.
3 You are apologising for something you have said to somebody.

4 You're telephoning your boss to say you're now better and will be returning to work on Monday.
5 Miranda has left dresses and blouses all over her room. Her mother is speaking. (wardrobe)
6 A bank official is telling you about the conditions attached to a bank loan.
7 On a walk you think you've lost your way.
8 You're explaining how long the return journey to the shops takes you.

6 Round

After verbs

go round (= rotate as a wheel does/see the various parts of a factory, a town etc./be sufficient for everybody (*There wasn't enough to go round.*))
show round (= show someone the different parts of a building)
look round (= go round looking at things generally, as in a large shop/look behind)
turn round (= turn to face the opposite way) (*He turned round and came back.*)/move something to face the opposite way (*Turn that chair round.*)
get (**a**)**round** (= spread (*News gets around.*) A person gets around when he/she visits many places.)
come round (= come to/regain consciousness)
bring round (= bring a person back to consciousness, revive him/her)
gather round (= come together round a person or object)

Other uses

PREPOSITIONAL
travel (all) **round** the world

ADVERBIAL
A roundabout moves **round and round.**
Taking a short cut is better than going **the long way round.**

Practice

What does each of the following do? Use one of the above expressions.

1 a person who has been under anaesthetic
2 a visitor to an exhibition
3 a person who hears his name called from behind
4 a stranger who finds himself in a cul-de-sac
5 the earth (the sun)
6 a guide
7 a first aid expert
8 a foreign correspondent
9 a rumour

Section G Prepositions out, off, away, towards, against

1 Out

General meaning

In almost all expressions, **out** suggests 'not in', and therefore 'not here' (actually or in the abstract), and so possibly non-existent, no longer existing. This also implies carried on to the end (as, for example, **work out** a problem).

Applications of this general meaning

a Indicating place:

go out/come out/walk out/run out/carry something **out**
fall out (of)/**lean out** (of)/**look out** (of) a window
get out of a car, train, (possibly) bus (see Part 3, Section G2)
see out/show out a visitor
turn out/throw out an unwelcome visitor
Get out! (a forceful way of asking someone to leave)
let out/put out the cat (**let the cat out of the bag** = give away a secret, usually unintentionally)
get out/take out something from a cupboard
set out for somewhere (= leave home to go somewhere)
stick out (a saucepan handle may stick out)
hang out the washing to dry

b Other meanings:

a flower/book **comes out** (= a book is published)
walk out (= go on strike (by leaving the factory) – **a walk-out**)
carry out a job (= do it)
fall out (with someone) (= quarrel)
Look out! (a shout indicating danger)
The weather **turned out** better than expected.
let out secret information
put out someone (= cause inconvenience or annoyance)
put out (ADJECTIVE) (= annoyed)
a teacher **gives out** books to the class

Indicating removal or disappearance

go out of fashion
a light/a fire **goes out**
turn out a light
blow out a flame
run out (of) (= have no more left)
supplies **run out/give out**
cross out/rub out/leave out a word
wear out clothes
worn out (= no longer wearable/tired out)
sell out (**sold out**) (= have no more goods left)
knock out in boxing (**a knock-out**)
do out of (= deprive of (sometimes by cheating))
out of breath/money/cigarettes

Suggesting the gathering and application of information

Meanings in this case are usually connected with the idea 'carried on to the end' included under the general meaning given above.

find out/**try out** a new idea
work out a problem
the idea **didn't work out** (= wasn't successful)
make out someone's writing/what someone is saying (= understand it)

Other verbal meanings

help out (= give extra help when this is needed)
carry out a job
an infectious illness/a war **breaks out**
shout out/**call out** loudly to attract attention
go out to work (= have a job outside the home) (compare: **go off to work** = set out for work)
set out

Other parts of speech

he's not in: he's **out**
the light's **out** (not on)
the fire's **out** (not burning)
out of fashion/**out of date**
a person may be **out of work**
a machine may be **out of order**
a car may run/be **out of control**
out of touch with other people/what is happening
she did it **out of kindness**/**gratitude**/**pity**
far enough away to be **out of the way**

The notice **out of bounds** may indicate that soldiers or the public may not enter.

Notes

1 **out**/**out of**
out is an ADVERB: *He went* **out.**
out of is a PREPOSITION: *He went* **out of** *the room.*

2 **out of**/**outside**
out of expresses movement: *He got* **out of** *his car.*
outside expresses position: *He is standing* **outside** *his car.*

Practice

a One or other of the above **out** forms appears in most of the following questions and for practice it should be included in the answer. Where there is no such expression, the answer should include a suitable one.

1 Why has Rosalie opened the wardrobe door?
2 What's the difference between **letting** the cat **out** and **putting** her **out**?
3 'Let me **show** you **out**, Mr Topman.' Describe what the speaker does next.
4 What could happen to you if you **leaned** too far **out** of a window?
5 When can't you see that a person's ears **stick out**?
6 What would **stand out** against the snow-covered slope of an almost bare hill?
7 What is Basil going to do with the pile of leaflets in his hand? (who will get them?)
8 Why is Gregory **calling out**?
9 'Long skirts have quite **gone out** now.' What have they gone out of?
10 Suggest a reason why factory workers may **walk out**.
11 What will probably happen to this rosebud tomorrow?
12 You hear a shout '**look out**!' Suggest a possible reason for looking out.
13 The TV weatherman forecast a dull day but proved to be wrong. What did the day **turn out** like?
14 What kinds of things do you **cross out**?
15 What do you do with things that are **worn out**?
16 What do you do when you find you're **running out** of petrol?

17 What did the police **find out** about the murdered man?
18 What group of people usually **carries out** the duty of making laws?
19 Suggest a reason why a riot might **break out.**
20 Why is it so cold in the sitting-room?
21 What might you have to do if you find the milkman (or the dairy) is **out of** cream?
22 When do people draw unemployment benefit?

b Answer these questions, using **outside** or **out of.**

1 Where do you stand when you knock at a door?
2 What do people do when there is an earthquake?
3 What did the canary do when the cage door was left open?
4 What do people do when a concert ends?

---

2 Off

General meaning

In most cases this adverb/preposition expresses the idea of moving away, departure, possibly coming to an end.

Expressing separation or movement away in space

take off one's coat
leave off one's overcoat in summer
run off usually without being followed (compare: **run away** in Part 3, Section G3)
get off a bus/a bicycle/a horse
see off (= say goodbye to someone at a station or airport)
go off (to work) (= leave home to go to work))
fall off a ladder
jump off a step
cut/break off a piece of chocolate
knock a cup **off** the table
an aeroplane **takes off**
They're off! (= they've started (at races))
We're **off** now. (= the train/aeroplane etc. has started moving)
he's **off** to Paris (= he's going to Paris)
off work (= away from work)
a day off (= a free day from work)
off limits refers to cafés, dance-halls etc. (similar to **out of bounds** – see Part 3 Section G1)

Other meanings

The idea of SEPARATION OR MOVEMENT AWAY is still present in most though not all of these cases, though the meaning may be more abstract or refer to time.

put off (= postpone/cause dislike (*The smell of the food* **put him off.**))
the party didn't **come off** (= didn't happen)
leave off (= stop doing something)
a bomb **goes off** (= explodes)
food **goes off/is off** (= becomes/is bad)
take off a person (= imitate him)
break off negotiations
give off an unpleasant smell
show off (= behave (often slightly foolishly) so as to attract attention)
well-off (= having plenty of money or other advantages)
badly-off
off-hand (= without notice (*I can't answer that question* **off-hand.**) (also: **off the cuff**))
off-hand (= showing little interest or concern: *He behaved in a very* **off-hand** *way when I tried to offer my advice.*)
off the record (= not to be quoted or printed)
off colour (= not well)
£10 off the price/the bill

Practice

a Here are possible objects to some of the verbs above. Together with a suitable form of the verb in question, use each of them in sentences of a reasonable length (not four words only). In some cases, more than one verb is possible.

EXAMPLE
her engagement
Philippa broke off her engagement to Ross after they had fallen out over the kind of home they wanted.

1 his motor-cycle
2 a high branch of a tree
3 a vase of flowers
4 the radio
5 people he found funny
6 my guests from America
7 filling in income tax forms
8 to a football match
9 diplomatic relations
10 shoes

b In this case subjects related to the above are suggested. Use them with suitably adapted verbs to make sentences of reasonable length.

EXAMPLE
the passengers in the aircraft
The passengers in the aircraft realised that after a long delay they were off at last.

1 most schoolboys
2 the sales manager
3 my secretary
4 this meat
5 the gun
6 his loud unpleasant voice
7 the international conference on new sources of energy
8 the bag-snatcher

c Answer these questions or complete the sentence opening.

1 Mr Sleek is fairly well-off. Suggest his annual income.
2 I feel a bit off-colour today. I think I'll . . .
3 'I can't answer that question off-hand.' What excuse is the politician giving for not answering the journalist's question?
4 When might you ask for a day off work?
5 When might you be off work for a week?
6 What time do you go off to work each day?

3 Away

General meaning This adverb (PREPOSITION: **away from**) is not unlike **off** in meaning, though there is a stronger idea of distance, of being 'not here'. While **off** may start from the moment of separation, **away** may refer more to a place elsewhere.
Compare: *He's off now.* (= He's leaving now.)
with: *He's away now.* (= He's somewhere else.)

move/walk/go/carry/send/drive/take/blow away (to some place that is not here)
get carried away (= get over-excited by some experience)
take-away food (= hot cooked food that can be bought and taken home to eat)
drive away (= repel, cause to go away)
take ten **away from** twenty
run away (from) (normally from someone running after you (compare: **run off** – without necessarily being followed))
get away (= leave, possibly with some difficulty/escape)
give away (= give without getting any payment/tell a secret)
throw away unwanted things

do away with (similar to **get rid of**)
put away money in a bank (*have a lot put away/put by*)
break away (= get free (*This province wants to break away from the federation.*))
turn away (= look in a different direction/from an unpleasant sight/too many people wanting to attend a performance)
keep away (= not go near/not allow people to go near)
stay away from school

Practice

Answer the following questions, introducing one of the above expressions in your reply.

1 Why is Hamish holding his hat as he watches the stormy sea?
2 Tom the cat and Jerry the mouse are crossing the room at great speed. What is each of them doing?
3 Why do some people keep a cat? (2 possibilities)
4 Suggest why Mrs Sweet wants to get away from her talkative neighbour and can't.
5 What kind of organisation do people give clothes away to?
6 Why are industrial firms careful not to allow outsiders to visit their research departments?
7 What common social custom would you like to do away with?
8 What do you have to throw away when you eat an orange?
9 How did Sid Slick get away from the policeman?
10 Why did Tommy Truant stay away from school yesterday?
11 Why are the people of the island of Solo refusing to pay taxes to the central government on the mainland?
12 What answer do you get if you take five away from nothing?
13 What excuse did the fans at the pop festival give for invading the stage?

4 Towards, against

Both of these are prepositions.

towards = in the direction of:
walk towards a bus

against =

1 using as a support:
lean against a bus

2 oppose/be in opposition to:
fight against an enemy
pass a law against misleading advertisements
turn against a former friend
refuse to act against one's principles

Compare: *show opposition/hostility to/towards the government*
with: *take action/demonstrate against the government*

Note
fight is often used without a preposition:
fight a battle/a duel/an opponent/injustice

Practice

In your replies to these questions, make use of either **towards** or **against**.

1 Which direction are you walking if you have your back to the sun at midday? (in the Northern Hemisphere)
2 Where did you leave the ladder?
3 What's a doctor's opinion of excessive smoking?
4 Why are so many Opposition members of Parliament making angry speeches? (Government bill)
5 Why shouldn't a public administrator take bribes?

Index

The following abbreviations are used:

adj	adjective	prep	preposition
adv	adverb	pron	pronoun
conj	conjunction	subj	subject
infin	infinitive	vb	verb
obj	object		